THE FIRST FAMILIES OF LOUISIANA

Volume II

Translated and Compiled

by

Glenn R. Conrad

Baton Rouge
CLAITOR'S PUBLISHING DIVISION
1970

Library of Congress Catalog Card No. 72-95549

Published and for sale by:
Claitor's Publishing Division
3165 S. Acadian at I-10, P. O. Box 239
Baton Rouge, La. 70821

TO

Sylvia, Martin, Alicia,
Margaret and Randolph
Conrad

INTRODUCTION

Between 1717, the year that Antoine Crozat abandoned his Louisiana concession, and 1731, the year the Company of the Indies returned operation of the colony to the French Crown, there occurred a most significant migration to Louisiana.

During those fourteen or fifteen years, thousands of Europeans, mainly Frenchmen and Germans but also Englishmen, Irishmen and Bohemians, quit their native land in search of a new life. Some of these immigrants voluntarily went to the colony, others did not. Some of the colonists were adventurers, a happy-go-lucky breed, but most were deluded farmers, soldiers and tradesmen. Still others were prisoners who were forced to go to Louisiana.

The fact remains, however, that regardless of why they sought the New World, these fearless people soon shared a common problem--survival. No matter their station in life, all of them--men, women, and children, freemen, <u>engages</u>, and prisoners--had to work hard to survive the perils of everyday colonial life.

Upon their arrival in America, after a hazardous journey across the Atlantic Ocean and the Gulf of Mexico, the colonists discovered that there was little more to greet them than a damp, forested land. Their task was obvious--begin the exhausting work of clearing the land. As the first and second years passed and their work of deforestation progressed, they experienced the simple joys of seeing their little homes become a reality and seeing their crops spring from the heavy delta soil. Tragedy, however, was always just beyond the horizon. Frequently they saw their ripened crops plundered by seemingly endless waves of blackbirds or they stood by helplessly as their grain, their homes, their meagre possessions were washed away by unpredictable floods and storms. Nevertheless, these hardy folk persevered between those years 1717 and 1732. They struggled for their new life and sometimes they failed. They died of overwork, malnutrition, fever, snakebite and the primitiveness of their enviornment. Some died of disappointment, pining for a France or a Germany they would never see again. Many colonists died fighting to protect their families and their homes from the first Americans.

Though death was a constant visitor, this intrepid group of minor noblemen, administrators, farmers, shopkeepers, soldiers, prisoners and vagabonds began the transformation of the wilderness they found into the heartland of America which they have bequeathed to their descendants.

What follows, then, are some of the lists which record the arrival, the pursuits, the joys and the sorrows of these first families of Louisiana.

These lists are copies of documents on deposit at the *Archives Nationales* in Paris. The author is aware that some of these lists have already appeared in several publications. It is the author's intention, however, to present in a single work, and as completely as possible, a compilation of the lists for the years 1717 to 1732. In order to document sources of information, the Table of Contents presents the French archival citation of each document employed in this work. All of the documents used can also be found in the Louisiana Colonial Records Collection of the University of Southwestern Louisiana at Lafayette, Louisiana.

The author must mention the inevitable problems that arose in the preparation of the work, particularly the problems of orthography and chirography. In order to solve the problem of different spellings for apparently the same personal name or place, the author adopted as his rule the spelling that appears on the document. Thus the alert reader will discover that the names "Kel," "Quel," "Quelle," and "Kelle" are probably different spellings for one person's name.

A greater problem was that of Chirography which rendered almost impossible, in some instances, a distinction between certain letters of the alphabet, but particularly between "u" and "n." For this reason a person's name may appear as "Fion" in one place and as "Fiou" in another place. Whenever it was impossible for the author to judge the correct spelling, the alternate spelling with a question mark is placed in parentheses following the supposed spelling. Furthermore, the French phonetic spelling of the German names has, in some instances, rendered these names almost unrecognizable from the correct German spelling. An aid to discovering the correct orthography of these German names can be found in J. Hanno Deiler's monograph on the German settlers of Louisiana.[1]

Now, a word of advice, particularly to the inexperienced genealogist. It is always wise to corroborate information from as many sources as possible. Presented here are some major sources of geneaological information for the given years. The author could not include, unfortunately, the hundreds, perhaps thousands, of names that appear individually or in small groups in the great number of documents pertaining to other aspects of colonial life during the period under investigation. Further research, therefore, could reveal additional information.

Finally, the author as taken the liberty of presenting

---

[1]J. Hanno Deiler, The Settlement of the German Coast of Louisiana and Creoles of German Descent (Philadelphia:1909). This author will be privileged to prepare an introduction to a new edition of Mr. Deiler's monograph to be published by the Claiter Publishing Company during 1970.

as the concluding item "The General Roll of Louisiana Troops from 1720 to 1770." Inasmuch as this list indicates the ultimate disposition of many of the soldiers who arrived in the colony between 1717 and 1732, the author believes that it should be included in this work. Indeed, it is the author's hope that his overall efforts will shed further light on those gallant pioneers--the first families of Louisiana.

University of South-
western Louisiana
Lafayette, Louisiana
June, 1969

Glenn R. Conrad

TABLE OF CONTENTS

Volume I

The Archives Nationales is the central repository for the archives and records of the French government. The archives from which the present material is taken is that of the Archives Colonies (abbreviated hereafter as AC).[1]

PASSENGER LISTS

---

[1]For a brief explanation of the arrangement of the French archives see chapter one, "The French Archives and American History," of J. Putney Beers, The French in North America: A Bibliographical Guide to French Archives, Reproductions, and Research Missions (Baton Rouge: Louisiana State University Press, 1957).

MILITARY OFFICERS

SOLDIERS[1]

[1]See also the lists of soldiers included with the passenger lists.

COMPANY OF THE INDIES

TABLE OF CONTENTS

Volume II

CENSUS REPORTS

BAPTISMAL AND DEATH REGISTERS

MISCELLANEOUS

NOVEMBER 24, 1721

CENSUS OF NEW ORLEANS AND ITS ENVIRONS

Name	Occupation	Wife	Children	French Servants	Slaves Negro	Slaves Indian
BIENVILLE	Governor			3	27	7
PAILHOUX	Commander				8	1
BANES	Major			2		
GAUVRIT	Captain	yes	1	1	5	2
PAUGER	Engineer				2	
DESCOUBLANS	Officer				1	
LA TOUR	Engineer				1	
BASSET	Officer				1	
COUSTILLAS	Officer			3	13	
DUPUY	Officer	yes	1		5	
ROSSARD	Notary				1	
BERARD	Surgeon				1	2
BERARD (the younger)	?	yes				
TRUDEAU	?	yes	7	2	31	1
SARRAZIN	Storekeeper	yes			2	1
BRULLE		yes	3		3	1
POIRE, Edmé Lucien	Gunsmith	yes			1	
BONNEAU	Captain of the NEPTUNE	yes				
DREUX, Pierre						
DREUX, Mathurin	(The DREUXS are brothers)			10	8	2
BELLEGARDE	Baker					
ROY, Mathurin	Gunsmith				1	
BUQUOIS, Henry	Miller	yes			3	
DUQUENOIS, Widow of						
RAYMOND, Jean		yes	1			
NIVET, Jacques	Ex-sargeant	yes			6	
AUBERT, Pierre	Locksmith	yes	1	1	2	
DELASSUS, Louis					1	
BERTIN, Germain	Shoemaker	yes	1	1	1	
DEMUN, Pierre	Tailor	yes				
DELUVER, Michel	Ex-soldier & carpenter	yes		1	2	
LEMAIRE, Jacques	Harness-maker					
VEILLON	Turner				1	
RIFFAUD	Stone-fitter					
BELAIR, Wife of	(Belair is a soldier)		2		1	
CARITON	Tailor	yes			1	
LEBRETON, Wife of						
TURPIN					2	2
ROY		yes				

Name	Occupation	Wife	Children	French Servants	Slaves Negro	Slaves Indian
TURPIN (the elder)	Canadian				2	2
VILLEUR						
ROY	Canadian	yes				
LA VIOLETTE		yes			1	
RICHAUME	Canadian	yes				
LA RIVIERE, Wife of						
TOMELIN	Miller		3			
DUFLEAU, Pierre Antoine		yes	1			
JOFFRE, Bertrand		yes			3	
HEBERT						
PROVENCHE	(Hebert & Provenche are associates)				5	
VIGER					7	
DULUTH					2	
BIGOT						1
SANS SOUCY, Widow of			1			
COSSINE, Jean	Tobacco Curer	yes	1			
FREYTAC, Jean Frederic		yes	1			
GRAVEUR, Louis Etienne		yes				
LE BLANC	Storekeeper			3	6	1
JOLLY	Miller					
FLAMANT, Adrien	Gardener	yes	1			
BONNAUD	Secretary to M. Diron & Inspector	yes	1		6	
TRAVERS	Tailor			1	1	
GODET					1	
BLANCHY		yes			1	
BARROY					2	
LEMPILEUR					1	
PATISSIER		yes	1		1	
BOUCHARD, Wife of						
CAYEUX, Called ST. GERMAIN	Cooper					
PINEAU, Pierre	Carpenter					
PEREAU	Carpenter					
BUREAU	Carpenter					
ROCHARD, Jacques	Carpenter	yes				
BIRRARD, Julien Called LA FORGE	Founder	yes				
FOUCHE, Pierre	Boatowner					
BEL Pierre,	Caulker					
VANGUEN, Jean	Caulker	yes				

Name	Occupation	Wife	Children	French Servants	Slaves Negro	Slaves Indian
LE FRANCOIS, Guillaume	Wagoner					
FIOU, François	Overseer	yes				
DE BRYE						
PASCAL	Boatowner	yes	3	1		
LA FRANCE	Boatowner	yes	1		1	
LABORDE	Boatowner	yes				
MERIE, Called SANS CHAGRIN	Boatowner	yes				
TAMESSE		yes	1			
MAZELIERE	Boatowner					
QUEMASION, François	Boatowner					
ROBERT, Pierre	Miller					
MOREL, Pierre	Miller					
ROBIN, Jean	Metal worker					
DU VALLE	Overseer of the Negroes					
HORSF	Edge-tool maker	yes				
DU FRESNE	Boatowner					
MARCHAND	Boatowner	yes				
MAIGRE	Boatowner					
MAGON	Boatowner					
MASSIERE	Boatowner	yes	2			
NANTOIS	Boatowner	yes	1			
DU ROCHER	Boatowner					
BLANCHARD	Boatowner					
VACHON	Boatowner					
CHERO, François	Boatowner					
DIONGUE	Boatowner	yes	1			
MARMANDE, Wife of			3			
LA BROSSE, Françoise						
MOUSSET, Jullien	Sailor					
LECLAIR, Claude	Sailor					
HORY, Gilles	Sailor					
CAYON	Sailor					
GUILLOUAS	Sailor					
LAPIERRE	Sailor					
ST. MICHEL	(A girl)					
GENDREAU	Sailor					
BOULEAU, François	Sailor					
LE VANEUR	Sailor					
VILLEUR	(A woman)					
CAMUS, Antoine	(The following are male convicts)					
GUILLAUME, Jacques						
RIBERT, Louis						

Name	Occupation	Wife	Children	French Servants	Slaves Negro	Slaves Indian
LA VIGNE						
FOISSARD, Thomas						
L'EPINIERE						
MARY, Pierre						
BONVOISIN						
TOURET						
LEGER, Joseph						
CAPET						
DURIVAN						
LA CLEF, François						
PERABON						
GUGU, Nicolas						
MONTEL, Nicolas						
BIDAUD						
FYSEAUX, Nicolas						
LE NOIR, André						
CRISTOPHLE						
DUPRE						
TEXIER, Charles						
LE GOF, Vincent						
MENAGER, Louis						
RENANDEAU (RENAUDEAU?)						
MORON, Antoine						
BASSE, Louis						
PIERRON						
PELLE						
DESMARRES, Thomas						
LA VIOLETTE						
CLERMONT						
VILLARD						
CORSEY, François						
LA ROQUETTE						
LA TERREUR						
BOURBONNOIS						
BOURGUIGNON						
LA FRANCE						
BELAVONE, Louis						
CASTANOUE, Guillaume						
LE GOF, Mars						

The Following are Female Convicts

JOLLY
BLANCHE
LA VIOLETTE, The wife of
CRISTOPHLE, The Mother of
TELLIER, Marguerite
LE TRILLARD, Jeanne

Name	Occupation	Wife	Childre	French Servants	Slaves Negro	Slaves Indian
Female Convicts (cont.)						
NAMONT, Anne						
LE NOS						
PONTON, Magdelaine						
FRONTEVEAU, Richard						
BOYER, Marie						
FONTENELLE, Louise						
HYVER, Suzane						
CENSUS OF THOSE LIVING IN THE VILLAGE OF BAYOU ST. JOHN						
RIVARD or LA VIGNE		yes	6		11	2
DUGUE, François					3	3
LANGLOIS		yes	1		8	1
GIRARDY, Joseph		yes	2		10	2
CENSUS OF THOSE LIVING IN THE VILLAGE OF COLASPISSAS						
DE BEAUNE, M.	Attorney General	yes	2	3	9	
CENSUS OF THOSE LIVING IN THE VILLAGE OF CHAPITOULAS						
DU BREUIL		yes	2	2	3	2
LANTEAUME				1	1	
DE LERY			3	1	33	4
LA FRENIERE				5	33	8
BEAULIEU					30	1
TRONION, Jean						
DOUBLET, Pierre					1	
Kolly, Concession of	62 men 12 women		5		46	2
DARCOURT (Widow of?)				2	11	
MASSY				5	8	
CENSUS OF THOSE LIVING IN THE VILLAGE OF GENTILLY						
SAINTON		yes	1	3	5	1
VIELLE VILLE		yes	1		1	
LA VIGNE		yes	1	1		
LANGEVIN					3	
CENSUS OF THOSE LIVING IN THE VILLAGE OF CANNES BRULEES						
DIRON	Inspector General	yes	6	20	20	2
DARTAGNAN, Concession of the Count	47 men 8 women		3		20	
ST. JULIEN	Ex-officer			3	8	1

Name	Occupation	Wife	Children	French Servants	Slaves Negro	Slaves Indian
CENSUS OF THOSE LIVING AT "LE PETIT DESERT"						
LE BLANC, Concession of M.	1 Man	5 women		7	9	
CENSUS OF THOSE LIVING AT ENGLISH TURN AND LES CHAOUACHAS						
DESLEAU					6	1
DUMANOIR, Concession of M.	3 men			6		
LE BLANC. Concession of M.	30 men	20 women	16	28	2	
LAW, Concession of M.	5 men	11 women	14	40		

RECAPITULATION

Men...........446
Women.........140
Children...... 96
Negroes.......533
Indian slaves. 51

MAY 1, 1722

CENSUS OF NATCHITOCHES

Name	Occupation	Wife	Children	Slaves Negro	Slaves Indian
ST. DENIS, M.	Commander			5	4
RECLOT, Sieur	Lieutenant				1
DUPUY, Sieur	Ensign			4	
CLAUSSEN, Sieur	Lieutenant (Half-pay)	He has 1 German servants with him.			
DERBANNE, Sieur	Storekeeper		3	4	3
JALLOT, Sieur					
COTOLLEAU, Pierre					
FAUSSE, Pierre					
LEON, Ives					
BERRY, François					
LEMOINE, François		yes			
LE ROY, Estienne					
DUBOIS, Pierre					
BENOIST, Marianne	Wife of a soldier				
GILLOT, Louise Françoise	Wife of a soldier				
LONGUEVILLE, Jeanne	Wife of a soldier				
DUPUY, Pierre Called GOUPILLON		yes			
GRENOT, Jeanne	Wife of a soldier				
POUTRE, Marie Catherine de	Wife of a soldier				
BONNET, Martine	Wife of a soldier		1		
AUDEBRANDE, Antoinette	Wife of a soldier				
MARIONNEAU, Pierre				3	
PIERRIER, Widow of			4	3	
CHAMPIGNOLE	Sargeant			1	

All of the above-named except Sieur DERBANNE and the Sieur JALLOT are discharged soldiers who have become farmers.

MAY 13, 1722

CENSUS OF THOSE PERSONS LIVING ALONG THE MISSISSIPPI RIVER FROM CANNES BRULEES TO THE TUNICA VILLAGES

Names	Men	Women	Children	Slaves Negro	Slaves Indian
GERMANS LIVING AT "LE GRAND DESERT" which is 1 1/2 lieues from New Orleans	3	3	7		
STE. REYNE CONCESSION, which is 7 lieues from New Orleans	12	1	1	2	
DUCLOS, Mathieu					
RIVIERE, Claude	(DUCLOS & RIVIERE are associates) 2 Negro slaves				
SAINTON	1	1	1	3	
TENSAS (Later known as the German Coast) which is 10 lieues from New Orleans					
DELAIRE, Sieur	2	1			
THE GERMAN VILLAGES which are also 10 lieues from New Orleans					
Village of Calstings					
D'ARENSBOURG, Cap.	1				
Village of Mariedal	26	30	26		
Village of Wen	25	29	40		
Village of Augsburg	17	20	33		
GRAND COLAS which is 12 lieues from New Orleans					
BESSON	1	1			
BISCORNET	1	1		1	
PETIT COLAS which is 19 lieues from New Orleans					
CHAVANE, Sieur	4	4		1	1

Name	Men	Women	Children	Slaves Negro	Slaves Indian
PETITS HOUMMAS which is 21 1/2 lieues from New Orleans					
COLLIN, François	1			2	1
CHENAL, François	1	1	1		
BORDIER, Jean	1	1	1		
LE COMTE, François	1	1			
PINEAU, Antoine	1	1			
GRANDS HOUMMAS which is 22 lieues from New Orleans					
DROCOURT, Pierre	2				1
BARRON, Pierre	1	1		4	1
CHAIGNEAU, Estienne	1		3		
ROUSSEAU, Louis	1	1		1	
LA CROIX, Widow of		1	1		
BUISSON, site of an old Chetimacha village, which is 29 lieues from New Orleans					
DUBUISSON, Sieur	8	3	2	18	4
MARTIN, Sieur	1	1		3	
DIRONBOURG, called Baton Rouge, which is 40 lieues from New Orleans					
DIRON, Concession of	10	5	2	6	
ECORES BLANC which is 43 lieues from New Orleans					
MEZIERES, Concession of M.	14	6		3	
POINTE COUPEE which is 45 lieues from New Orleans					
Ste. Reyne Concession	15	5	2	19	
TUNICA Villages which are 60 lieues from New Orleans					
ROMAND, Jacques	1				
ROUDEAU, Jean	1	1			
ASSELIN, Thomas	1	1			
KIMPER, François Nicolas de	2	1	1		
POUZET, Louis	1	1			
RAYMOND, Thomas	1	1			

Name	Men	Women	Children	Slaves Negro	Slaves Indian
TUNICA Villages (cont.)					
GEORGE, André and another Frenchman	2	1			
CHARON, Jean	1				
BONHOMME and another Frenchman	2			5	
GERMAIN, Pierre	1	1	1		

NOVEMBER 12, 13, 1724

CENSUS OF THE GERMAN VILLAGES LOCATED ON THE MISSISSIPPI RIVER ABOVE NEW ORLEANS

Name	Age	Comments
BEGINNING WITH THE GERMAN RESIDENT FARTHEST FROM NEW ORLEANS ON THE WEST SIDE OF THE RIVER		
LAMBERT, Simon	40	Native of Doberebesheim, Bishopric of Spire. Roman Catholic. Farmer. His wife and son, aged 18 years, are with him.
FREDERIC, Conrard	50	Native of Rotemberg, Bishopric of Spire. Roman Catholic. Farmer. His wife and five children are with him. The eldest child, a girl, is 13, the youngest is a boy of 5 years.
TROUSTER, Jean Georges	26	Native of Listamberg in Alsace. Roman Catholic. Mason. His wife is with him.
POCH, Jean Georges	35	Native of Golcher which is about 2 1/2 miles from Fort de Relle and from Strasbourg. Roman Catholic. Weaver. His wife and an infant child are with him.
ZIRIAC, Guillaume	50	Native of Ilmestat, near Mayence. Roman Catholic. Farmer. Formerly coachman for King Stanislaus. His wife and a daughter of 7 years are with him.
CALLANDRE, Jean	26	Native of Anbrequin in the Paltinate. Roman Catholic. Farmer. His wife, a daughter aged 14 years, his sister-in-law and mother-in-law are with him.
KISTENMACH, Etienne	39	Native of Cologne on the Rhine. Roman Catholic. His wife and a daughter of 10 years are with him.
WAGNER, Jeremie	27	Native of Orendoff, marquisate of Ansbach. Lutheran. Farmer and hunter. His wife, an infant, and his sister-in-law are with him.
MAGDOLFF, Leonard	45	Native of Hermunse in Wittemberg. Roman Catholic. Farmer. His wife and an orphan child of 10 years that he adopted are with him. (The child was a boy).

Name	Age	Comments
SCHANZ, André	25	Native of Kochausen in Franconia. Roman Catholic. Miller. His wife, an infant, and his sister-in-law, aged 15 years, are with him.
PETZ, Jean Georges	32	Native of Weibstalle, Bishopric of Spire. Roman Catholic. Butcher and prévot. His wife, an infant son, and an orphan girl of 9 years are with him.
MATERNE, Jean Adam	26	Native of Rosenheim in Upper Alsace. Roman Catholic. Weaver. His wife, an infant son, and two sisters-in-law, aged 18 and 20 years, are with him.
TOUBS, Gaspard	40	Native of Eche in Switzerland. Protestant, Farmer. His wife and two sons, aged 10 and 12 years, are with him.
HESDEL, Ambroise	22	Native of Neukirchen, Electorate of Mayence. Roman Catholic. Baker. His wife; his brother, aged 18; and his crippled brother-in-law, aged 13; are with him.
REITER, Jacques	28	Native of Lustnen in Wittemberg. Roman Catholic. Shoemaker. His wife is with him.
VOGEL, Michel	40	Native of Aldorff. Roman Catholic. Cooper. His wife and a son are with him. A daughter,aged 18 years, is in New Orleans.
FUNCK, Sebastien	30	Native of Haguenalle in Alsace. Roman Catholic. Farmer. His wife, an infant son (about 1 year old), and an orphan girl of 16 years, are with him.
HORN, Michel	39	Native of Limbac, near Mayence. Roman Catholic. Farmer. His wife and a daughter of 5 years is with him.
MENTHE, Baltazard	42	Native of Tropau in Silesia. Roman Catholic. Farmer. His wife and a daughter of 18 months are with him.
ROEZER, Jean George	37	Native of Biringrus, Electorate of Mayence. Roman Catholic. Marshal. His wife and an orphan girl of 18 years are with him.

Name	Age	Comments
BEBLOQUEL, Jean Jacob	36	Native of Lamberloch in Alsace. Lutheran. Farmer and Hunter. His wife, two sons, and a daughter are with him. Of the children, the eldest is 13, the youngest is 2.
ERIZMAN, Jean	46	Native of Routh(Ronth?) in Switzerland. Calvinist. Farmer. His wife and a son of 5 years are with him.
MARX, Baltazard	27	Native of Wullemberg in the Palatinate. Roman Catholic. Nail-maker. His wife, aged 22 years, is with him.
WICH, Bernard	46	Native of Teinlach in Wittemberg. Lutheran. Farmer. His wife, one son, and two daughters are with him. Of the children, the eldest is 13, the youngest is 2 months.
ROMEL, Jean	24	Native of Kinhart in the Palatinate. Roman Catholic. Tailor. His wife is with him.
WELLERIN, Catherine	49	Native of Helbron. Lutheran. Widow of Auguste PAUR, a tailor. She has no children and is alone.
COHN, Anne	?	Widow of Jean Adam ZWICKE, a Roman Catholic, who died in Biloxi. She has one daughter of 12 years.
FROMBERGER, Madelaine	50	Widow of Georges Mahyer, a Roman Catholic, and native of Inquelepille in Swabia. Her son, Nicolas MAHYER, 20 years old, is crippled but he is a good cooper. An orphan girl of 20 years lives with him.
REYNARD, Margueritte	46	Native of Baourbuque, Bishopric of Spire. Roman Catholic. She is separated from her husband, Jean Zenck, who lives along the Mississippi River. She has a seven-year-old daughter by her first marriage.
HENECKE, Catherine	?	Native of Horenbourg in Brandenburg. Widow of Christian GRABER, a Roman Catholic who died at Biloxi at the age of 50 years. She has a daughter, 14, who is with her. Both are sick.
GRABER, Cristian	23	Native of Brandeburg. Roman Catholic. Farmer. His wife and an orphan boy, aged 13 years, are with him.
NEIKER, André	36	Native of Dettenhausen in Wittemberg. Lutheran. Miller. His wife is with him.

Name	Age	Comments
OBERLE, Jacob	33	Native of Saverne in Alsace. Roman Catholic. Weaver. His wife is with him.
SENCH, André	35	Native of Saxony. Lutheran. His wife and a son of two years are with him.
TIL, Marc	43	Native of Bergwidz in Silesia. Lutheran. Shoemaker. His wife is with him.
KOBEL, Maurice	64	Native of Bern in Switzerland. Calvinist. Butcher. He has served 30 years in the Swiss Regiments of France. His wife is with him. He asks to return to France.
ARENSBOURG, M.	31	Half-pay Captain. Native of Sweden. An orphan boy of 10 to 12 years lives with him.
TREGUE, André	37	Native of Donaller in Bavaria. Roman Catholic. Hunter. His wife and an infant son are with him.
SENEK, Jean	45	Native of Banbergue, Bishopric of Weissebourg. Farmer. Separated from his wife.
HOFFMAN, André	27	Native of Aure, Principality of Ansbach. Roman Catholic. Farmer and butcher. His wife and a daughter of 7 years are with him.
FREDERIC, Mathieu	29	Native of Weillerheim in Alsace. Roman Catholic. Farmer. His wife, an infant son, and an orphan girl of 15 years, are with him.
RAUESCH, Bernard	52	Native of the Palatinate. Roman Catholic. Tailor. His wife, a son of 15 years, and a daughter of 11 years, are with him.
KLOMP, Paul	30	Native of Beauerbaque, Bishopric of Spire. Roman Catholic. Farmer. His wife, a son of 2 1/2 years, and an orphan boy of 12 years are with him.
SMITZ, Adam	44	A widower. Native of Isnen in Swabia Lutheran. Shoemaker. A daughter of 9 years is with him.
RODLER, Jean	35	Native of Rastat, Principality of Baden. Roman Catholic, Metal worker His wife is with him.
DISTELZUE, Antoine	29	Native of Selz in Alsace. Roman Catholic. Farmer. His wife and a son of 1 1/2 years are with him.

Name	Age	Comments
PICTOT, Guillaume	50	Native of Moncontour in Brittany. Roman Catholic. Farmer. His wife is with him.
MELQUET, Frederic	30	Native of Kaltensverche in Wittemberg. Roman Catholic. Butcher. His wife is with him.
MUNICK, Pierre	40	Native of Dobricheim in the Palatinate. Roman Catholic. Carpenter. His wife, one daughter of 14 years and another daughter of 12 days are with him.
STRIMPHLE, André	33	Native of Ottirsuir, near Fort de Kehl on the Rhine. Roman Catholic. His wife and son of one year are with him.
RIEL, Jean Adam	45	Native of Hatzweir, Basle, Switzerland. Roman Catholic. Carpenter. His wife and a daughter of 5 months are with him.
POCHE. Jacques	45	Native of St. Omer in Artois. Roman Catholic. Shoemaker. His wife is with him.
WAGUEPAK, Joseph	23	Native of Schwobse in Upper Alsace. Roman Catholic, Farmer. His wife is with him.
HEILE, Sibille	37	Widow of WEIDEL. Native of Helchingue in Swabia. Roman Catholic. She is alone.
EDELMAYER, Jean Adam	50	Native of Reiheim in the Palatinate. Calvinist. Cooper. His wife and two sons, aged 14 and 10 years, are with him.
ZONN, Philippe	26	Native of Groshoefflein in Hungary. Roman Catholic. Farmer. His wife is with him.
FOLTZ, Jean Jacob	26	Native of Ramestin in the Palatinate. Roman Catholic. Shoemaker. His wife and an infant son of 1 year are with him.
ANTOINE, Bernard	30	Native of Ehweigen in Wittemberg. Farmer. Lutheran. His wife and a son of 10 years are with him.

DECEMBER 20, 1724

CENSUS OF THE PERSONS LIVING ALONG THE MISSISSIPPI RIVER BETWEEN NEW ORLEANS AND THE GERMAN VILLAGES.

Name	Age	Comments
BEGINNING ON THE EAST SIDE OF THE RIVER (approximately in the present-day area of Napoleon Avenue, New Orleans. Ed. note.)		
LARCHE, Jacques	30	Native of Quebec. Brick-maker. Lives on M. Bienville's concession. His wife and two small children are with him. Three Negroes and an Indian work for him. His place is next door to that of M. Bienville.
LE QUINTREC. Jean Joseph	27	Native of the Bishopric of Quimper in Brittany. He lives on land owned by M. Bienville. His wife is with him. He also serves in the Swiss Company.
HECHLE, Gaspard	35	A Swiss from Lucerne. Roman Catholic. Lives on M. Bienville's concession. His wife, a daughter, and two orphan boys are with him. He has been on the land for two years.
HOUBER, Jacob	45	Native of Swabià. Roman Catholic. Lives of M. Bienville's land. Farmer. His wife, a son of 16 years, and a servant are with him.
KRESTMAN, André	45	Native of Augsburg in Bavaria. Wheelwright. His wife, two sons of 16 and 18 years, and an orphan girl of 15 years and another of 5 years are with him. He is a good worker.
ROY, Sieur Etienne	33	Nephew of M. CHAUVIN. Native of Montreal. Lives on M. Bienville's land. His wife and and Indian woman are with him. He has lost about 20 arpents of sugar cane in a fire.
KUHN, Simon	50	Native of Wissembourg, Duchy of Auspabe. His wife, his daughter, and his brother-in-law, Daniel YOPF, aged 20 years, are with him.
MILHER, The widow	?	Her husband, a brick-maker, died 8 days ago. She has two daughters, the eldest being 14 years and the youngest being 3 years.

Name	Age	Comments
WEYBER, Jean	28	Native of the area of Kehl, near Strasbourg. His wife, his mother-in-law and an orphan girl of 16 years are with him. He has made 20 barrels of rice this year.

CONCESSION OF M. CLAUDE JOSEPH DUBREUIL (Nephew of the CHAUVINS)

Name	Age	Comments
DUBREUIL, Claude Joseph	30	Native of Dijon in Burgundy. He came to Louisiana in 1719 aboard the COMTE DE TOULOUSE. His wife and two sons, aged 9 and 11 years are with him.
PARENT, Sieur Mere Son	17	
MOREAU, Jacques	47	Native of Paris
REFFAIT, Pierre		Native of Orleans, Master carpenter.
LANGLOIS, Joseph		Native of Vendome. Edged-tool maker.
DE LATTES. Antoine Joseph		Native of Douay. Carpenter
WAGON, Henry		Native of Maynault
PASSERA, Pierre		
46 Negroes		
2 Indians		

CONCESSION OF M. CHAUVIN DE LERY

Name	Age	Comments
CHAUVIN DE LERY, M.	50	Native of Montreal. He has three sons, aged 15, 13, and 11 years.
WILLARD		Carpenter
BEAUPRE		Indigo worker
59 Negroes		
1 Indian hunter		

CONCESSION OF M. CHAUVIN DE BEAULIEU

Name	Age	Comments
CHAUVIN DE BEAULIEU, M. Louis	46	Native of Montreal. His wife is with him.
43 Negroes		
2 Indians		

CONCESSION OF M. CHAUVIN DE LAFRESNIERE

Name	Age	Comments
CHAUVIN DE LAFRESNIERE, M.	48	Native of Montreal. His wife and nephew, M. BELAIR, are with him.
LANGEVIN		Indigo worker
MOUSSIGNAC		?
GIRAUD		Carpenter
77 Negroes		
5 Indians		

Name	Age	Comments
STE. REYNE CONCESSION		
CEARD, M.		Director
DUPLESSIS, M.		Assistant Director
DALGUERAY, M.		Employee
FLOT, The widow		Old storekeeper. She has 2 children
CANDIE		Carpenter. His wife is with him/
ANNETIALL (?)		Carpenter
SOISSONS		Carpenter
DECOUS		Cooper. His wife and 1 child are with him.
DUBOIS		Carpenter
DAUBLIN		Edged-tool maker
LA JOYE		Edged-tool maker
POURCEAU	17	Orphan. He is a domestic servant.
Two girls	10 & 6	Both orphans
71 Negroes		
1 Indian		

The following names are concession workers who have been discharged.

Name	Age	Comments
AUSSY		His wife and 1 child are with him.
PAILLARD		Leather worker
CALAIS		Two sons are with him.
ALLARD		His daughter is with him.
L'EMBREMONT		His wife is with him.
LEGROS, Albert		His wife and one child are with him
DORGEAU		His wife is with him.
BONNET		His wife and 2 children are with him

(End of the Ste. Reyne Concession)

Name	Age	Comments
VERETTE, Joseph	29	Native of Quebec. His wife and one _engagé_ are with him. He has harvested 40 to 50 quarts of rice.
DARTIGUIERE and BENAC		24 arpents of land
PELEGRIN, Henry	25	Native of Grace in Provençe. Farmer on the concession of Count Dartagnan. His wife and two children are with him. He has decided to stop farming since he cannot make a living.
PELLERIN, M.		This is the farm of M. Pellerin, a Company employee, which he bought from M. ST. JOSEPH.

Name	Age	Comments
CREPE. André	25	Native of Grace in Provençe. Farmer on the concession of Count Dartagnan. His wife is with him. He lost his crop to a flood. He is a good worker but he is miserable and has decided to quit farming.
COUSIN, Pierre	38	Native of Vienne in Dauphiné. His wife and an infant son are with him. He has two engagés, Jacques GENETEL, aged 52 years, and François DAUPHINE, COUSIN has been on the land two to three years. He is a good worker.
VAQUIER, Guillaume	27	Native of Opercy. His wife and a child of 2 years are with him. He works hard but wants to quit farming because he cannot make a living.

CONCESSION OF M. DIRON

DESJEAN, M.		Director. Absent.
LEJEUNE, Michel	17	
25 Negroes		

This concession is very beautiful, well situated and is in an excellent state.

CONCESSION OF THE COUNT DARTAGNAN AT CANNES BRULEES

DARTIGUIERE, M.		
BENAC, M. de		
BOUSSIGNAC, Sieur		Surgeon
PATU, Sieur		Employee
COUDERC		Carpenter
IMBERT		Metal worker. His wife is with him.
30 Negroes		

(End of Count Dartagnan's Concession)

CHANTREAU DE BEAUMONT, M.		His wife and four children are with him.
PUJEAU, Jean	30	Native of Lerac, near Bordeaux. Brick-maker. Roman Catholic. Works on the Dartagnan concession.
HARASSE, Joseph	23	PUJEAU's associate. Native of Paris. His wife and 1 child are with him. Together PUJEAU AND HARASSE have bought 4 arpents from Chantreau de Beaumont.

Name	Age	Comments
MERAND, Claude	28	On Dartagnan's concession. Native of Paris. Roman Catholic. Shoemaker. His wife is with him. He has bought 24 arpents of land from Edmé BONNON.
FERANDON, Denis	?	Native of Moulins in Bourbonnois. Roman Catholic. Weaver. His wife is with him.
MONGE, François DOUNON, Edmé		Formerly associates of FERANDON.
BOUETTE, Sebastien	40	Native of Varade, Bishopric of Nantes. Roman Catholic. Tailor. Was sent to Louisiana was a illicit salt dealer. He has about 15 arpents cleared.
CHEVAL, François	35	Native of Chantaise in Dauphiné, near Grenoble. Farmer. His wife and two children, aged 3 years and 3 months, are with him. He has 8 arpents of land.
CHESNEAU, René	33	Called DUCHESNE. Native of Lude in Anjou. He came to Louisiana from Canada. His wife is with him. He served 5 to 6 years in the army. He is a good subject.
DAUNY, Philippe	22	Native of Louarge in Flanders, near Douay. His wife is with him. The six arpents he occupies were abandonned by BERTHEL who left for New Orleans at the beginning of the year in order to go to Canada.
BROUT, Pierre	37	Native of Tours. Roman Catholic. Cooper. His wife is with him. He harvested 40 barrels of rice this year.
[illegible]ierre	24	Native of Belfort in Alsace. Roman Catholic. Farmer. His wife and two sons, aged 2 years and 1 year, are with him.
[illegible]	22	Native of Annecy(?) in Savoy. Roman Catholic.
CEZARD, Pier	25	Called LA BRYE. Native of Brye in France. Roman Catholic. His wife and one child of about 1 year are with him.

The CEZARD family is the last family on the east bank of the Mississippi before reaching the German villages.

Name	Age	Comments
FIRST RESIDENT BELOW THE GERMAN VILLAGES ON THE WEST SIDE OF THE MISSISSIPPI RIVER ABOUT EIGHT LIEUES ABOVE NEW ORLEANS.		
SAINTON, Pierre	28	Native of Chatelrault. Son of an attorney. His wife and two sons, aged 4 years and 2 years, are with him. He harvested 60 barrels of grain this year.
MARSEILLE, Dizier de	?	Roman Catholic. Barber on the Diron concession. His wife and a daughter of 3 years are with him. He bought 6 arpents of land from Sieur ST JULLIEN.
ST. JULLIEN	?	He has bought 12 arpents of land from François GOBERT and LA COSTE who have gone to New Orleans
DEJEAN, M.		Director of the Diron Concession.
PELLOIN, Pierre	40-45	He works M. DEJEAN's farm. Roman Catholic. Farmer. One of the best workers in the colony. His wife is with him.
SMITH, Pierre	34	Native of the Palatinate. Roman Catholic. Farmer. His wife and brother-in-law, aged 17 years, are with him. He bought three arpents of land from Barthelemy YENS, his neighbor.
HYENS, Barthelemy	25	Native of Cologne. Roman Catholic. Brewer. His wife and one infant child are with him. He is on the land less than a year and has only a garden.
THE ST. JULLIEN PLACE		
ST. JULIEN, M. St. Pierre		
DAUNY, Jean François		His German wife and an orphan girl are with him.
PIQUET, Remy		
8 Negroes		
1 Indian woman		
(End of the ST. JULIEN Place)		
GOBERT, François	28	Native of Dieppe in Normandy. His wife and an infant son are with him.
ROUX, Antoine	30	Called LAFLEUR. Native of Castelnaux, near Grace in Provençe. He is a gardener on the Dartagnan concession. He has twelve arpents of land upon which he has live for the past two years. Good worker.

Name	Age	Comments
CAUTION, Henry	25	Native of Grace in Provençe. Gardener on the Dartagnan concession. His wife is with him. He has bought six arpents from Antoine ROUX.
GUICHARD, Thomas	30	Native of Lyon. His wife and one child of ten years are with him. He has two <u>engagés</u>. He bought 6 arpents from BERTHEL three years ago.
PIQUERY, Pierre	31	Native of Mons in Haynault. Baker. His wife and two small children are with him. His harvest was very small this year because of destruction by the blackbirds. He has decided to quit farming and move to New Orleans.

<u>The PETIT DE LIVILLIERS Place</u>

Name	Age	Comments
PETIT DE LIVILLIERS, M.	22	An officer from Canada.
THIERRYSON, M.		
5 Negroes		
2 Indians		

(End of the Petit de Livilliers Place)

Name	Age	Comments
DUCROS	35 to 40	Native of ________ in Provençe. His wife is with him.
LANTHEAUME, Bernard	50	Native of Valence in Dauphiné. His family is in France.
RITTER, Joseph	52	Native of the Principality of Dourlick. Carpenter. His wife and a son of 20 years are with him. Two orphan girls, aged 14 and 18, also live with him.
BAILLIF, Claude	58	Native of Picardy. Farmer. His wife and a daughter of 18 years are with him. Another daughter is married and living in France.

Note: Ritter and Baillif are on the lands of the late M. DE LA TOUR.

Name	Age	Comments
BAILLIF, Joseph	22	Native of Dieux in Lorraine. German. Farmer. His wife is with him. He has bought 8 arpents of land from a man named PROVENCHE.
SMITZ, Nicolas	40	Native of Frankfort. Roman Catholic. His wife and two daughters, aged 18 and 6, are with him. He bought 8 arpents of land from a man named MALBOROUK.

Name	Age	Comments
BAYER, Pierre	23	Native of the vicinity of Philisbourg. Roman Catholic. Farmer. His wife is with him.
FOUX (that is to say RENARD), Jean	38	Roman Catholic. Native of Bern. His wife and infant daughter are with him. He has bought 4 arpents of land from LANGLOIS who lives at Bayou St. Jean.
RITTER, Laurent (son)	20	He has 8 arpents of land that he bought from François DUGAY who live at Bayou St. Jean.
DAIGLE, Estienne	27	Native of Quebec. Called MALBOROUK. His wife and three orphan children are with him. He has bought 12 arpents of land from ST. AMANT.
VIGIER, Louis	35	Native of Montreal. His wife and infant son are with him. He has seven Negroes and one Indian on the place.
RICHAUME, Pierre	26	Native of Quebec. His wife and two children, aged 2 and 1, are with him. He has two Negroes on the place.
LARCHE, Joseph (the younger)	28	Native of Quebec. He has harvested 150 barrels of rice after being on the land only one year. His brother lives on the other side of the river.
CARON, Jean	20	Native of Peronne in Picardy. His wife and two orphan children, aged 2 and 3, are with him.
PAILHOUX, M. de		The farm of M. de Pailhoux, who came to Louisiana on the CHAMEAU.

MARCH, 1725

CENSUS OF THE RESIDENTS OF DAUPHIN ISLAND, MOBILE AND PASCAGOULAS.

Name	Negroes	Women (Wives)	Children
AT DAUPHIN ISLAND			
RENAULT	7		
HERVIEUX		1	3
AT MOBILE			
LA TOUR	23	1	
BOURGIGNON			
TALON			
LUSSER	9	1	2
LES CHACTO			
DU BREUIL	12	1	4
OLLIVIER	15	1	2
ROCHON	15	1	5
CABEL			
MIRAGOIN	6	1	4
HUET	4	1	4
BARREAU		1	
AT PASCAGOULA			
LA POINTE, Joseph	5	1	3
LAVERGNE	5		2
LA MOTTE	10		
GRAVELINE	17		2
ST. LAURENT	1		1
BONON		1	
BRASSELIE		1	2
LAGARDE	19		
CRISTIAN		1	2

JANUARY 1, 1726

CENSUS OF THE INHABITANTS OF LOUISIANA

Name	Wife	Children	Engagés or Domestics	Slaves Negro	Slaves Indian	Land Cleared in arpents
BEGINNING WITH M. BIENVILLE'S LANDS AT NEW ORLEANS AND GOING UP THE EAST SIDE OF THE MISSISSIPPI RIVER TO CHAPITOULAS.						
On M. Bienville's land are his two nephews and M. DE MOUY	?	?	2	4	2	100
GERMAN RETAINERS ON M. BIENVILLE'S LAND						
GASPARD	yes	2				4
OUNERE, Jacques	yes	1				5
SECREMENT, André	yes	2				4
IGOUETTE, Jacques (homme de force)						2
LE ROY & BELLAIR (associates)	yes		1	1		15
COMME, Simon	yes		2			5
POPE, Daniel	yes	1				3
LAISNE, Thomas	yes		1			3
CREPE, André	yes	1				6
VERRET, Joseph	yes		2			4
BONNAUD, Sieur (former Storekeeper)			1	8		10
CHAPITOULAS						
VECONOME, Dulude of the Ste. Reyne Concession		2	10	83		150
DUBREUIL, Sieur. Concessionary	yes	2	5	48	2	200
CHAUVIN DE LERY		3	2	95	2	150
CHAUVIN LAFRENIERE	yes	3	2	115	3	150
CHAUVIN BEAULIEU	yes	3	2	44	4	150
PROVIDENCE						
L'ARCHE, François	yes	1				6
SOUDRET, Jean and an associate	yes	1				4
PELLEGRIN, Henry	yes	2				4

Name	Wife	Children	Engagés or Domestics	Slaves Negro	Slaves Indian	Land Cleared in Arpents
PROVIDENCE (cont.)						
COUSIN, Pierre	yes	1				4
LAMALATIE, Louis and an associate						4
CANNES BRULEES						
DIRON'S Concession			2	23		80
DARTAGNAN'S Concession. M. BENAC, director			3	29	4	80
DAUPHIN, François (père)	yes	1				6
DAUPHIN, François (fils)	yes					4
PUJAULT, Jacques	yes					4
CHENAL, François	yes	2	1			4
DUCHESNE, René	yes					4
POCHES, Jacques and an associate	yes					4
QUINDRE, Joseph and and associate	yes	2				5
VILLAGE OF COLAPISSAS						
DATON, Philippes and an associate	yes	1				4
BELLEAUDAU, Pierre	yes	1	1			5
LA COSTE and an associate	yes	2				6
CEZAR, Pierre	yes	1				6
SOMMIER, Pierre	yes	2				6
GOUIS, Augustin and an associate	yes					5
LAMAURY, Pierre and an associate	yes					6
OUMAS						
COLIN, François	yes			2	3	6
BARBEAU, Jean	yes	2				6
LA CHEVALIER						
BARON, Pierre	yes	1	5			8

Name	Wife	Children	Engagés or Domestics	Slaves Negro	Slaves Indian	Land Cleared in Arpents
POINTE COUPEE						
POULAIN, Gabriel	yes		3			8
LEGROS, Albert	yes	2				6
DE CUIR, Albert and		3				
an associate			1			9
DOEGON, François and an associate, his brother-in- law	yes	3				6
THE TUNICA VILLAGE						
RENCOU, Thomas	yes					4
CHANTIN, ?	yes	1				4
GOURON, Paul	yes	1				6
GERMAIN, Pierre	yes	1				4
LEMOINE, Pierre	yes		1			6
RONDEAU, Jean	yes	1				6
BARBIER, Pierre	yes	2				5
DUPRE, Jacques	yes	1	1			7
HEBERT, Nicolas	yes	1				4
PAILLARD, Nicolas and an associate			2			7
HAURY, Pierre	yes	1	1			7
CARTAN, Joseph	yes	2				4
PERRET, Jean	yes	2				4
JOLICOEUR and	yes	1				
an associate						4
CONRANT, André	yes	3				6
INHABITANTS ON THE WEST SIDE OF THE RIVER DESCENDING FROM THE TUNICA VILLAGE						
BAYOUGOULA						
Concession of PARIS DU VERNEY. M. LE VERTEUIL, his wife, his (her) sister and DU BUISSON			6	15	1	70
THE GERMAN VILLAGE						
RAVILLE, Jean	yes					6
LAMBERT, Simon	yes	1				6
FREDERIC, Conrad	yes	5				6

Name	Wife	Children	Engagés or Domestics	Slaves Negro	Slaves Indian	Land Cleared in Arpents
THE GERMAN VILLAGE (cont.)						
PECK, Jean Georges and	yes					
PECK, Jean Georges (fils) associates	yes	1				6
VIQUE, Bernard	yes	3				6
MAGRE, Claude	Mother					4
QUERJAC, Guillaume	yes					4
CALENDRE, Jean	yes	(Mother-in-law & sister-in-law)				6
MARON, Baltazard	yes	1				6
RISTAMPER, Etienne	yes	1				6
VAGUER, Jeremie	yes	(and Sister-in-law)				6
MADOLFE, Leonard	yes	1				6
SCANTIER, André	yes	2				6
PITOCH, Georges	yes	2				6
ADAM, Jean	yes	2 (and his sister-in-law)				6
TOUK, Gaspard	yes	2				6
KIER, Ambroise	yes	1 (his brother & brother-in-law)				6
RITTER, Jacques	yes					4
TOQUET, Michel	yes	2				4
FAISIQ, Sebastien	yes	2				4
KONE, Michel	yes					4
SOREUR, André	yes	2				4
D'ARENSBOURG, Frederik	yes	1	1			10
DARQUER, André	yes					4
ROLLIER, Jean	yes					4
RODOCHE, Bernard	yes	2				4
KAMPLE, Paul	yes	1				4
SOHUL, Adam	yes					4
THIEL, Marçon	yes					4
ORISMAN, Jean	yes	2				6
MERQUERLA, Frederik	yes					4
MUNIQUE, Pitre	yes	1				4
ROZERE, Jean Georges	yes	3 (and his brother-in-law)				6
VAGUEUR, Joseph	yes	1				6
SAUMSEL, André	yes	1				4
EDETMER, Jean Adam	yes	3				6
RABELLE, Jacques	yes	4				6
FREDERIK, Mathias	yes	3				6
FORETS, Jacques	yes	1				4
ANTOINE, Bernard	yes	1	1			6
HOKMAN, André		2				4
JUIN, Philippes	yes	1				4
GRABERT, Cristian	yes	(and his sister-in-law, his mother-in-law and his sister)				6
DE MEUVES Concession at Tensas, Sieur DELAIRE, Director			2			?

Name	Wife	Children	Engagés or Domestics	Slaves Negro	Slaves Indian	Land Cleared in Arpents.
ON THE WEST BANK OF THE MISSISSIPPI RIVER BETWEEN THE GERMAN COAST AND OPPOSITE THE CITY OF NEW ORLEANS,DESCENDING THE RIVER.						
SAINTON, François	yes	3	1			6
CHEMIN	yes	1 (and his brother-in-law)				4
ST. JULIEN, M.			1	8		12
MOULAYE, François	yes	1			1	4
LE ROUX, Antoine						2
BAILLIF, Joseph	yes	1	1			6
VERNAY, Jean	yes	2	1			4
QUELLE, Laurens	yes					4
BAILLOU, Claude	yes	1				4
On the farm of M. PETIT DE LIVILLIERS			1	2		18
CHEMIN, Nicolas	yes	2				6
FOUQUET, Jean	yes	1				6
CHESNE, Jean	yes					4
L'AIGLE, Etienne	yes		1			6
VIGIER, Louis	yes	1				6
RICHAUME, Pierre	yes	3	1	3		8
L"ARCHE, Sieur	yes	2	2	3	1	8
LA GOUBLAYE	yes	2	1	2	1	6
On the farm of the late M. PAILLOUX				16		60
ON THE COMPANY'S FARM ACROSS THE RIVER FROM NEW ORLEANS.						
PERRIE, M. director			1	25		60
ON M. BIENVILLE's OTHER FARM ABOUT 5 MILES BE-LOW NEW ORLEANS ON THE WEST BANK			1	45		100
PROVENCHE			1	2		25
EMMERY	yes					30
LA PIERRE	yes					12
PAUL	yes					?
BOURBEAU	yes	2		4	1	?
PLAISANCE	yes			1		6
PERRY's farm	---	-	-	-	-	-
FAZENDE's farm	---	-	-	-	-	-
MASSY			3	19		80
BARRE				1		25
BALCONS				4		30
COUSSINE	yes	3				?

Name	Wife	Children	Engagés or Domestics	Slaves Negro	Slaves Indian	Land Cleared in Arpents
DESCENDING THE WEST BANK OF THE RIVER TOWARD THE MOUTH (cont.)						
BIGOT						?
TREPANIER, Widow		5		17	2	180
LABRO	yes			16		80
St. Catherine Concession. M. DUMANOIR director				20		100
DASFELD Concession				23	1	100
FARMS ON THE EAST BANK OF THE MISSISSIPPI RIVER GOING FROM THE MOUTH TO NEW ORLEANS						
DRAPEAU	yes	4				20
DESLAUS				5		190
CARRIERE, François				30	9	70
FAGUIER, Joseph and NOTSET, Nicolas	yes					6
CARRIERE, Jacques	yes			4		50
CARRIERE, Joseph	yes	3		13	1	60
TIXERANT	yes	4		42	6	60
BOYER			2	1		18
CHENAL		1				15
On Bruslé's farm				2		15
FILLARD, Sieur			1			12
LEONARD and his son						10
CHAMILLY				9		20
MANADE	yes					40
LA LOIRE JOUSSET	yes			5	1	20
ROCHON			1	3		25
CHAPERON				5		50
LA LIBERTE	yes			6		50
On Mandeville's farm			1	6	1	15
On Raguet's farm			1	17		100
On the Maretz brothers' farm				4		30
Raphael (Free Negro)						3
DALCOUR	yes	1		16		90
ON Dupuis Planchard's farm			1	4		250
TRUDEAU				25		300
COUSTILLAS				11	2	140
SENER, Rex	yes	2				10
DARBY			2	11		60
On Chavannes' farm				2	1	16
The brewery of the DREUX brothers			2	2		

Name	Wife	Children	Engagés or Domestics	Slaves Negro	Slaves Indian	Land Cleared in Arpents
NATCHEZ						
The TERRE BLANCHE Con cession of the Marquis Dasfeld, Sieur BROUTIN, director			7	31		100
The STE. CATHERINE Concession of M. Kolly and associates, M. DE LONGRAYS, director			22	25	4	150
The concession of PELLERIN and his associate			3	4		21
The concession of LA PAGE				2	3	5
CHAUVEAU DE BEAUMONT		2				?
PAPIN, René	yes	2	1			3
ELOY, Etienne	yes	3				2
ROUSSEAU, Jean						2
VILLENEUVE, Hardy	yes					5
LE FRET, Jacques	yes					3
GOUPILLA, Mathurin						2
HURLOT, Laurent (called LA SONDE)			1	1		4
BARA, Jean	yes					4
GUIBARA (called BEAU-SOLEIL)						2
HENRY, Louis	yes	1				4
SOILEAU, Noël	yes					2
MARTIN, Guillaume (called LA LANDE)						1
MONTUY, Simon		1				4
PINSONNEAU, Michel (called BIGNON)						2
JOUARD, Antoine	yes		1	2	1	12
ROUSSIN, Jean	yes	2				2
FRETIN, François	yes	1				3
VERNET, Jean	yes	1				4
FLANDRIN, Jean	yes	2				3
CORDELIER, Louis	yes					3
LOUET and MANSEAU, associates						4
RIVE, Etienne	yes	2				2
LA COUR, Nicolas	yes					3
BEAU, Michel	yes					3

Name	Wife	Children	Engagés or Domestics	Slaves Negro	Slaves Indian	Land Cleared in Arpents
NATCHEZ (cont.)						
BIDEAU, Simon						3
DEVEL, Jean	yes	2				2
HAMBAR, Jean François	yes					?
CHARTIER, Julien	yes	1				4
CHIT, Jean (called ALLEMAND)	yes					3
FOUCAULT, Anselme	yes	1				2
ROUSSEAU, Nicolas and an associate		1				4
MIRAULT, Louis	yes	1				1
MORON, Urbin	yes	2				1
FRONIN, Sebastien	yes				1	2
DEPART, Jean	yes	2				1
DILLON, Jean	yes					2
DANTIN,Philippes	yes					
BOITET, Guillaume			1			1
HAYNAULT, René	yes					2
RICHARD, Allain and an associate	yes					?
Retainers on the Terre Blance Concession			9			
Retainers on the Ste. Reyne Concession			10			
RAGUET, Sieur						?
YAZOO						
POUVALAIN,Etienne and	yes					
PEZE (called LE BLONS) and LE COUREUR	yes					9
ILLINOIS						
On the farm of MM. BOISBRIANT and LALOIRE			2	22		100
RENAUD, M.			3	20		80
LA CROIX	yes	5		1		5
ROLLET	yes	2				5
NEAU	yes				2	30
GIARD						4
PREE	yes	2				4
RICHARD						3
BONTEMS	yes	1				2
NICAPORT						4

Name	Wife	Children	Engagés or Domestics	Slaves Negro	Slaves Indian	Land Cleared in Arpents
BARON	yes	1				4
DARBONNE	yes	1				4
CHAPU	yes			2	3	6
LOISEL	yes			2	1	?
HEBERT	yes			4		6
SANS CHAGRIN	yes	2				10
FABUS						?
TIMONIER						20
DUTRON	yes					4
BOURGMONT						4
BAPTISTE (Negro)			1			6
L'ESPAGNOL, Joseph	yes	2				5
L'ESPAGNOL, Antoine						5
BIRON		1				4
ST. JEAN	yes					?
LA FOREST						10
BECQUET	yes	2				4
LAJEUNE LALANDE						?
PRADEL				2		?
BARCELONE						5
DUSABLON	yes					5
DES ESSARTS						?
ROBILLARD	yes				1	10
DRAGON						5
CHASSIN	yes	2			2	10
LA JEUNESSE (called LEGROS)					2	8
LA PLUME		1		3		8
BELLEGARDE		2		1	2	20
LANGEVIN	yes					?
ST. PIERRE	yes	1			1	7
LANTURLU	yes					5
GARDON	yes	1				6
ANTOINE	yes					5
CANAREL and associate						8
ROBIN and associate				1		8
DANIEL						6
CAPITAINE	yes			1		4
ST. JACQUES	yes	1				6
PIERRE						6
GOUVERNEUR & LEBRUN						4
BELHUMEUR	yes					8
MARIN	yes	1				4
DAUPHINE	yes	2				3
BEAUSEJOUR & associate						8
THOMAS						6
BELLEROSE					1	5
LE NORMAND						4

Name	Wife	Children	Engagés or Domestics	Slaves Negro	Slaves Indian	Land Cleared in Arpents
ILLINOIS (cont.)						
TEXIER	yes	1				8
LA POINTE	yes	1		2		20
HEBERT, Ignace						10
TURPIN, Widow		2			1	?
Four Priests			2	9	2	100
GIRARDEAU	yes	1	1	1	1	33
MELIQUE (officer) & LA JEUNESSE	yes	1			1	70
LA FATIGUE	yes	2				35
DES VIGNES	yes	2		5	2	24
LALANDE LAISNE	yes	4	1	1	4	50
DU LONGPRE	yes	2	3	2	4	50
CARRIERE	yes	2	1	11	1	80
LE VIEUX POTIER	yes	4		1	2	80
DESLAURIES	yes	1	2		1	20
LEJEUNE TURPIN	yes	4	2	2	2	30
BAILLARGEON	yes	2	3	3	2	30
COLLET						10
DE LAUNAY	yes	2	1		2	40
LAMY	yes	3	1 (and his nephew)			150
PHILIPPES, Michel	yes	6	2	5	3	100
ST. PIERRE	yes	2		2		30
LA SONDE	yes	1	2		1	56
BOURBONNOIS	yes	3		2	5	150
BOSSEROT, Leonard	yes	4	1	7	2	100
MERCIER	yes	1	1			35
OLLIVIER	yes					?
CLIVET	yes	2				?
POTIER (the younger)	yes	1	1	4	2	40
LA RENAUDIERE	yes	2				?
MALET	yes					12
CADOUINET	yes			1	1	20
BEAUJOLY						10
LALANDE (the younger)	yes	3	1	6	6	150
FRANCHOMME (officer)	yes		1	3	1	20
LA RIGUEUR	yes		1			10
BIENNANT (the younger)					1	20
ADAM						5
DE NOYON						?
GAUTIER	yes					?
HEBERT	yes			1		15
BOISSEAU	yes	2				?
LIBERGE						?
ST. CERNAY						4
LA BONTE (Tailor)			1			
TAILLOUX	yes	2				?
PORTIE	yes					?
ST. JEAN	yes	4				?
PIGNET (PIGUET?) (gun-smith)						
LA VIGNE						10
DU LUDE						?

JULY 1, 1727

CENSUS OF THE DEPARTMENT OF NEW ORLEANS

Name	Wife	Children	Engagés or Domestics	Slaves Negro	Slaves Indian	Comments
PERIER, M. Governor of the Province	yes		4	5		
CHAMBELLAN, M.						Perier's sons.
PERIER, M.						
MONDROLLOIS, Sieur						Perier's Secretary
LA CHAISE, M. de Commissary of the King						
BOISBRIANT, M. de Lieutenant of the King						
GRAU, Sieur Director of the Hospital						
<u>PERSONS IN THE HOSPITAL</u>						
LE FEUVES, Jacques						sailor
VIEL, Jean; Child of						
CHAMPION, Guillaume						
LE JET, Pierre						Cooper
FORGERON, Jaria						
JOHANNE, Jean						Carpenter
ALLEMAND, Pierre						
BALTAZARD						A German
JEMETEL, Jacques						Farmer
KOBOCK						Swiss farmer
LOEIL, Joseph						Laborer
MOUSSET, Jacques						Indigo worker
RINGAL, Wife of		2				
LORIN, Wife of						
LA VIOLETTE, Wife of						
BOURDON, Wife of		1				
BALTAZARD, Wife of		1				
LA PIERRE, Wife of						
ST. JEAN, Wife of						
LALAFOND, Wife of						

Name	Wife	Children	Engagés or Domestics	Slaves Negro	Slaves Indian	Comments
QUAY STREET						
DAMARON, Sieur	yes			2	1	apothicary
RAGUET, Sieur	yes	4		4		
BELLEVEUE, M.	yes	1				Concierge
DURIVAGE, Sieur	yes	1	3	2	1	Shopkeeper
DUVAL, Sieur François	yes	1		2	1	Head Cashier
MAISSONNEUVE, Sieur						DUVAL's clerk
PREVOST, Sieur						Head Bookkeeper
BAILLY, Sieur						Assistant
PELLERIN, Sieur						Head Storekeeper
MORISSET, Sieur						Employee
BLANPIN, Dame						Washerwoman
CARITOIN, Sieur	yes	1	4			Tailor
ROY						Founder
ROGER						
LOEIL, Chartier	yes	3				At the hospital.
BORDIER, Michel			2			Baker
BONNEAUD, M.			2	1	1	Former Storekeeper
BROUTIN, M. and GOUNICHON, M.			2	2		
NOYAN, M. de (elder) and his brother				9		
PICH, Jean Georges	yes	2				A German
MUNIER, David	yes					Carpenter
BOELLE, Estienne						Carpenter
ADAM, Nicolas						Barber
LE BRISSON, Gilles						
ADRIEN, M.						Carpenter
ROTUREAU, Honnoré						Miller
DORE, Julien						Carpenter
CHARTRES STREET						
GAMBIE	yes					Carpenter
DUBOIS						Carpenter
LE BLANC, M.				2	1	
MORAND, M.	yes			7	1	Inspector of workers
ST. MARTIN, M. de						
BIMONT, M. and BERNOUDAT, Sieur			1			
FOST, Jean	yes	1				
BRUSLE, M.	yes	1				Councilor
MANDEVILLE, M.	yes	1				Major
PRAT, M.						Doctor

Name	Wife	Children	Engagés or Domestics	Slaves Negro	Slaves Indian	Comments
CHARTRES STREET (cont.)						
ROBERT, Bonnaventure	yes					Tailor
FACIR, Antoine						Apprenticed Tailor
SARAZIN, Sieur	yes	3				
VALLERAN, Sieur	yes	1	1			Block-maker
LA GARDE, M. de						Director of CHAUMONT's Concession
LEMOINE, Charles François	yes					Carpenter
PENIGAULT, Toinnette Zambon		1				
DUBUISSON, Sieur						Employee of the Council
ROSSARD, M. and			2			Recorder of the Council
DROY, M.						Rossard's Clerk
An Indian Woman					1	Belonging to M. Renaud, Cap.
DECOUR, Sieur and TESSON (associates)						
CLAIREFONTAINE, Sieur						Employee at the Company store
RECHE, Arnaud	yes	3				Called BEL-LAIR
OZANNE, Jacques						Edged-tool maker
LE MAIRE, Simon						Edged-tool maker
PASSERAT, Pierre						Gardener
THOMELIN, Pierre	yes	2				Carpenter
BRUSLE, M.	yes			1		
CONDE STREET						
RAPHAEL, Father			1	1	1	Grand Vicar
THEODORE, Father						
SIRIET, Brother						
ASSELIN, Thomas	yes	1				
FASARD, Marie (Widow)		1				
LASSUS, M. de			2			Engineer
CARON, Jean	yes		1			Baker
CHERNU, Jean Baptiste						
STE. LUCE						A German Carpenter
PERAUL, Toussaint						

Name	Wife	Children	Engagés or Domestics	Slaves Negro	Slaves Indian	Comments
CONDE STREET (cont.)						
MOREAU, Joseph		3				Metal Wor
MALOT, Antoine	yes					Tailor
PONYADON						Surgeon
HEN, Claude						
VILLEUR, André						
PROVENCHE, Jean Baptiste	yes			1		
PECHE, Claude Imbert	yes	1				
CHEVALIER, Barbe						
TRUDEAU, Madame		4	1	4		
VUIME, Jean	yes	1				Carpenter Called CA PENTRAS
DOYART, Marie Magdelaine						Wife of René MALA Called SA CHAGRIN
MERANGUIER						
ROBERT, Pierre						Carpenter
ROYAL STREET						
MUGUET, François						
BRETON, Marie Louise (Widow)		2				
LATULIPE, Jean						Ex-soldie stationed at Mobile
FONDELCK, Albert		2				A German farmer.
TOURNELOTTE, Marie (Widow)		2				
GRANDJEAN						
CHEVALIER, Marie						Wife of S GRAU
GOMMET, Claude	yes	1				Called CO TOIS. Com mander of Fortifica tions.
FICHON, Nicolas	yes	2				Candlemak
BARTHELEMY, Antoine		2 (one orphan)				
CHESNAU, Hilaire		1				Gunner
MICOU, Antoine						Carpenter
MICHAU						Day-labor
ABUCOIN, Simon						Carpenter
BONNAVENTURE, Françoise (Widow)		3	1	2		
BLANVILAIN						Day-labor
AUBERT	yes	1				
GONBIN, Charles						

Name	Wife	Children	Engagés or Domestics	Slaves Negro	Slaves Indian	Comments
ROYAL STREET (cont.)						
GRESLIN						Formerly on Law's Concession.
PETIT, Joseph	yes	2		1		Tiler
POIRIER, Livien	yes	1				Gunsmith
LEBOULAN, Francois	yes	2 (one an orphan)				Called SANS REGRET
ORSE, François						Edged-tool maker
MARIN, Claude François			1			
MONDAUBAN, Wife of		1				Her husband is a soldier
LE MOINE, Guillaume	yes	1				
LA RIVIERE, Antoine			1			LA RIVIERE is a sailor and is at Mobile
FONTAINE, Claude	yes	2				"Voyageur"
MICHEL, Roch	yes	4				Employee of the Council
BINARD, Julien	yes	1				Edged-tool maker
PERRIER, Guillaume	yes	2				Overseer on the Company farm
L'EVESQUE, Jean						
AUFRERE, Antoine	yes	1				
BOUSQUERAT, Guillaume						"Voyageur"
SERVAY						
BESSON	yes	1				"Voyageur"
JOBELIN, Antoine	yes					Called SANS SOUCY. "Voyageur."
CAILLON, Pierre	yes	1				Mason
PIERROT, Nicolas						Called VENDOME
LE VENNE, Antoine	yes	1				
PINVILLE, Marianne						Wife of de BREDA, soldier
JARRY, Louis	yes				1	Innkeeper
JARRY, Jean Baptiste	(Brother of above)					
LAJOYE						
ROGER, Charles						
BEAUPRE, Jean Baptiste						
A Negro Domestic belonging to M. DE MOUY.						

Name	Wife	Children	Engagés or Domestics	Slaves Negro	Slaves Indian	Comments
FAZENDE, M.	yes	1				His mother, Madame MOLIES is with him.
HARPIN, Claude						Merchant
DAUVILLE, Florent	yes	2				
DUPUY PLANCHARD, M.	yes	1				Officer
A Negro belonging to M. DEMERVEILLEUX				1		
VINCENT, Jacques	yes					Doorkeeper for the Council
DUMANOIR, M.				1	2	
LANGLOIS, Sieur						
LA LIVAUDAIS, M. de						
ESTIENNE, M.						
PERILLAUT, M.						
PAQUIER, M.						
<u>BOURBON STREET</u>						
LEBLEU, Paul	yes	1				
L'ANTIC, Gratien	yes	3				Worker
VITREQUIN, François		2				Called COUILLARD. He is at Natchez
LARTAUD, Pierre Sebastien	yes	1				
PICQUERIC, Pierre	yes	2	1			Baker
SAUNIER, Jacques						Founder
DETRONQUIDY, M.	yes	2				Captain of the <u>LOIRE</u>
PATIN, Antoine	yes	4				Carpenter
FONTAINE, Baptiste						Apprenticed carpenter
BERTEAUD, André	yes		1			
OUDAR, Catherine						Widow of the late BEAULIEU, sargeant.
DORMOIS, Claude	yes	2				Day-laborer
MANSIAN, François	yes	2 (Children are for PHILIDOR)				Carpenter
PHILIDOR, Louis	yes	2 (Which are the above)				Carpenter
LA CLAYE, François	yes					Major of the Company.
LA VALLE, Christine (Widow)						
CALLAIR, François	yes					Carpenter
ALIX, François	yes					Brewer. Called LA ROSE
GERNAY, Renaude	(An orphan living with ALIX)					

Name	Wife	Children	Engagés or Domestics	Slaves Negro	Slaves Indian	Comments
<u>BOURBON STREET</u> (cont.)						
LE DUC, Philipes	yes					Metal worker
POULIN, Estienne	yes					Day-laborer
FERAND, Pierre						At the Houmas
GAUTIER, Wife of						He is a soldier.
THOMAS, Christophe						Laborer
EVRARD						Carpenter
RONDEAU, Jean	yes					Carpenter
RAFLAUD, Daniel	yes	2				Tiler
NEGRIER, Antoine	yes					
BABAS						Currier
AUJIBEAU						Carpenter
BROSSET, Michel				1		Surgeon
COQUELIN, Jacques	yes	1				
FRONTIER, François	yes	1				Metal worker
L'ANGLOIS						Metal worker
DARTEL, Nicolas	yes					Hunter
DUPRE, Jacques	yes	1				Carpenter
BERNARD, Wife of						He is a soldier
CARDON, Joseph	yes					Farmer
LEQUESNE, Pierre						Tiler
GARNIER, Marie Geneviève		1				Wife of SANNUE
ST. QUENTIN						He is at Natchez
MARIE, Joseph						Employed by a fisherman
BOURDON, Jean François	yes	3				Carpenter
BUNEL, Antoine	yes	1				Wheelwright
BRANTANT, Nicolas						Gunsmith
LEON						Nail-maker
GAPAYEL						Nail-maker
MONSIGNAC						"Voyageur" Called PIPIC
BLOQUIN, Jean			1			
CARON, Michel	yes					
ROCHE, Jean						Carpenter
DIDIER, Gaspard	yes	2				Carpenter
DUTOUR, Sieur						
BUSEAU						
BORE, Jean Baptiste	yes					
VINCENT, Charles						Sailor
LAJEUNE, Anne Margueritte						Wife of Charles VINCENT
BAGUETTE, Wife of						

Name	Wife	Children	Engagés or Domestics	Slaves Negro	Slaves Indian	Comments
A STREET WHICH INTERSECTS THE END OF BOURBON ST.						
BAUDOUIN, Pierre	yes	1				Day-laborer
HUPE, François	yes	1				Former sailor
BOUCHER			1			
BARRE, Gilbert	yes	2				Sailor
DUPUIS, Charles						Called ORLEANS. He is hunting in Arkansas.
FOUCHER, Guillaume	yes	1				Nail-maker
LECLERC, Pierre	yes	1				
SERPILLON, Jean	yes					
ON THE BAYOU ROAD						
MARCHAND, Nicolas	yes					
LAFONTAINE, Martin						Sailor
SILARD, Jacques						"Voyageur"
GENTILHOMME	yes	1				Canoe owner
COUTOIS, Pierre	yes	2		1		
MEGNEUX, Antoine						Nail-maker
CONTI STREET						
CHAVANNES, M. de				2		Secretary to the Council
FLEURIAU, M.	yes			8		Attorney-General
MANADE, M.	yes					Surgeon
GENOT, M.						
SET, Antoine	yes	2				A German
BOULANGER, Magdelaine		2				Wife of Sr. Vauvray
GAGNEUR, François	yes	1				Fisherman
THULIE, Jazabelle			1 (an orphan)			Wife of BONPART
LE BOURGEOIS						Wife of DELAURIERS
REINE						
ALEXANDRE, M.	yes		1	3		Surgeon
COSSARD, Joseph		(Lives with ALEXANDRE)				
ROBIDON, Sebastien						Builder
FAUVAU, Magdelaine						
SOISSONS		1				Carpenter
LOTTIER, Baptiste						He is at Natchez
MARTIN						

Name	Wife	Children	Engagés or Domestics	Slaves Negro	Slaves Indian	Comments
CONTI STREET (Cont.)						
BAYAN		1				They are a Natchez
C_____, Maurice	yes					A German
CHRISTIAN, Nicolas	yes					
ST. LOUIS STREET						
DUPLESSY, Sieur						
COMANT (COURANT?), Sieur						
STE MARIE						
PETACHE						
ST. AMANT, Jean François	yes	2			1	
JET, Ignace	yes					Carpenter
BACHELET, Marie Magdelaine (widow)						
DELATTES, Antoine Joseph						Carpenter
LAMBERT, Wife of						He is a soldier
PICHOT, Therese						
AVOT, Gilles	yes	1				Founder
SAUNIER, François						Sailor
TOULOUSE STREET						
DIZIER, François	yes	2				Barber
CHAPE Claude						
BARBE						
DUGUES, Louis	yes	2		3		Surgeon
LA GOUBLAYE	yes	2		3		Bookkeeper at the Co. Store
FILASSIER, Etienne						
CORDON, Nicolas						
VINANTE (VIVANTE?), Jean						Fisherman
CHATEAU, Nicolas M artin du						Shoemaker
CARNET, Pierre	yes	1				Sawyer
BOURELLIER, Toussaint						Carpenter
BRUNEST, François						Founder
LOT, Pierre						Carpenter. He is at Natchez
DAVRIL, Michel						
CARIE, Marianne						
DUMAS, Jean						
LOUISSON, Claudine						Wife of a soldier.
ST. PETER STREET						
GELARD, François	yes	5		1		
HUMBERT, Nicolas	yes	1				Founder
LEFORGE, Marianne		1				

Name	Wife	Children	Engagés or Domestics	Slaves Negro	Slaves Indian	Comments
ST. PETER ST. (cont.)						
VALENVINNE, Therese		1				
ROCHER, André	yes					"Voyageur"
SINNARD, Mathurin			1			Sailor
VIGNOLLE, Anne						Wife of SINNARD
POTIER, François			1			Sailor
RAGUETTE, Pierre						
PROUET, Nicolas	yes	1				Wheelwright
BARBIER		2				He is at the Tunica village
PINET, Yves						Gunsmith
JOU, Jacques						Soldier. His sister is with him.
ROBERT, Jean		3				A soldier
CONARD, André	yes	2				Wheelwright
MENEROLLE, Maturin	yes					Metal worker
LE COMTE, Pierre						Wheelwright
METAYER, Wife of Jean						He is a corporal, called LA NIVIERE
OUDIN, Jean						Called LAFONTAINE
LARZILLIERS, Marie		1				Wife of CARDON
VAQUIER, Jean						Tiler
BAILLY, Vivien	yes	1				Sailmaker
SENET, M.		1				Captain of the port.
ORLEANS STREET						
GARGARET, Pierre	yes	1				Doorkeeper for the Council
JOUTEUR, François	yes	1				
MARTINOT, Pierre	yes	1				
LEGER, Jean						Carpenter
BELAIR, Wife of						He is a soldier
VANEUL, Jean						Gunsmith
AMELOS, Joseph		1				Fisherman
CANTEREL, Jacques	yes					
CAFFE, Françoise		1				Widow of SAMSON

Name	Wife	Children	Engagés or Domestics	Slaves Negro	Slaves Indian	Comments
ORLEANS STREET (cont.)						
LOUIS, Jean						Canoe owner
GOFFION, Antoine						Day-laborer
FONDER, François	yes		1			His sister is with him.
BION, M.			2			
HONNORE			(He is an Engagé)			Overseer
LAMBERT	yes	1				Overseer
TYET, Pierre						Cooper
FONTAINE, Pierre François	yes					Tailor
LE HOUX, Pierre	yes	1				On his way to Arkansas
BOCHE, Nicolas		2				He is a resident of Yazoo
COURSAN, André	yes	3				Butcher
LEDAIN, Louis						Tailor
COURSAN, André	yes	1				Farmer
DAUSSEVILLE, M.				3		Councilor
GUILLAIN, Robert	yes	1				Shoemaker
NOISET, Nicolas	yes	1				
ST. ANN STREET						
ALARD, Christine		3				Wife of Jean LABE
DELISLE, Pierre Joseph	yes	1				Called DUPART
LAZON, Joseph	yes					
DURAND, Charles						Called LAFUILLADE
DEJERBOIS, François						
HERISE, François (Wife of)		2				He is a soldier
LOM, Antoine	yes	1	1			Tailor
PERON, Louis	yes		(He is an engagé)			Sailor
JEANDRAU			(He is an engagé)			Sailor
VIVIER, Guillaume			(He is an engagé)			Sailor
MARLESGOF			(He is an engagé)			Sailor
MELAIN, Jean	yes					Founder. Called D'ORANGE
MAIRAIN, Wife of Claude						He is a soldier.
JARDELA, Alain	yes	1				Charcoal maker
CLERAU, Pierre						Founder
DANIEL						Whitewasher

Name	Wife	Children	Engagés or Domestics	Slaves Negro	Slaves Indian	Comments
ST ANN STREET (cont.)						
BODESON, Claude				1		Founder
LA GONSALEAU						Wife of a soldier at Mobile.
COURTABLEAU, Wife of		2				Her husband deserted 5 years ago.
TOUZE, Nicolas			(He is an engagé)			Sailor- Called RI-CHARD
GAUTIER, Julien			(He is an engagé)			Sailor. He is at Mobile
DUMAINE STREET						
MUNIER, M.						A Canadian
GUYON, M.						A Canadian
BERLIN, Isabelle		1				Wife of Jean PASCAL
BIGUARD, Jean	yes	1				Cooper
CHARLES, Claude						Tailor
JELIZOT, Wife of Jean						He has gone to France
BARRATON, Estienne	yes	1	They live on Chermont St.			Wagon-maker
NAVES, Jean						Day-laborer
CLAIREMONT STREET						
VEILLON, Jacques						Turner
LA DUSABLON						Her husband is in Ill.
LAPRERIE, Jean Philipe	yes					
FREDERICK, Wife of Jean de						He is called LAFONTAINE, and is a drummer.
MUGUET, Françoise						
FONDELICK, Albert	yes	2				A German farmer
BRETON, Marie Louis (Widow)		2				
TOURNELOTTE, Marie (Widow)		2				
CHEVALIER, Marie						Wife of Sr. GRAU
GOMET, Claude	yes	1				Commander of Fortifi-cations
FICHON, Nicolas	yes	2				
BERTHELEMY, Antoine		2	(One child an orphan)			Called LA GARENNE
CHESNAU, Hilaire		1				Gunner
MICHAUX						Day-laborer

Name	Wife	Children	Engagés or Domestics	Slaves Negro	Slaves Indian	Comments
CLAIREMONT STREET (cont.)						
ABINION, Simon						Carpenter
LEFEVRES, Françoise (Widow)		3				
BROUET, Louis		1				Wheelwright
LE MOINE, Marie		1				Wife of Charles MERCIER, called SANS CHAGRIN
LAVIOLETTE, Wife of		1				Her husband has been on the other side of the ocean for a long time.
GUIDON, Nicolas	yes	1	(He is an engagé)			Sailor
BERNOUDY, Sieur						Bookkeeper
MANE, Therese		(An orphan girl)				
COLIER, Wife of		2				He is a sargeant, called JOLLYCOEUR
RESIDENTS ON THE BAYOU ROAD AND CHANTILLY						
GODET	yes					
CONGO, Louis	yes					
GAUVRIT, M.	yes	3		5	1	Captain
LANGLOIS	yes	3		7		
JOSEPH	yes	4		15	2	
FRANCOIS			1	6		
RIVARD, M.	yes	5		22		
LAVIT	yes	2				
SAUBANNIER, M.	yes	2	1	5		
DREUX Brothers			1	12	2	
CAZIMBERT, Jean	yes	1				Lives on a farm owned by the Dreux Bros.
PARTIAL CENSUS OF THE INHABITANTS ON THE EAST SIDE OF THE MISSISSIPPI RIVER BETWEEN BALIZE AND NEW ORLEANS						
DUVERGIER, M						Commander at Balize
GASPARD, Father						Capuchin

Name	Wife	Children	Engagés or Domestics	Slaves Negro	Slaves Indian	Comments
FROM BALIZE (cont.)						
ST. MICHEL						Storekeeper
BALDIE						Surgeon
FIOU, François	yes	2				Chief Pilot
TRIET, Pierre	yes					2nd. Pilot
PINAULT						
LEBAS, Mathurin						Carpenter
DELAURIERS, Resin						Carpenter
LIGNY, François						Knacker
BUREAU, Jean						Knacker
GAY, Joseph						Called DAUPHINE
BAUGREMONT, Vincent						Knacker

End of the Census

AFTER 1731

LIST OF LANDOWNERS ALONG THE MISSISSIPPI RIVER FROM ITS MOUTH TO THE GERMAN VILLAGES WITH THE AMOUNT OF LAND EACH OWNS FRONTING ON THE RIVER.

Name	Comments
BEGINNING ON THE EAST SIDE OF THE RIVER JUST OUTSIDE OF NEW ORLEANS AND PROCEEDING DOWN STREAM TOWARD THE RIVER'S MOUTH.	
DREUX (the elder)	6 1/2 arpents. Two arpents by grant. 2 bought from Sieur LAGARDE and 2 1/2 bought from Sieur CHAVANNE.
D'ARBY	1 1/2 arpents bought from Sieur CHAVANNE.
CANTILLON	8 arpents by grant. 6 bought from Sieur BANESSE.
COUSTILLAS	19 arpents received in three grants.
LAPOMMERAY	6 arpents belonging to the Widow LABOULAY whom he married.
TRUDEAU	18 arpents acquired in three grants.
GAUVRIT	6 arpents bought from Estienne L'ANGLOIS.
DE LA CHAISE	10 1/2 arpents bought from Sieur DUPUY PLANCHARD
D 'ALCOURT	12 arpents bought from the estate of Sieur LE BLANC.
MARETS DUPUY	7 1/2 arpents acquired through grant.
MARETS DE LA TOUR	7 1/2 arpents acquired through grant.
RAGUET	5 arpents bought from the MARETS'
BROUTIN	10 arpents belonging to Widow DE MANDEUIL whom he married.
FLEURIAU	8 arpents received through grant and 6 arpents bought from Sieur MORAND.
JORY GIBERY (called ST. MARTIN)	8 arpents bought from the DREUX brothers.
The Ursulines	8 arpents received through grant.
D'AUSSEVILLE	7 arpents through grant and 12 bought from BERTRAND JAFFRE, called LA LIBERTE. 4 arpents from TERREBONNE
DEMORIERE	7 1/2 arpents received through grant.
The Capuchins	7 1/2 arpents received through grant.
JAFFRE, Bertrand	Called LA LIBERTE. 15 arpents by grant.
VAUPARIS	8 arpents by grant.
LA PRADE	8 arpents by possession and 4 bought from Joseph GIRARDY.
LOUBOYE	3 3/4 arpents by grant.
D'ESQUEIRAC	3 3/4 arpents by grant.
CHAPERON	12 arpents bought from ROCHON, 4 bought from LARCHEVEQUE and 8 by grant.
LALOIRE JOUSSET	10 arpents received in two grants.

Name	Comments
BACHEMIN	10 arpents bought from Sieur MANADE and 3 received by grant.
CHAMYLY	9 arpents by grant.
LEONARD	8 arpents by grant.
LIVETTE	12 arpents bought from the late Sieur SCHEPART (DECHEPART?)
MORISSET	12 arpents bought from Jacques and Romain ROFINAC
D'ALCOURT	9 1/2 arpents received from the Council.
MASSY	10 arpents bought from Sieur D'HAUTERIVE
BRUSLE	12 received by grant.
BALCOURT	4 arpents by grant and 4 bought from D'ARTELLE
PERARBE (Called TRACE MONTAGNE	4 arpents by grant.
FILLARD	9 arpents by grant and 6 bought from FAGUIER.
CHEVAL	4 arpents by grant and 6 bought from Nicolas NOISET.
BROSSET	5 arpents by grant.
BOYER and the late CLAIRE FONTAINE	16 arpents by grant.
TIXERANT	15 arpents belonging to the Widow CARRIERE whom he married and 4 belonging to him by grant.
CARRIERE, Joseph	11 arpents by grant.
CARRIERE, François	11 arpents by grant.
CARRIERE, Jacques	14 arpents by grant.
MEUNIER	8 arpents bought from Augustin L'ANGLOIS
SAUCIER, Widow	8 arpents by grant.
RIVART (son)	16 arpents received in 2 grants.
TRUDEAU (son)	12 arpents bought from DELAYE and 3 by possession
ARNAUD	18 arpents by grant and 2 by possession.
SAUCIER BROTHERS (4)	18 arpents by grant.
L'EMPILEUR	4 arpents by possession
LAMY	4 arpents by possession
PAQUET (the tailor)	4 arpents bought from the freed negro, Jean Baptiste.
PINET	4 arpents by grant and 4 by possession.
ROUGOT	6 arpents bought from ARNAUD.
ROBIN	12 arpents belonging to Sieur DELOT which he received after marrying DELOT's daughter.
ALEXANDRE (Surgeon major)	6 arpents bought from Nicolas PROUEST and 16 bought from Sieur ESTIENNE.
BUSSON	12 arpents by grant,
DRAPAUX	10 arpents by grant.
CARRIERE, François	8 arpents bought from LORRIN, 4 bought from ST. JOSEPH and 3 by possession.
BEAUPRE	4 arpents bought from François TRIBOULOU.

Name	Comments
MONTIGNIE	12 arpents by possession.
LUNELLE	6 arpents which he has abandoned. He has returned to France.
CASTEL (Called LILOIS)	8 arpents (abandoned).
RENAUD, Claude (called AVIGNON)	4 arpents by grant.
FAUCHEUX (called FRANCOEUR)	6 arpents by possession
COLLETTE, Louis (called JOLY COEUR)	6 arpents by possession
LA LIBARDIERE	6 arpents by possession
ROBIN	8 arpents bought from Gabrielle MARTIN
TRONQUIDY	12 arpents by grant
GUILLAUME	6 arpents by possession
FIOU (pilot at Balize)	8 arpents by possession
MADRE	8 arpents by possession

WEST SIDE OF THE RIVER BEGINNING DIRECTLY ACROSS FROM NEW ORLEANS AND PROCEEDING DOWN STREAM

Name	Comments
For the King	18 arpents
BOURGEOIS, Charles	8 arpents bought from M. BIENVILLE
BIENVILLE	44 arpents received as a concession from the directors of the Company of the Indies
BALDIC	10 arpents bought from AUBUCHON
PROVANCHEZ	8 arpents by contract with M. BIENVILLE
L'ANGLOIS, Augustin	9 arpents through agreement with M. BIENVILLE
RIVARD	6 arpents bought from Pierre EMERY
L'ANGLOIS, Etienne	7 arpents by contract with M. BIENVILLE.
L'ANGLOIS, Louis	8 arpents through permission of M. BIENVILLE.
RAGUET	10 arpents by possession
JORY GUIBERRY (called ST. MARTIN)	18 arpents belonging to the Widow DUGUAY whom he married. Duguay received 10 by grant and 8 through contract with M. BIENVILEE.
VIENT, Michel	10 by grant.
TRUDEAU & D'ALCOURT	18 arpents from BOURBOT and 6 from Paul ALLEMAND
BUQUOY (called PLAISANCE)	9 by possession for 8 years.
BAULNE	8 bought from M. FAZENDE, acting for the Sieur PERRY
FAZENDE	9 arpents by grant
DEMORIERE, Widow	6 bought from BOURBOT
PELLERIN	22 arpents bought from Sieur MASSY
CHAPERON	8 arpents bought from PROVANCHEZ
BARRE	8 arpents bought from Sieur PRAT.
COUSSINE	8 arpents by grant
FLEURIE	12 arpents bought from BIGOT

Name	Comments
AUBERT, Widow	4 arpents by grant
GRASSE	4 arpents by grant
DUMANOIR	8 arpents bought from Sieur VEILLON
MARCILLY	18 arpents belonging to the Widow TREPAGNIER whom he married.
LEBRO	18 arpents belonging to the Widow BACHERRE whom he married.
MARCILLY	6 by possession
CARRIERE, Joseph	6 by grant
MEUNIER	4 by possession
TIXERAND	10 by grant
BROUTIN	8 by grant
TREPAGNIE, Ignace	10 arpents by grant
TREPAGNIE, François	10 arpents by grant
Ste. Catherine Concession	36 arpents
D'ASFELD concession	72 arpents
ROQUIGNIE	15 arpents by grant
PERRIER, Jacques	4 arpents by grant
MASSY	4 arpents by grant and 4 bought from Sieur ROSSARD.
ROBIN	8 by possession
THOMELIN	12 arpents bought from JOYAUX, LACOSTE and CONSTANT

THE EAST SIDE OF THE MISSISSIPPI RIVER, ASCENDING THE RIVER FROM NEW ORLEANS (Ed.'s note: Beginning about at present-day Napoleon Ave.)

Name	Comments
The Jesuits	25 arpents bought from BIENVILLE.
D'HAUTERIVE	12 arpents belonging to the Widow DUVAL whom he married and 10 arpents by contract with BIENVILLE.
VILLAINVILLE	10 1/2 arpents in estate. He held this land by contract with BIENVILLE.
D'ARBY	6 arpents bought from BERGERON and MALLO.
BONNAUD	12 arpents bought from LARCHE LAINNEE.
CARRIERE	8 arpents bought from DAUPHIN (father) and 4 bought from DAUPHIN (son).
LIVAUDAIS	6 arpents bought from VIGIER.
ROYE	6 arpents bought from HOUVRE, the German.
VOISIN	6 arpents bought from Sieur BUCHER
DE BLANC	8 1/2 arpents by contract with BIENVILLE
PAQUIER	8 1/2 arpents by contract with BIENVILLE
LE SUEUR	8 arpents by contract with BIENVILLE.
BELLAIRE	18 arpents by contract with BIENVILLE And 3 bought from CONNE (CONUE?).
BLANPAIN	7 arpents bought from Joseph CHAMEE.
CHAVANNE	4 arpents bought from Sieur LA CHAISE (son), 6 arpents from Rodolfe GUILLAIN and 6 by contract with BIENVILLE.

Name	Comments
ADAM (called BLONDIN)	3 arpents bought from François DONNE and 3 by possession.
PRADEL	10 arpents bought from Sieur PREVOST.
LA FRENIERE	17 arpents by possession
DE MOUY	12 belonging to Widow BEAULIEU whom he has married.
DUBREUILLE VILLAR	26 arpents by concession.
DE LERY	6 arpents by grant
DE MOUY	6 arpents belonging to Widow BEAULIEU whom he has married.
LA FRENIERE	6 by grant and 6 bought from Pierre CHAUVIN.
Ste. Reine Concession	24 arpents bought from MASSY and GUENOT, 3 by grant, 8 bought from Sieur DUBREUILLE VILLAR and 8 by grant.
DE LERY (the oldest son)	6 by grant.
DE LERY BOISELEIRE	6 by grant.
DE LERY DES ISLETS	6 by grant.
DE LERY	8 arpents in the estate which were bought from Louis DASLENNE.
VERRETTE	6 arpents bought from HUGOT and 8 by grant.
BELLEVUE	12 arpents bought from Hubert DE LA CROIX and 12 from Jean HUBERT.
LA FRENIERE	6 arpents by grant
BENAC	16 arpents by grant and 8 bought from Sieur DEROCHE.
D"ARTAGUETTE	Major at New Orleans. 6 arpents bought from VAQUIER and 6 from LA PIERRE and 6 from PELLERIN
D'ARTAGUETTE's Concession	20 arpents in two grants.
D'ARTAGNANT's Concession	32 arpents by grant.
BENAC	6 arpents bought from DAUPHIN and 2 from PUGEAU
CRESPE, André	3 arpents by grant, 2 bought from M. BENAC and 2 from Joseph ARASSE.
BARRE, Jean (Called LIONNOIS)	5 arpents by grant.
HUET (called DULUDE)	12 arpents bought from Claude MEIREAU.
SANSON	12 arpents bought from AUFRERE
YZET	12 arpents bought from SANSON.
ROYE, Antoine (called LA FLEUR)	6 arpents bought from FERANDON.
YZET	12 arpents bought from MALABISE and FREDERIC and 8 by grant.
ANTOINE	A sargeant. 6 arpents by possession.
VEBURE, Jean	6 arpents by possession.
DUSALLE	8 arpents by possession. He is presently at Chetimachas and has abandoned this land.
MARY, Joseph	8 arpents bought from LE MESLE, called BELLEGARDE.
LE MESLE, François Called BELLEGARDE)	12 arpents bought from POUPART, called LA FLEUR and 8 arpents from POUDRET and 2 by grant.
TOUBS, Louis	8 arpents by possession
TOUBS, Gaspard	8 arpents bought from Sieur GAULLAS.

Name	Comments
HEYDEL, Ambroise	5 arpents bought from GAULLAS and 10 by possession.
VILLAR, Jean (called LIONNOIS)	6 arpents by possession
HOTION, Henry and FERANDON	16 arpents by possession
BROUE, Pierre (called BELLODOT)	15 arpents by possession
SERIGNON, Jacques	6 arpents by possession.
DOMAR (called DAUPHINE	8 arpents by possession.
LA CHAMPAGNE, Louis	6 arpents by possession.
CHEVAL, François	8 arpents by grant and 4 bought from DUBUISSON.
LE BORNE, Jacques Antoine	10 arpents by possession.
BOUCHARANT, Antoine	5 arpents by oral consent.
CHAMPIGNEUL	6 arpents by grant
BOQUET	8 arpents bought from Henry HOTION and FERANDON
D'ORVIN, René	10 arpents bought from LE BORNE.
POMMIER, Pierre	8 arpents by grant
VIENER, Nicolas	4 arpents bought from Jacques PAUCHER
POPF, Daniel	8 arpents bought from Joseph de KENTERECK, called DUPONT.
MASSE, André	12 arpents bought from KENTERECK, 4 from POPF, and 4 from LAVERGNE.
BOUCHARANT, Antoine and LAMATIE	5 arpents by grant
PAUCHER (called LA CHAPELLE)	6 arpents by possession
MONPIERRE, Jean Bapt.	8 arpents by possession
LACOSTE, Jean	8 arpents by grant. (After this landowner is La Colapissas.

WEST BANK OF THE MISSISSIPPING BEGINNING DIRECTLY ACROSS FROM THE CITY OF NEW ORLEANS AND ASCENDING THE RIVER.

Name	Comments
PERIER	15 arpents bought from the estate of M. DE PAILLOUX, 10 from Sieur BIZOTON and 10 by grant.
LA CHAISE (estate)	10 arpents by grant.
L'EMPILLEUR	2 arpents by grant
LARCHE (the elder)	10 arpents bought from ROYE and 6 from LA GOUBLAYE.
LARCHE, Joseph	5 arpents from LEMPILLEUR and 1 1/2 by grant.
BIMONT	10 arpents belonging to Widow RICHAUME whom he has married.
VIGIER	10 arpents by grant
MALBOUROUCK	12 arpents bought from MEUSLION
MAREILLY	10 arpents bought from JUDICE.
JUDICE	8 arpents through permission of the Council and possession.
RIXNER	10 arpents bought from SCHEMITTE.
STE. TERESE	6 arpents by grant and 8 bought from M. DE BOISBRIANT.

Name	Comments
BESLILE	6 arpents by grant and 6 bought from Claude BAILLY
LIVAUDAIS	8 arpents by possession
SIMON (Mulatto)	4 arpents by possession and 2 bought from SCIPION, a free negro.
GUCHOT	6 arpents by possession
SENET	12 arpents bought from Sieur BELLAIRE
DASFELD Concession	14 arpents at Petit Desert.
DE MOUY	6 arpents belonging to Widow BEAULIEU whom he has married.
MIKELLE	16 arpents bought from Sieur DUBREUILLE VILLAR.
DUBREUILLE VILLAR	18 by concession
LA FRENIERE	20 bought from MASSY and 12 by grant.
DE LERY (estate)	20 bought from MASSY and 6 by grant.
DE MOUY	12 arpents belonging to Widow BEAULIEU whom he has married.
PETIT LIVILLE	7 arpents by grant and 12 bought from TIERRY.
COULLANGE	6 arpents by grant and 6 bought from IMBERT
SENET	8 arpents by grant
BAILLY	4 arpents by grant
RERNION	6 arpents by possession
LAVERGNE (the Canadian)	12 arpents bought from Sieur ST. JULLIEN
ST. JULLIEN	55 arpents by possession
BARRON (at the Houmas)	6 arpents bought from SENET
CONNE, Simon	4 arpents by grant and 6 bought from Gaspart AYGLY.
PUGEOL	14 arpents bought from LE BAT and RERNION.
NOYON	4 arpents by grant and 4 by possession.
DARTAGUET	Major of New Orleans. 8 arpents by grant.
BEAU, Jacques	Sargeant. 4 arpents by possession
DUPRE, Jacques	4 arpents by possession
CHRISTMAN, Henry	6 arpents by possession
CHRISTMAN, André	6 arpents by possession
CHRISTMAN, Jacques	12 arpents by possession
WANDERECK	12 arpents by possession
NEYGLY, Jacques	6 arpents by possession
SONT, Philipe	4 1/2 arpents by possession
DONNE, François	6 arpents by possession
CROISIEZ, Jacques	4 arpents by grant
ROUSSEAU	4 arpents bought from Jean DUPRE
FOLTZ, Jacques	6 arpents by possession
OFFEMANNE, André	5 arpents by possession
GRAIVER, Christianne	6 arpents by possession.
CLEIROT, Pierre	7 arpents by possession
DESLANDE, Jean	4 arpents by possession and 4 bought from LAVERGNE.
LAVERGNE	5 arpents by possession
AEICKLY, Gaspart	5 arpents by possession
LABEE	4 arpents by possession
MOREAU (called PARISIEN)	4 arpents by grant
MEUNIER, David	8 arpents by possession

Name	Comments
LABEE	4 by grant and 4 by possession.
ST. TON	10 arpents by grant (Here is vis-a-vis Lake Outarde)
RABELLE, Jacques	6 arpents by possession
VEISCRAME, Jacques	2 arpents by possession
ADAM, Jean	8 arpents by possession
TROTSLER, George	9 arpents by possession
ROEFER, George	8 arpents by possession
HOUBRE, Jacques and Christofle (father and son)	12 arpents by possession
ANTOINE, Bernard	8 arpents by possession
FREDERICK, Mathias	6 arpents by possession
WAGENSBACH, Joseph	6 arpents by possession
MEUVE Concession	4 lieues
BOURGEOIS, Jean Bapt.	3 arpents by possession
STUMPHLE, André	6 arpents by possession
KAISER, Christofle	3 arpents by possession
MUNIGUE, Pierre	2 arpents by possession
BERLINGUE, Simon	3 arpents by possession
SCHEMITTE, Adam	1 1/2 arpents by possession
ANDRE, Joseph	3 arpents by possession
LE PRESBITAIRE	6 arpents by possession
DRACGUER, André	5 arpents by possession
DARRANSBOURG	12 arpents by grant
MAYER, Claus	8 arpents by possession
RITTER, Jacques	6 arpents by possession
MATERNE, Adam	8 arpents by possession
MAGDOLFE, Leonard	6 arpents by possession
MARX, Baltazar	6 arpents by possession
CHANTZE, André	8 arpents by possession
CIRIAQUE, Guillaume	4 arpents by possession
SCGSNEIDER, Albert	4 arpents by possession
VIQUE, Bernard	6 arpents by possession
FREDERICK, Conrat	6 arpents by possession
ROMMELLE, Jean	6 arpents by possession
GUILLAND, Rodolfe	4 arpents by possession
CALLINDRE, Jean	4 arpents by possession
POQUE, Jean George	2 arpents by possession
GAULLOIS, Michel (called LANGOUMOIS)	5 arpents by possession
VOGUEL, Michel	6 arpents by possession
LAMBERT, Martin	5 arpents by possession

1731

CENSUS OF FARMS AND CONCESSIONS ALONG THE MISSISSIPPI RIVER

Owner of farm or concession	Male person living on the land	Wife	Children	Engagés	Negroes
BEGINNING AT THE MOUTH OF THE MISSISSIPPI AND ASCENDING THE RIVER ON THE EAST SIDE TO NEW ORLEANS					
MADRE	MADRE	yes	1		2
CONTANT	CONTANT	yes	1		
FIOU	FIOU	yes	4		1
TRONQUILLY	TRONQUILLY	yes	3		4
LA RIBARDIERE	LA RIBARDIERE				
ROBIN	ROBIN	yes	1	2	11
FAUCHEUX	FAUCHEUX	yes	2		
JOLICOEUR	JOLICOEUR	yes	2	2	1
MONTIGNY	MONTIGNY	yes	3		2
CASTEL	CASTEL	yes			
BEAUPRE	BEAUPRE	yes	1		2
DRAPEAU	DRAPEAU	yes	2	1	3
BUISSON	BUISSON	yes	2		8
PERIER	PERIER, Jacques	yes		1	16
PINET	PINET	yes		1	5
PASQUIER	PASQUIER	yes	2		1
LEMPILEUR					
SAUCIER					
ARNAUD	ARNAUD				
TRUDEAU (son)	TRUDEAU (son)				
SAUCIER	SAUCIER, Widow		3		7
MEUNIER	MEUNIER				4
CARRIERE	CARRIERE, Jacques		1		8
CARRIERE	CARRIERE, François	yes	1	3	17
CARRIERE	CARRIERE, Joseph	yes	4		12
TISSERANT	TISSERANT	yes	5	1	33
BOYER	BOYER			1	2
CHEVAL	CHEVAL				12
PERALBE	PERALBE, François				1
FILART	FILART				8
BRUSLE	BRUSLE				5
LIVET	LIVET	yes	4		7
LEONARD	LEONARD	yes			6
CHAMILLY	CHAMILLY				4
BACHEMIN	BACHEMIN, Corbin	yes	7		4
LA LOIRE	LA LOIRE JOUSSET	yes	4		7
CHAPERON	CHAPERON	yes			16
FLEURIE	FLEURIE				4

Owner of farm or concession	Male person living on the land	Wife	Children	Engagés	Negroes
RICARD	RICARD				4
LOUBOEY					
LA PRADE	LA PRADE	yes			1
VAUPARIS					
LA LIBERTE	LA LIBERTE	yes			14
The Capuchins					5
DESMORIERS	DESMORIERS				1
DARBONNE	DARBONNE	yes	3		2
DAUSSEVILLE				1	25
The Ursulines	VAUPARIS	yes			16
ST. MARTIN				1	17
FLEURIAU	FLEURIAU	yes	2	1	16
BROUTIN		yes	3	1	34
RAGUET	RAGUET	yes	2	1	15
LA TOUR	MAREST DE LA TOUR				7
DUPUY	MAREST DUPUY				8
DALCOURT	DALCOURT and the Demoiselle MILON	yes	6		30
LA CHAISE (est.)	BISOTON				29
GAUVRIT		yes	2		7
TRUDEAU	TRUDEAU (father)				30
LABOULAY		yes	2		11
COUSTILLAS	COUSTILLAS				38
DES KAIRAC	DES KAIRAC				6
DARBY (the elder)	DARBY				10
DREUX					3
NEW ORLEANS					
The Jesuits				2	29
D'HAUTERIVES					36
VILLAINVILLE (est.)				1	7
DARBY (the younger)					2
BONNAUD					12
DAUPHIN (father)					8
DAUPHIN (son)	DAUPHIN (son)	yes	1		6
LIVAUDAIS				1	12
ROYE	ROYE, Louis	yes	4	1	2
VOISIN	BORE				6
DE BLANC	DE BLANC	yes		1	8
PASQUIET	PACQUIET				10
BELLAIRE	BELLAIRE	yes	3		22
BLANPIN				4	9
CHAVANNES	CHAVANNES				26
BLONDIN	ADAM (called BLONDIN)	yes			4
PRADEL					6

Owner of farm or concession	Male person living on the land	Wife	Children	Engagés	Negroes
CHAPITOULAS					
GUYOT	GUYOT and ST. GERMAIN	yes	1		5
DUBREUIL	DUBREUIL (father)				
	DUBREUIL (eldest son)	yes		4	76
	DUBREUIL (youngest son)				
DE LERY	DE LERY (father)	yes	3		
	DE LERY (eldest son)			1	58
	DE LERY (2nd son)				
	DE LERY (3rd son)				
DE MOUY	DE MOUY	yes	5		51
LA FRENIERE	LA FRENIERE	yes	4	6	76
LE SUEUR	LE SUEUR				
KOLLY Concession				1	46
CANNES BRULEES					
VERET	VERET, Joseph	yes	2	1	8
CANTEREL	CANTEREL	yes	3	1	4
DARTAGUIETTE				2	39
ISET	ISET				4
DARTAIGNAN Concession	GALIMACHE	yes		1	58
CRETZ	CRETZ, André	yes	2		3
LIONNOIS	JAMBART LIONNOIS	yes	2		1
DULUDE	DULUDE		1		7
NOYON	NOYON				4
SANSON	SANSON	yes		1	6
ST. AMANT		yes	2		4
ROUX	ROUX, Antoine	yes	3		1
FAVROT					2
MACE					5
ANCE AUX OUTARDES					
ROUSSEAU	ROUSSEAU	yes	3		8
LA COSTE	LA COSTE	yes	2		3
ALLEMANDS or ANCEAUX OUTARDES					
TOUPS	TOUPS & 2 grandsons	yes			3
HEILD	HEILD, Ambroise	yes	2	1	3
BROU	BROU, Pierre	yes	3		3
BOURGEOIS	BOURGEOIS, Jean	yes	3	1	1
CHEVAL	CHEVAL, François	yes	5		4
BORNES	BORNES	(2)	3	4	4
DORVEINKS	DORVEINKS, René and his brother	yes			1
DAUPHINE	DAUPHINE	yes			1

Owner of farm or concession	Male person living on the land	Wife	Children	Engagés	Negroes
POMMIER	POMMIER	yes	1		2
WITNER	WITNER, Nicolas	yes	1		2
QUINTREL (called DUPONT)	QUINTREL, Joseph	yes	5		1
LOF	LOF, Daniel	yes	2		3
DONAY	DONAY, Philippe	yes	3		2
LA CHAPELLE	POCHE, Jacques (called LA CHAPELLE)	yes	1		
MONTPIERRE	MONTPIERRE	yes	5		2
<u>OUMAS</u>					
LEGRAS	LEGRAS, François	yes	1		2
PERRET	PERRET	yes	1		1
ROMAN	ROMAN			5	5
CHAMPIGNOLS	CHAMPIGNOLS	yes	2		2
BARON	BARON	yes	2		7
MAIGRE	MAIGRE	yes			
<u>ECORES BLANCS</u>					
MEZIERES Concession	PAILLARD				15
<u>POINTE COUPEE</u>					
COUILLARD	COUILLARD	yes		1	3
JAPPIOT	JAPPIOT	yes		1	2
BAU, Michel	BAU, Michel	yes			4
BARA, Jean	BARA, Jean	yes	1		1
LA COUR	LA COUR	yes	2		2
LA FACINNE	LA FACINNE				1
LE GROS	LE GROS	yes	1		
<u>CROSSING TO THE WEST SIDE OF THE MISSISSIPPI AT POINTE COUPEE AND DESCENDING TOWARD NEW ORLEANS</u>					
DUPONT	DUPONT	yes	1	1	2
MATELOT	MATELOT				1
AVIGNON	AVIGNON	yes			1
GAUSSERAN	GAUSSERAN	yes	2		1
BONHOMME	BONHOMME				
LE COUREUR	LE COUREUR	yes			
RAIMOND	RAIMOND	yes			3
BERGERON	BERGERON	yes			3
CASTILLON	CASTILLON	yes			1
GUICHARD	GUICHARD	yes			1
GERMAIN	GERMAIN	yes			9

Owner of farm or concession	Male person living on the land	Wife	Children	Engagés	Negroes
DUPLECHIN	DUPLECHIN	yes	1		
LE NORMAND	LE NORMAND	yes	3		2
MAYEUX	MAYEUX	yes	3		1
SOISSONS	SOISSONS	yes	1		4
HOUMAR	HOUMAR	yes	3		2
RONDEAU	RONDEAU	yes	2		4
DECUIR	DECUIR, Jean				1
DECUIR	DECUIR (father)			1	4
ANOTIAU	ANOTIAU	yes	2		3
HAUSSY	HAUSSY	yes			2
ALLARD	ALLARD, Widow		3	1	
LE PERCHE	LE PERCHE, Widow				
BIENVENAU	BIENVENAU				
HAYNAU	HAYNAU				
LE PERCHE	LE PERCHE, Pierre				5
ALAIN	ALAIN				1
DECOUX	DECOUX	yes	7	2	2
<u>CHETIMACHAS</u>					
DUSABLAY					4
BELLEHUMEUR		yes	1		2
CORDONIER		yes			1
JOUBART					1
LANDERNAU		yes	2		
MARON		yes	2		1
<u>BAYAGOULAS</u>					
DUBUISSON	DUBUISSON MONFERIER	yes	5	1	6
LA GARDE	LA GARDE			5	48
<u>ALLEMANDS</u>					
LAMBERT	LAMBERT, Jean Martin	yes	1		
FOUQUEL	FOUQUEL, Mikel	yes	2		1
GAULOIS	GAULOIS, François	yes	1		1
HORN	HORN, Mikel	yes			
QUISTENMAHER	QUISTENMAHER, Etienne	yes	1	1	1
KALENDRE	KALENDRE	yes	1		1
ROUSSEL	ROUSSEL, Jean	yes	3		
FREDERIC	FREDERIC, Conrard	yes	1	1	2
HUIKS	HUIKS, BERNARD	yes	2	1	1
ALBERT	ALBERT	yes	1		1
SIRIAK	SIRIAK, Guillaume	yes			
POK	POK, Jean Georges	yes	3		
CHANTS	CHANTS, André	yes	2		3

Owner of farm or concession	Male person living on the land	Wife	Children	Engagés	Negroes
MARCK	MARCK Baltazar	yes	2		1
MACKDOLF	MACKDOLF, Leonard	yes			
MATERNE	MATERNE, Adam	yes	3		5
REITHER.	REITHER, Jacques	yes			
MAYER	MAYER, Nicolas	yes	2		1
DARENSBOURG	DARENSBOURG	yes	4	1	3
DREIKER	DREIKER, André	yes	3		2
A Capuchin	Father Philippes			3	1
BERLING	BERLIN, Simon	yes			
VENDERHEK	VENDERHEK	yes	1		5
MUNIK	MUNIK, Pierre	yes	2		
STRUNFS	STRUNFS, André	yes	3		
DELAIRE	DELAIRE				2
VAGUENBAC	VAGUENSBAC, Joseph	yes	3		1
FREDERIC	FREDERIC, Mathis	yes	3		
FOLET	FOLET, Jacques	yes	2		
ANTOINE	ANTOINE, Bernard	yes	3	1	
CREBERT	CREBERT, Cristianne	yes	3		
OFMAN	OFMAN, André	yes	4		
OUBERT	OUBERT, Jacques	yes	2	1	2
REUZER	REUZER, Georges	yes	1		
TROUCHELER	TROUCHELER, Georges	yes	2		1
ADAM	ADAM, Jean	yes	5		1
LIONNOIS	LIONNOIS	yes	1		
RABLAU	RABLAU, Jacques	yes	5		
ANCE AUX OUTARDES					
SAINTON	SAINTON	yes	4		5
LABE	LABE	yes	4		9
DAVID	DAVID &	yes			
	PARISIEN	yes		1	5
GASPARD	GASPARD	yes	2		3
LA VERGNE	LA VERGNE	yes	3		2
DESLANDES	DESLANDES, Jean	yes			5
CLERAUT	CLÉRAUT	yes			2
SOM	SOM, Philippe	yes	3		1
LA THULIPPE	LA THULIPPE				
DAUNAY	DAUNAY, François	yes	2		
CRISTIANNE	CRISTIANNE	yes	5		
ROZIER	ROZIER, Jacques				
KRESMANE	KRESMANE, Jacques	yes	1		
KRESMANNE	KRESMANNE, André	yes	1	1	4
DUPRE	DUPRE	yes	2		
CANNES BRULEES					
LANGEVIN	LANGEVIN	yes			
PUGEOL	PUGEOL	yes	3		1

Owner of farm or concession	Male person living on the land	Wife.	Children	Engagés	Negroes
CONE,	CONE, Simon	yes	1		3
DUPUY GOUPILLON	DUPUY GOUPILLON	yes	3		5
ST. JULLIEN	ST. JULLIEN, Chevalier			1	17
LA VERGNE	LA VERGNE	yes	5		4
QUERNION					4
BAILLIF		yes			1
PETIT	PETIT	yes	4	1	31
BELOW CHAPITOULAS					
DE LERY's Mill					3
SERINGUE	SERINGUE, Mikel	yes	3	1	12
DASFELD Concession		yes	1	2	12
SENET	SENET, François			1	13
SCIPION	SCIPION (Free Negro)				
SIMON	SIMON (Free Negro)	yes			1
PETIT	PETIT	yes	1	1	16
STE. THERESE	STE. THERESE DE LANGLOISERIE				11
RISTENER	RISTENER (son)				3
JUDICE	JUDICE	yes	4	1	6
LARCHE	LARCHE GRANDPRE	yes			6
DAIGLE	DAIGLE, Etienne	yes	3		5
VIGER	VIGER	yes	4		11
BIMON	BIMON	yes	4		7
LARCHE	LARCHE, Joseph	yes	2	1	10
LARCHE	LARCHE (the elder)	yes	5		15
LA CHAISE (est.)		yes	2	1	12
PERIER	LANGE			1	72
Co. of Indies	LE PAGE			2	201
BOURGEOIS	BOURGEOIS	yes	3	1	9
BIENVILLE	SERVAY				33
BALDY	BALDY			1	10
PROVENCHE	PROVENCHE	yes		2	7
LANGLOIS	LANGLOIS, Augustin	yes	4	2	6
LANGLOIS	LANGLOIS, Etienne	yes	5		15
LANGLOIS	LANGLOIS, Louis				5
DUGUAY				1	24
VIEN	VIEN, Michel	yes	1	1	4
CHAUVIN	CHAUVIN, Jacques				1
PLAISANCE	PLAISANCE	yes	2	1	5
BEAUNE	BEAUNE	yes	5		10
FAZENDE	FAZENDE	yes	4	1	15
PELLERIN	LA JANGE	yes	4	1	20
BARRE	BARRE, Paul	yes	2		5
COUSSINNE	COUSSINNE	yes	4		2

Owner of farm or concession	Male person living on the land	Wife	Children	Engagés	Negroes
FLEURIE	BONNE, Pierre				3
GRACE	RODOLPHE				5
MARSILLY	MARSILLY	yes	6		23
TREPANIER	TREPANIER, François				
LABRO	LABRO	yes	3		17
TREPANIER	TREPANIER, Ignace				4
Ste. Reine Concession	DUMANOIR		2	1	27
Dasfeld Concession	ROUJOT	yes	4	4	98
ROCQUINY	ROCQUINY	yes	3	1	8
MASSY	MASSY	yes		2	30
THOMELAIN					1
DREUX	DREUX (the younger)				10
HARANG	HARANG				1
PRAT	MANIGME				27
Capuchins	GUILLAUME	yes	2		10
RIVARD	RIVARD, Widow	yes	4	1	16
RIVARD	RIVARD (son)	yes			
GIRARDY	GIRARDY, Joseph	yes	3		15
TOURENJEAU			2		3
BOISSIER	BOISSIER	yes			10
MORAND	MORAND	yes			45

RECAPITULATION

MEN	377
WOMEN	209
CHILDREN	390
ENGAGES	119
NEGROES (men only)	2529

1732?

LIST OF THOSE PERSONS WHO OWN LAND IN THE CITY OF NEW ORLEANS

1 BIENVILLE
2 BIENVILEE
3 DASFELD
4 BONNEAU
5 PARIS (at Bayagoulas)
6 LA CHAISE
7 TIXERAND
8 CO. OF THE INDIES
9 LA FRESNIERE
10 BELLISLE
11 DE LERY
12 MANDEVILLE, Widow
13 DREUX BROTHERS
14 DAUSSEVILLE
15 DUVAL, Widow (bought from BEAULIEU)
16 DUVAL, Widow
17 ROSSARD
18 SAINT MARTIN
19 DARBY
20 DE MONIC
21 DE LERY
22 AUGARD
23 CO. OF THE INDIES
24 STOREHOUSE
25 CHANTIER
26 STOREHOUSE
27 STOREHOUSE
28 DARTAGUET
29 PETIT DE LIVILIER
30 DAMARON
31 PELLERIN
32 GAUVRIT
33 PROVANCHET, Madame
34 DE VILLEUR
35 COMPANY OF THE INDIES
36 LAZOU
37 RAGUET
38 CO. OF THE INDIES
39 TRUDOT
40 LE BLANC
41 MORAND
42 DAUBLIN
43 AUFRAIRE
44 MORISSET
45 VANDOME
46 BRULE
47 CO. OF THE INDIES
48 - - - - - - - -
49 BRUSLE
50 MANADEL
51 ST. HILLAIRE
52 VALLERANT
53 SARAZIN, Widow
54 VILRI
55 PIGRE
56 LA GOUBLAYE, Widow
57 COUPARD
58 JARI, Widow
59 FAVRE
60 LA FRENIERE
61 LA TOUR (estate)
62 DELATTE
63 ARNAUDROYE, Called BELLAIRE
64 BELCOUR
65 L'HOMELIN
66 BRULE
67 BENAC
68 Concession of MEZIERE
69 CHAMILLY
70 BEAUSEJOUR
71 OZANE
72 SANFASSON
73 RIVARD
74 LOUBOIS
75 TREPANIER, Widow
76 CARRIERE, Joseph
77. HANRY
78 CARRIERE, François
79 CARON
80 MARIN
81 ALLIN
82 LE NORMAND
83 Co. OF THE INDIES
84 L'ANGLOIS, Augustin
85 RIVARD, Widow
86 The Capuchins
87 ARNAUD
88 MOREAU
89 - - - - - -
90 MALO
91 DRIAND, Widow
92 BARASSON
93 MALO

94 BLANCVILLIN
95 ROBERT, Widow
96 CHAVANNE
97 CARDINAL, Widow
98 BIGOT
99 DALCOUR
100 CARPENTRAS, Widow
101 SABLON
102 BRETONNE
103 GRANDJEAN
104 GRAND COUR
105 MONROUGE
106 LA PIERRE
107 ST. MARTIN
108 LIVAUDAIS
109 MORISSET
110 CHEMITTE
111 BONPART, Demoiselle
112 ALEXANDRE
113 CHEMITTE
114 BONNET
115 DAUVILLE
116 CHASTANT
117 ANDROUIN, Children of
118 LA LIBERTE
119 TRONQUIDI
a LA VIGNE, Widow
120 ST. HILLAIRE
121 LA ROSE (the Brewer)
122 MICHEL
123 L'EMPILLEUR
124
125 SANTIER
126 ROCHER
127 ROBERT
128
129 DURANTAI
130 FONDER
131 LE MAIRE
b ROBERT
132 VITRE, Paul
133 FRANCOISE, Marie
134 CORNMERCY
135 THOMAS
136 SENET
137 AVIGNON
138 FRANCOEUR
139
140 SAUSSIER, Widow
141 VANDOME
142 FORESTIER
143 DARGARET
144 ROUSSEAU and FONDER
145 LA RIVIERE
146 PINET
147 LE MAIRE
148 DU PART
149 ANGLOIS
150 JEAN LOUIS
151 LA COSTE AND FRANCOISE, Marie
152 ORLEANS
153 CHENIER
154 MANCELLIERE
155 CHENIER
156 JOSEPH
157 BIGNARD (female)
158 BAIME
159
160 AUVERGNAT
161 Marie (N egro)
162 BRUNET
163 BRUNET
164 BOURBON (female)
165 LA MAURI
166 BOUCHARDIERE
167 POIRE
168 BROUET
169 ST. JOSEPH
170 GUIDON
171 VINCENT
c CAPE
172 FLACON
173 CARON, Widow
174 JELIZO (female)
175 VOISIN
176 TOURNEL, Marie
177 FILARD
178 CHAPRON
179 LA PALINE
180 (Abandoned)
181 ST. JEAN
182 DESLORIERS
183 FOUTRE, Jean
184 LEGER, Thomas
185 REITER
186 LA ROCHE CASTEL
187 BEQUET
188 BARBEAU
189 MANSEAU
190 FAVIER
191 ST. JACQUES
192 MARTIN

193 - - - - - - - -
194 CRISTINA
195 LA CLEF
196 ROSSARD
197 CANEL
198 LE DUC
199 POUSSORT
200 GAUTIER, Pierre
201 LA ROZE, Alix
202 GUILLAUTEL
203 SARROT
204 FILASSIER
205 RENAUD, Pierre
206 BROSSET
207 RAFFLOT
208 LA PIERRE
209 MARTIN
210 BAILLY, Widow
211 NEGRIER
212 TOURANGEAU
213 DUPRE
214 DAUSSERVILLE
215 MARCOUSTIL
216 AUBRUN, Nicolas
217 BALLE
218 BRUNELLE
219 JADELA
220 BOTSON
221 FLAMANT
222 L'ARTEAU, Widow
223 BUISSON
224 MOIN
225 GRATIEN LANLIER
226 BOURGUIGNON
227 LAMBERT
228 LOYSEL
229 LA ROZE
230 BOURGUIGNON (female)
231 MARCHE A TERRE
232FAVIER, Nicolas
233 PENTUREAU, François
234 CHEREAU, François
235 - - - - - -
236LARCHE
237 HUPE
238 NANTIER
239 FAUCHER, Guillaume
240 GAUTIER, Julien
241 BOURGUIGNON
242 SAINT GERMAIN
243 L'EMPILLEUR
244 - - - - - - -
245 - - - - - - -
246 PARISIEN
247 ST. MICHEL
248 BELLEROZE
249 - - - - - -
250 LANTURLU
251 REINE (female)
252 LARCHE
253 - - - - - -

JANUARY, 1732

CENSUS OF THE INHABITANTS OF NEW ORLEANS

HOME OWNER	RESIDENT	Wife	Children	Orphans	Negroes
ON THE QUAI					
Hospital	DUCHEMIN, Attendant				
	PRAT, Doctor	yes			3
	BIZOTON		1		
RAGUET					
LAZOU	LAZOU, Captain	yes		1	7
PELLERIN	PELLERIN, Storekeeper	yes	2		6
	LANTEAUME				
	DESCHAMPS				
	GAUTHEREAU				
DAMARON	DAMARON, Apothicary	yes	2		6
DARTAGUIETTE	DARTAGUIETTE				
	SALMON	yes			4
	LE BRETON	yes			
	DERLIN, Servant				
	CHARLES, Cook				
	LAPOMERAY, treasurer				1
	PREFONTAINE				1
DAUTERIVES	D'HAUTERIVES, Madame		1		3
DUVAL (estate)	PREVOST				8
	ARBAUD				2
	COUTURIER				
	ADAM				
DAUSSERVILLE	DAUSSERVILLE				
MICHEL	MICHEL, baker	yes		1	1
	TOUZAY, Jean				
DREUX	DREUX				
The King	BROUTIN, Engineer				
	SAUCIER, Draftsman				
TIXERANT					
DE LA GARDE	DE TROHOIS, Clerk				
DASFELD Concession	CAUSSY, Financier				2
BONNAUD	BONNAUD	yes	1		2
DE NOYAN	DE NOYAN, Captain				1
	ST. MARTIN, Servant				
The King's Mill	KYSERR (?), Miller	yes	2		
The Jesuits	Father PETIT				
	Father PARISET				
CHARTRES STREET					
KOLLY (Estate)	Six Ursulines				
The Ursuline Convent	Six Boarders				
	27 orphans				
DUBREUIL	DUBREUIL, Madame				1

HOME OWNER	RESIDENT	Wife	Children	Orphans	Negroes
CHARTRES STREET (cont.)					
BRUSLE	LIVAUDAIS, Captain of the Port				2
The King	MANADE, Surgeon	yes			12
ST HILAIRE	ST. HILAIRE, Carpenter	yes	2		3
VALLERAN	VALLERAN, Turner	yes	3		
BORDELON	BORDELON, Madame		4		2
VITRY	SONGY, François	yes	3		
PICQUERY	PICQUERY, Baker	yes	3	1	4
BELLAIRE	BELLAIRE	yes	3		3
BALIOUS	PRADEL, Madame				1
	LAYRAC				
THOMELAIN	THOMELAIN, Carpenter	yes	1		5
BRUSLE	BRUSLE, Madame		1		3
	BALCONS, Director of Fortifications				2
The Capuchins	Father RAPHAEL			2	4
	Father HIACINTE				
	Father PIERRE				
MARSILLY	PAQUET				
CARIER	MARQUIS, Clerk				
MARSILLY	HENRY, Clerk	yes			1
CARIERE	FORCADE, Tobacco curer.				
CARON	CARON, Butcher	yes	1	1	2
ARNAUT	RUEL, Mason	yes			
	HENRY, Widow				
MOREAU	MOREAU	yes			1
BLARD, Louis	BLARD, Louis (Called ST. LOUIS)	yes			
	DIMANCHE, Widow				
CHARTIER	MULON, Tailor				3
DRILLAN, Widow	CHEVALIER, Widow				
DRILLAN, Widow	VEILLON, Turner				
	LA BAPTISTE	yes			
PROVENCHE	LA FONTAINE, Tailor				
	BOUTONNIER, Ex-soldier				
	TISON				1
VILLEUR	VILLEUR				
The King	LEONARD, Gardener	yes			
	LEONARD, Frederic				
	CAP, Georges, Cooper				
	ROYE, Jacques				

HOME OWNER	RESIDENT	Wife	Children	Orphans	Negroes
CHARTRES STREET (cont.)					
LE MOINE	LE MOINE, Carpenter	yes	3		
	PATIN, Carpenter				
BLANPIN	BLANPIN				
BROUTIN	AMELOT				
	SONGARION				
ROYAL STREET					
CHMIT	CHMIT	yes	1		
CHMIT	STE. HERMINE, Madame		1		
BONNET	BONNET	yes		1	
DAUVILLE	DAUVILLE	yes	2		3
MICHEL	MICHEL, Clerk	yes	4		4
LEMPILEUR	DUMAS, Called LEMPILEUR	yes	2		2
BERTAUD	BERTAUD, Carpenter	yes	1		
SAUTIER	SAUTIER, Carpenter	yes	1		
	Marie, the Bohemian				
SAUCIE	POUSSINNE, Tailor				
	MANSIAU, A boy				
	BOUTON				
VENDOME	VENDOME	yes	2		
FORESTIER	FORESTIER	yes	3		1
LEMAIRE	LEMAIRE, Innkeeper				2
	Elizabeth, Wife of LA PIERRE				
JACQUET	JACQUET	yes	2		
MANIERE, Children	PATRON, Joseph Marie	yes	2		
CHENIER	CHENIER	yes			2
JOSEPH					
AVILLE	LABOUCHARDIERE	yes	1		
POIRE	POIRE, Gunsmith	yes	2		
BROUET	BROUET, Wheelwright	yes	1		2
	PLAISANCE	yes	1		
	SANS CHAGRIN, Widow		1		
ST. JOSEPH	ST. JOSEPH	yes	3		5
	FRANCOIS				
VOISIN	VOISIN		5		4
	VOISIN (son)				
ST ANDRE, Widow	GIRAUD, Carpenter	yes	2		
3 Houses for VOISIN					
CHAPRON					
PANTINET	PANTINET, Widow. A Bohemian		1		
DUSABLON	DUSABLON	yes			
MOUTARD, Baptiste	MOUTARD, Baptiste Carpenter	yes	2		
MERLE, Jean	MERLE, Jean				

HOME OWNER	RESIDENT	Wife	Children	Orphans	Negroes
ROYAL STREET (cont.)					
LA GRANDCOURT	VALADE, Sailor	yes			
FINEAU	FINEAU	yes	2	2	2
AUBERT					
CHAVANNE	VUE (?), Nicolas	yes	2		3
MONTAUBAN	ALAIN, Ex-sailor	yes	1		
DROUILLON	DROUILLON	yes	3		1
LANGLOIS	DARGURET	yés	2		1
BEAUSEJOUR	BARY, Coppersmith	yes	1		
	LA RIVIERE, Jacques Ex-sailor				
	LA TELLIER (female)				
OZANNE	OZANNE, Cooper	yes	2		3
	TESSON				
SANS FACON					
JARRY	JARRY, Widow		3		3
FABRE	FABRE, Gunner, & his mother-in-law	yes			1
LA FRENIERE	LAVIOLETTE, Widow				
BRUSLE					
BELLAIRE	BELLAIRE, Carpenter	yes	5		
MORICET	DURIVAGE, Mason				
DAUPHIN					
BOURBON STREET					
DAUPHIN	LAFORGE, Widow				
LA SONDE, Widow	LA SONDE, Widow		1		2
DESLAURIERS					
LA ROCHE CASTEL	LA ROCHE CASTEL Founder	yes	1		1
BECQUET	BECQUET, Metalsmith	yes	3		1
BARBAUD	BARBAUD	yes	4		6
MANICAN	MANICAN	yes	2		
LA CLEF	LA CLEF	yes	1		
CANELLE	CANELLE, Carpenter	yes			
LE DUC	LE DUC, Metalsmith	yes			
BELHUMEUR	BELHUMEUR	yes	3		1
GAUTIER	GAUTIER, Mason	yes		1	
	SADOT, Jean. Ex-soldier				
LA ROSE ALIX					
RENAUDOT	RENAUDOT, called SANS CHAGRIN	yes			
BROSSET	BROSSET, Surgeon				
RAFLOT	RAFLOT, Tiler	yes			2
LA PIERRE	LA PIERRE, Barber	yes	3		

HOME OWNER	RESIDENT	Wife	Children	Orphans	Negroes
BOURBON STREET (cont.)					
DUPRE	DUPRE, Carpenter	yes	2	1	1
BOURGUIGNON	BOURGUIGNON				
MARCHEATERRE	MARCHEATERRE	yes			
XAVIER	XAVIER (Free Mulatto)				
ROTUREAU	ROTUREAU	yes			
ST. GERMAIN	LE NORMAND				
BARRE	BARRE, Jean Bapt.	yes	2		
PARISIEN	LAUVERGNAT	yes	2		
LAUVERGNAT	BARRE				
MARIE	Marie (Free Negro)				
BRUNET	LA COUTOIS (female)		1		
FLACON	MATE, Jean Louis Called FLACON	yes	4		4
LA ROCHE	LA ROCHE, Carpenter	yes	2		1
AVIGNON	BEAUCOURT				
LEMAIRE					
VITRE	VITRE, Paul	yes			
ANGEBAUD	ANGEBAUD, Carpenter				
COMMERCY	COMMERCY, Cutler	yes	1		
LA CROIX					
FRANCOEUR	FRANCOEUR, Baker	yes			
HERPIN	HERPIN, Clerk				
NELLE, Jean	NELLE, Jean. Carpenter				
MATE	MATE, Wagon maker	yes			
FACING THE WOODS					
GAUTIER	GAUTIER, Julien				
FAUCHE	FAUCHE, Guillaume	yes	1		
	VALET, Nicolas				
	LA COURTABLEAU (female)				
NANTIER, The late					
MENAGER	MENAGER	yes			
	MATHURIN				
LARCHE	LARCHE				
	COUTOIS	yes			3
	LEBODET				
ST. PHILIP STREET					
TRUDEAU	TRUDEAU, Madame		3		
	LAVAU				
DALCOURT					
GAUVRIT					
ST. MARTIN	ST. MARTIN				

HOME OWNER	RESIDENT	Wife	Children	Orphans	Negroes
ST. PHILIP STREET (cont.)					
LA ROSE	LA ROSE, Wagon-maker	yes	1		
LA PRAIRIE	LA PRAIRIE, A Bohe- mian	yes	1	1	
GUIDOU	GUIDOU	yes	1	2	
	FONDELAY, Widow				
VINCENT	VINCENT	yes			
ST. MICHEL	ST. MICHEL				
DUMAINE STREET					
BARRE	CHENEAU, Gunner				
ASSELIN	ASSELIN	yes			1
	LA BIGNARD				
MARIN	MARIN	yes	2		2
MEUNIER					
BIGOT	BIGOT				2
	LA AUBERT (female)				
BRUSLE	BRUSLE	yes	5		11
ST. ANN STREET					
The King	PERIER	yes	3		6
	TERLIN, Mlle.				
	LEMAITRE				
	LABBE, Boat owner				
ASSELIN	ASSELIN, Thomas	yes			
	HUBERT, Catherine				
	VIEL, Marie Jeanne				
DUPARC	DUPARC, Interpreter	yes	3		4
LAMORY	LAMORY				
BOURBON	BOURBON	yes		1	
JEAN LOUIS					
LARVE	LARVE, Tailor	yes	2		
BRANTAN	BRANTAN, Gunsmith				
LOISEL	ROMAYOUX, Metalsmith	yes	3		1
BOURGUIGNON	BOURGUIGNON				
JULLIAU	JULLIAU				
BUNEL	BUNEL	yes	1	1	6
JARDELA	JARDELA	yes	1		
BOTSON	BOTSON, Founder	yes	1		4
ORLEANS STREET					
LOUIS, Jean	LOUIS, Jean			3	3
LA COSTE	LA COSTE				

HOME OWNER	RESIDENT	Wife	Children	Orphans	Negroes
ORLEANS STREET (cont.)					
DARGAREY					
SABANNIER (estate)	PICQUARD	yes			
MARIE FRANCOISE	MARIE FRANCOISE				
BALLE	BALLE, Carpenter	yes			
DUBUISSON	DUBUISSON				
LAMBERT	LAMBERT				
	BELLAIRE				
VINCENT					
GALOIRE	GALOIRE				
	CARQUOT, Nicolas Called PIPY				
DAUSSEVILLE	GRACE	yes			
CHAMILLY	CHAMILLY, Madame		2		1
	ST. MARTIN, Mlle.				
	CHAMILLY, Mlle.				
PINET	PINET, Gunsmith	yes			
ROCHER, André	ROCHER, André	yes			
	SIMART, Sailor	yes	1		
	RACQUETTE				
ROBERT	ROBERT, Sargeant	yes	3		1
DURANTAY	DURANTAY				2
JACQUILLON	JACQUILLON, Ex-soldier	yes	4		
BAILLIF	BAILLIF, Widow		1		
AUBRUN	AUBRUN, Mason				
	LA DUPRE				
NEGRIER	NEGRIER	yes			1
	ROBERT, Tailor				
SKIL	SKIL, Marc	yes			
TOULOUSE STREET					
TOURENJEAN	TOURENJEAN, Gardener	yes			1
FRANCOEUR					
LA CHENAY	LA CHENAY, Sawyer				
TOURENJEAN	DIGNY, Carpenter				
	DUCROS, Widow				
FILASSIER	FILASSIER	yes			
	DAUVERGUE				
AVIGNON	AVIGNON	yes			2
SAN FACON	SANS FACON				2
PIOZAT	PIOZAT, Barber				
	MILET, Mason	yes			
COUPARD	COUPARD, Carpenter	yes			4
MORICET	MORICET	yes	2		4
LOUBOEY	LOUBOEY, Lt.				6
ROSSARD	ROSSARD	yes			5

HOME OWNER	RESIDENT	Wife	Children	Orphans	Negroes
CONTY STREET					
DE LERY	GISCARD, Louis Called BENERIS	yes	1		2
DAUSSEVILLE					
DE MOUY					
DESLATTES	DESLATTES, Carpenter	yes	1		
	DESLATTES, Michel				
The King	MARQUET, Sail-maker	yes			
SAROT	SAROT				1
RICARD	RICARD				
	LIOTAUR				
ST. JACQUES	HERVE				
ST. LOUIS STREET					
REITER	REITER	yes		1	1
CRISTINA	CRISTINA	yes			
LAGE, Thomas	LAGE, Thomas	yes	2		
CONRAT	CONRAT	yes	1		
	COSSET, Jean. Carpenter				
ALEXANDRE	ALEXANDRE, Surgeon	yes	1		7
BONPARD, Madame	BONPARD, Madame				1
AUFRERE	AUFRERE	yes	3		
BELLEGARDE	BELLEGARDE	yes	1		6
DE LA CHAISE	DE LA CHAISE				2
	DEBAT				
DAUBLIN	DAUBLIN, Founder	yes	1		
	BRU, Agent for the Co. of the Indies				3

RECAPITULATION

Total Whites	626
Total Negroes	267

AUGUST 8, 1720 TO SEPTEMBER 4, 1723

LIST OF THOSE WHO DIED AT OLD FORT BILOXI DURING THE ADMINISTRATION OF M. DAVION

Name	Date of Death	Comments
BREVAL, Pierre	August 8, 1720	
DEMOLISSE, Pierre	13	
CHAPUY, Antoine	14	Convict
CADET	15	
REQUETTE, Louis	17	
BOUTVILLE, Michel	19	
PINDELIGUE, Guillaume	22	
COTTINOT	25	Soldier
BESOIN, Louis	26	
DUVAL	27	Soldier
MARCHAND, Nicolas	30	
USEL, Alain		
CARRET, Urbain	Sept. 2, 1720	
LA CONDAMINE	3	Soldier
SUICHEG, Jacques	3	
DAROSEE, Mariane	3	
LE ROUX, Claude	4	
PHILIPINE, Catherine	5	
PHILIPE, Henry	6	
BERGERON, François	8	Soldier
GAUTHIER, Jullien	8	
GIBERT, Nicolas	10	
NIVEAUX, Wife of	10	
LA BELLE, Guillaume	11	
FER, Edmé de	11	
LA ROSE	12	
MORVANY, Jean	13	
LOUVART, Pierre	17	
MATTER, J. B.	17	
BERMONT, Jacques	17	Convict
SAOGT, Michel	18	Convict
MASSON, Jacques	19	Soldier
CORBAN, Adrian Joseph	20	
GUERIT, Guillaume	20	Convict
RAYMOND, Pierre	21	Convict
HAVET, Jean	22	
FORINAT, Thomas	23	
LERMINE, François	23	Convict
GUILDET, René	23	
DUCHENET, Jean	23	
ALEXANDRE, Pierre		

Name	Date of Death	Comments
DAUSTRICE, Fredericq Paul	Sept. 24, 1720	
(There are no listings for October and November, 1720)		
DUBOIS, Jerome	Dec. 9, 1720	Soldier
ARSELLE, Jacques	9	Soldier
MARTELLE, Charles	9	Mason
DIACRE, Salomon	9	
AUBIER, Antoine	10	
BELAIN, Antoine	10	
AUSTRONE, Jean	11	
BARRE, Child of	11	
VACHON, Marguerite	12	Wife of the late COURTEAU
BATEMENT, Marguerite	12	Wife of ALEXANDRE
L'ANGLOIS, René	13	
CHAPELIER	13	Soldier
COUTEAU, Marie	13	Wife of LYONNOIS
BOURDY, François	13	
GALOCHET, François	13	
CULVAR, Jean	16	
DUPUYS, Marguerite	16	
LE VESRIER	16	
CALLIET, Pierre	19	Soldier
THOMAS, Henry	19	Soldier
HAN, Jacques de	20	Volunteer
RIGAULET, Nicolas	20	Soldier
PILAIN, Wife of Antoine	20	
CORDIER, Wife of	20	
LAVERDURE, Pierre	21	A child
DANIEL, Ollivier	21	Convict
PICART, Pierre	24	Corporal
LA ROCHE	24	Owner of a chaloupe
PINART, Pierre	24	
BOISSIERE, Pierre	25	
VOISIN	25	
HUBERT, François	25	
PARISIEN, Wife of Jacques	25	
MARTIN, Jacques	28	Silk-worker
VOISIN, Pierre	Jan. 6, 1721	Soldier
LA BOISSIERE, François	6	Soldier
IMBERT, François	7	Soldier
VINCENT, Gille	9	
BRETON, Adrian	11	
Wife of DE HAYT (le fils)	11	
METIER, Claude	13	

Name	Date of Death		Comments
REQUIEM, Wife of	Jan.	14, 1721	
MARTIN, Charles		16	Worker
LEVESQUE		16	
HEM, Nicolas		20	
MORN, Elizabeth		20	A child
GRIMALLE, Antoine		22	
DUBOIS, Jean		27	
VANEUIL, Wife of Jean		27	
MORISSEAUX		28	
FILLE, François		28	
PRIMART, Antoine		30	
GILLES, François		30	Soldier
LAMBALLE, Margueritte	Feb.	1, 1721	
COLOMBELLE, Marie		1	
GUERELLE, Jeanne		3	
TREVILLON		4	Soldier in LE BLANC's company
FRESNE, Thomas du		6	
ROMENNAU		17	Convict
DIVIER, Antoine		21	From Artois
BELLISLE, François	Mar.	2, 1721	Soldier
PARISIEN, Jacques		10	Soldier
DUFOUR, Bernard		11	Soldier
DESSESSARTS, François		13	Storekeeper for the Company.
SIMONIN, Jean		13	Convict
COURTE, Marie		25	
MARGUERITTE	Apr.	3, 1721	
DUBUISSON, Gabrielle		26	Girl, aged 16 years.
ALLAIN, Jean	May	24, 1721	Edge-tool maker
LE BEAU, Louis		25	Carpenter
DULILLET, André		25	Age 22
BERNARD, Charles	June	21, 1721	
L'EPRON, Simon		21	Carpenter
ARLUT, Angelique	July	10, 1721	
ROUGEAUT (ROUGEANT?) Anne	Aug.	22, 1721	
DUVERGER, Nicolas		24	
RISBOURG, Jean	Sept.	1, 1721	Convict. Aged 20 years
REYON, Louise		4	German

Name	Date of Death		Comments
LA LANCETTE	Oct.	11, 1721	Soldier and barber
BALNON, Jean		19	
DURAND		23	
LALO, M.		24	Ensign
BRAQUIGNY, Mathieu		25	Owner of a chaloupe
MARIE		28	
SAUCE, Pierre		28	
LE BEAUREPERT		30	Daughter of COUVENT
MICHEL, Philipe		30	Child of Pierre VERNIER
DOUBLAIN, Jean		31	
LAVALLE, Pierre	Nov.	3, 1721	
VIVIER, Nicolas		7	
BARBIER, Pierre		9	
LA VILLE, Margueritte		23	Wife of Henry LA VILLE, soldier
COUDRAY, Izac du	Dec.	18, 1721	Soldier. Age 33
DEVIN, Jean		18	Edge-tool maker. Age 46
BAUDAC, Anne		20	Wife of Jacques BAUDAC
JACQUOTOT, Denis		25	Avocat of the Parlement of Paris
LA BAR, Anne		26	Wife of Jacques GOUY. Age 30
GOUANE, François	Jan.	6, 1722	Age about 15
MELANIE, Marie		7	Came on the Baline
BOISSIMOND, Jacques		7	Master of a vessel
BELSAGUNY, Dominique		13	From Bayonne. Age 35
QUEROL, Valtre		22	From Prague in Bohemia. Age 40
NETCH, Marie	Feb.	4, 1722	Widow of TROBAS, a German. Age 40
LAMAUL, Noël		5	From Switzerland
JANNETTE, Jeanne		24	Wife of Jacques SAVIGNON. Age 20.
PISTOLLE, Marte		25	Wife of Cristophe BRIE. Age 42.
DESAUNAY, Vincent Le Clerc		25	Officer on MAZIERES' concession
KERON, Jacques		28	Sailor. Age 25
HIBERT, Prime		28	German. Age 30
BLANQUET, Marie Angelique	Mar.	2, 1722	Daughter of Robert BLANQUET
JOURDAN, Nicolas		13	Cadet. Age about 28
BALSER, Magdelaine		14	Wife of Jean BALSER. Age about 40.
D'OUBLANT, Jean Catherine		16	
ELIE, Laurent		18	German. Age 20
GOURON, Jeanne		20	Wife of Jean FUMA. Age about 28.

Name	Date of Death		Comments
BARON (?), Marie Louise	Mar.	28, 1722	Daughter of Madame BARON
MIOL, Jean Bernard		29	
BOGUE, Catherine Joseph	Apr.	30, 1722	From Douery in Flanders
BOIE, Cristophe	May	11, 1722	From Orleans. Age about 40.
VILLETE, Pierre	Aug.	7, 1722	Storekeeper for the Company
AUDRIOT, Nicolas		13	Major in the army.
CARIERE, Jean	Sept.	19, 1722	"Habitant". Age 35
BLANPIN (fils), Pierre	Oct.	9, 1722	
TRIBOULOTE, Anne		11	Daughter of François TRIBOULOT
VIEIL, Marie Françoise	Nov.	14, 1722	Wife of Jean VIEIL, a sailor. Age 28.
QUARTIER, Jean	Jan.	27, 1723	From Bezier. Age about 35
FORES, Michel		31	From La Rochelle. Cooper. Age about 22 years.
PENIL (PEUIL?), Marie	June	25, 1723	Wife of HENRY, a soldier. Age 33.
JUBIT, Marie	July	18, 1723	Wife of Guillaume GUITTON, a baker.
JAVOTTE, Marie Joseph	Aug.	19, 1723	
ROY, Louis Pierre		25	
LA COMBE, Sieur de	Sept.	4, 1723	Officer in M. LE BLANC's company.

1722-1723

LIST, BY FATHER PHILIBERT DE VIANDEN, CAPUCIN MISSIONARY, OF THOSE WHO DIED IN THE DISTRICT BETWEEN CHAPITOULAS AND POINTE COUPEE.

Name	Date of Death	Comments
TORDEUR, Jean Baptiste	October 31, 1722	Native of Ponce in Flanders. Worker on the Ste. Reyne Concession
ZOON, Pierre	December, 1722	
ZOON, Marie Marbe	December, 1722	
NAIGELLE, Martin	December, 1722	
ZINCHEN, Chat	December, 1722	
RITTER, Chate	December, 1722	
FREDERIC	December, 1722	Son of Conrad Frederic
GREVERINNE, Anne Marie	December, 1722	
MUNICH, Barbara Regina	December, 1722	Daughter of Pierre MUNICH
DRAGUER, Margueritte	December, 1722	
SCHMID, Fronica	December, 1722	Wife of Ausdant SCHMID
LEGROS, Ignance	December, 1722	Stone-cutter
SCHIDZON, George	1723	
HARTMAN, Philipe	1723	
MAZANAU, Gaspard	1723	
DUBOIS, Anne Marie	1723	Wife of Barthelemy JANTEN

1724-1725

LIST OF THOSE WHOSE DEATH WAS REGISTERED AT NEW ORLEANS BETWEEN JANUARY 1, 1724 AND JANUARY 14, 1725.

Name	Date of Death	Comments
DUHALLET, René	January 1, 1724	Native of Lorient, Bishopric of Vannes in Brittany.
ROGER, Jean François	January 11, 1724	Son of Mathurin ROGER and Catherine BLANCHART.
AURARD, Simon	January 16, 1724	Master of the port at New Orleans.
RICHARD, Marie	February 8, 1724	Native of Melun in Brie. Wife of Louis GALLES, soldier, who died at the hospital on the 7th.
ROB, Martin	February 8, 1724	Company worker, died at the hospital.
SAINT JEAN	February 9, 1724	From Chartres in Beauce, soldier.
BONNEAUD, Edmé Guillaume	March 9, 1724	Captain of the Company's ship <u>LE DROMADAIRE</u>.
FOURCHE, Louis	March 16, 1724	Son of Louis FOUCHE and Jeanne LE NOBLE.
Therese	March 18, 1724	Daughter of Cecile, Indian slave of Sieur LAGOUBLAYE.
KECBSENDHEM, Marie Elizabeth	May 29, 1724	Wife of Jean George KECBSENDHEM, German resident established on the Mississippi River.
JARRY, Marie Anne	June 1, 1724	Daughter of Louis JARRY and Anne SOULETIER, aged 15 months.
CHARDON, Jeanne	June 18, 1724	Wife of Antoine BUREL and LA BRANCHE, a miner.
DUBOIS, Joseph	July 15, 1724	Son of Joseph DUBOIS, Aged 14 to 15 years.
FIDEL, Jean Baptiste	July 29, 1724	Aged 6 months. Son of Pierre FIDEL and Marie ThereseLIVILLIER.
LA FORGE, Marie Anne	August 5, 1724	Daughter of Jacques LA FORGE and Marie Anne BOURGUENET.
HUGOT, Jean	August 19, 1724	Aged 53 years. Resident, former employee on the Le Blanc Concession.
PICARD, Pierre	Sept. 20, 1724	Called RUDE AUX POULES. Native of Burgundy. Died at the hospital.
LA CROIX, Laurent	Sept. 20, 1724	Native of La Rochelle. Died at the hospital.
LANGLOIS, Marie Louise	Sept. 23, 1724	Daughter of Etienne Langlois and Catherine BOUDEROT, resident, aged 3 days.

Name	Date of Death	Comments
PREVOT, Etienne	Sept. 24, 1724	Native of Dumarien, Bishopric of Langres. Died at the hospital.
VALLERAUD (VALLERAND?)	Sept. 24, 1724	Child of VALLERAUD, worker and resident.
BARRASSON, Child of	Sept. 24, 1724	
DEMAING, Child of	Sept. 24, 1724	The father is a tailor.
ST LEGER. Wife of	Sept. 29, 1724	ST. LEGER is a soldier and a native of Versailles.
SCIPION	Sept. 29, 1724	Freed Negro. Sailor on the Company's ship LE DROMADAIRE.
DUFLOT, Child of	Sept. 29, 1724	Posthumous child of DUFLOT and Marie Margueritte CHARTIER.
CARMELET, Wife of	Oct. 3, 1724	CARMELET, called JOLLY COEUR, is a soldier. His wife died at the hospital.
DUPUY, Christine	Oct. 20, 1724	Native of Brittany. Aged 35 years. Died at the hospital.
BARRE, Mathurin	Oct. 5, 1724	Son of Gilbert BARRE. Aged 19 months.
MARTIN, Child of	Oct. 1, 1724	Child of Gabriel MARTIN, resident.
RINCHE, Gertrude	Oct. 9, 1724	Wife of André SANNE, coppersmith.
AIME, Catherine	Oct. 9, 1724	Wife of Estienne GIRAU, carpenter.
FLAMANDE, Therese Capet	Oct. 28, 1724	Wife of Nicolas CAPET, soldier. (Note: the "Flamande" here probably indicates that she was a native of Flanders, rather than it being her maiden name.)
DESMARAIS, Francois	Oct. 28, 1724	Native of Flanders. Aged 45 years.
AMELOT, Marie Elizabeth	Oct. 30, 1724	Daughter of Joseph AMELOT and Catherine RUESEN.
TREPANIER, Claude	Nov. 21, 1724	Aged about 50 years. A resident of this parish. He died around the mouth of the Mississippi.
FERRET, Françoise	Nov. 28, 1724	Wife of Charles Gaigné de DUPLESSIS. Native of St. Jacques Damiens in Picardy. Aged 45 years.
Antoine	Nov. 25, 1724	Called LA ROSE. Corporal. Native of Allinghen de Boulogne in Boulonnois.
VINAIGRIES, Louis	Nov. 27, 1724	Native of Langres. Aged 55 years.
SEGUIN, Michel	Nov. 6, 1724	
FERRCE, François	Nov. 27, 1724	

Name	Date of Death	Comments
Chistina (CHRISTINA?)	Nov. 17, 1724	A German, aged 40 years.
MARTIN, Etienne	Nov. 28, 1724	Native of Angers. Aged about 40 years. Died at Biloxi and was buried by the chaplain of the ship PROFOND which was calling at that port.
DESMARAIS, Jean François	Nov. 21, 1724	Native of Chalet, county and diocese of Liège. Aged 28 years.
GILBERT, Jean	Nov. 3, 1724	Native of Querqueville, Bishopric of Coutances in Normandie. Son of Jacques GILBERT, aged 46 years.
BEAULIEU, Catherine	Nov. 1, 1724	Native of St. Jacques de la Boucherie. Aged about 36 years.
GALFAT, Jullien Robert	Nov. 7, 1724	Native of St. Quas de St. Malo.
BEGON, Jacques	Dec. 2, 1724	Called BELLAIR. A soldier. Native of Sedan. Aged 40 years.
LARNAU, Bertrand de	Dec. 2, 1724	Native of Pau in Bearn. Aged 45 years. Died at the hospital.
HEMERY, Alexandre	Dec. 28, 1724	Son of Jean Pierre HEMERY and Anne Catherine CHRIC. His parents are residents of the lower Mississippi .

ADDITION TO THE MONTH OF OCTOBER, 1724

Name	Date of Death	Comments
BORDIER, Marie Cather-	Oct. 7, 1724	Wife of Jean BORDIER, resident. Aged 23 years. Native of the parish of St. Nicolas in La Rochelle.
AUGRAND, Nicolas	Oct. 10, 1724	Master mason employed by the Company. Aged 63 years. Native of Dieppe in Normandy.
MAUART, Marie	Oct. 15, 1724	Aged 18 years. Daughter of François Mauart and of Marie Catherine MANERA.
MANERA, Marie Catherine	Jan. 5, 1725	Native of Nanir, Aged 25 years. Wife of Jean François MAUART who is from Marsienne sur l'Escarpe, Diocese of Arras.
BIDOT, Jean Baptiste	Jan. 14, 1725	Crippled child of Jean Baptiste BIDOT, a goldsmith of Paris.

1725

LIST OF THOSE PERSONS WHOSE DEATH WAS REGISTERED AT NEW ORLEANS DURING THE YEAR 1725.

Name	Date of Death or Burial and Comments
BIDOT, Jean Baptiste	Died January 14, 1725. Native of Paris. Aged 23 years. Son of Jean Baptiste BIDOT, a goldsmith of Paris. Died at the hospital at 2:a.m. Death certificate signed by François DUVAL and Sieur BEAULIEU, a resident of Chapitoulas.
MONDAIN, Laurent	Died January 14, 1725. Called LAVERDURE. Native of Pomelin, Bishopric of Quimper in Brittany, resident of New Orleans. Aged about 37 years. Death certificate signed by Charles CAYEUX, resident of New Orleans; Sieur Gilbert DUMAS, called L'AMPILEUR; and Jacques GUY, called ST. ANDRE.
LUMAUX, Marie	Buried January 30, 1725. Native of St. Jean d'Angely, Diocese of Bordeaux. Wife of the late Jacques SALAN (SALAU?) who died on the 2nd of this month. Buried in the presence of Sieur Jacques CICILE, cadet in the naval regiment; Sieur Gilles PIGEON, Surgeon in the same regiment.
LE VASSEUR	Buried January 16, 1725. Native of Venencour, Bishopric of Amiens. Wife of Sieur Nicolas Charles BOURGEOIS, resident of New Orleans. Died January 15. Aged 25 years. Died suddenly.
AYET, Antoine	Buried January 17, 1725. Ten-day-old son of Antoine AYET and Claudine GRISON, residents of this parish.
GIRARD, Elizabeth	On the deposition of the undersigned witnesses, I, Frère Hyacinte de Verdun, Capucin missionary, certify that the body of Elizabeth GIRARD, native of Rouen, aged about 22 years, was buried at Natchez, November 24, 1721. Signed: BLOUIEN (?), Claude LA CROIX, BARRIE, and Frère Hyacinte.

Name	Date of Death or Burial and Comments
DAUDENAU, Marie Anne	On the deposition of the undersigned witnesses, I, Frère Hyacinte de Verdun, Capucin missionary, certify that the body of Marie Anne DAUDENAU, native of St. Severin, near Paris, Aged about 24 years, was buried at Natchez on September 29, 1722. Signed: BLOUIEN, Claude LA CROIX, and Frère Hyacinte.
MOREAU, Jacques	Died January 19, 1725. Buried January 27, 1725. Worker on M. Dumanoir"s concession. Native of Ville Neuf, parish of Montigny sur Nugin, Diocese of Langres. Aged about 25 years. Witnesses: TOUSSAINT BOURLIER who has made his cross.
ANDRONIQUE, Honoré	Died and buried January 23, 1725. Native of Riesse in Provençe. Aged about 48 years. Witnessed by Pierre COUILLERET who has made his mark.
DAUPHIN, François	Died and buried February 7, 1725. Native of Neon in Poitou, parish of St. Vincent, Bishopric of Poitiers. Workers on the Diron concession. Aged about 40 years. Died at the hospital.
DELACHAUME, Marie Françoise	Died and buried February 17, 1725. Daughter of Monsieur and Madame DEZONY. Native of the parish of Jouy, Bishopric of Sausse in Burgundy. Aged 25 years. Came to Louisiana on the DEUX FRERES, commanded by M. FERRET. Died at the hospital.
GERMAIN, Claude	Buried February 5, 1725. Negro boy aged 6 days.
LANGEVIN, Jacques	Died March 7, 1725, buried March 8, 1725. Native of La Coste St. Paul, parish of La Chine. A voyageur, aged 28 years. Witnesses: ROCHOT and J. B. BERGERON.
POIREE, Françoise	Died March 19, 1725, buried March 20, 1725. Daughter of Louis POIREE, resident of New Orleans. Aged 17 months.
BONHOMME	Buried March 18, 1725. Native of the parish of St. Jean in the vicinity of Quebec. Aged 60 years. Sone of the late BONHOMME and the late Françoise UGE. Died at the hospital.
BOURGEOIS, Nicolas Jean Baptiste	Buried March 2, 1725. Aged 16 months. Son of Nicolas BOURGEOIS, resident of New Orleans.

Name	Date of Death or Burial and Comments
PIERRE	Buried May 25, 1725. Aged 14 months. Son of an Indian slave belonging to Sieur SAINTAMAN, a resident of New Orleans.
VILLEROY, Marie	Buried May 28, 1725. Wife of Pierre PELONIN, resident of Cannes Brulees. Aged about 30 years. Died at the hospital.
MARSANSOLEIL, Capt.	Died February 6, 1725. Buried February 7, 1725. Naval captain in the service of the Company of the Indies. Native of Audaye. Aged about 50 years.
FRANCOISE	Buried June 8, 1725. Negro woman belonging to M. DE VERTUEIL of the Bayougoula concession. Aged 15 years.
DAMOURETTE, Jeanne	Died and buried June 9, 1725. Wife of Joseph MOREAU, master locksmith in New Orleans. Witnesses: GIRAUT, ROY, and LE BLANC.
MARCHAND, Mathurine	Died June 9, 1725. Buried June 10, 1725. Native of Vannes in Brittany, parish of St. Paler (?). Wife of Pierre CLERC, resident of New Orleans. Aged 32 years.
ILENEF, Jean	Died May 25, 1725. Buried May 26, 1725. Native of Camberge. Aged about 60 years.
DUHAMEL, Martellin	Died and buried September 16, 1725. Called LA POMPE. A block-maker. Native of Paris, parish of St. Louis on Notre Dame Island. Son of Antoine DUHAMEL, wine merchant, and the late Heleine Elizabeth SAUVAGE. Aged about 30 years. A soldier in Mandeville's company. Died at the hospital.
DUMONT, Adrien	Buried June 10, 1725. Son of Sieur DUMONT of St. Honoré Street in Paris, parish of St. Roch. Died at the hospital. Wittness: PREVOT.
GIRAULT, Denis	Died June 28, 1725. Buried June 29, 1725. Native of Paris, Montmartre Street, parish of St. Joseph. Master clerk and notary of the Company of the Indies. Aged 45 years. Witnesses: BONNEAUD and DUVAL.
FOURNAU, Marie Jeanne	Died July 7, 1725. Buried July 8, 1725. Wife of Antoine DURANT, shoemaker and resident of this parish. Witnesses: STENSTEL, Laurent CHENCOLY, and Antoine DRIGNY.

Name	Date of Death or Burial and Comments
DRILLANT, Denis	Died July 8, 1725. Buried July 9, 1725. Native of La Rochelle. Clerk at the store of the Company of the Indies. Witnesses: BONNEAUD, GAUVRIT, CEARD, François DUVAL.
OUALLE, Guillaume	Died July 14, 1725. Buried July 15, 1725. Clerk at the store of the Company of the Indies. Native of Paris, Mortellèrie Street, parish of St. Gervais. Witnesses: CREPIN, BRANTAN, SAGARENNE, LEGAC, CHEVAL.
VITREQUAIN, Marie Louise	Buried August 10, 1725. Aged 18 months.
LABOULAYE, Michel	Died August 6, 1725. Buried August 7, 1725. Native of Dieppe. Sailor on the ELEPHANT. Died at the hospital. Aged about 23 years.
DIVAN, Marie Nicolas de	Died August 12, 1725. Buried August 15, 1725. Pilot of the ship ELEPHANT. Son of Julien de DIVAN. Died at the hospital. Aged about 36 years.
SONTINE, Agatte	Died August 18, 1725. Buried August 19, 1725. Native of Romsac in Alsace. Wife of Gaspard HULUIN, a German resident on the Mississippi above New Orleans. Aged 35 years.
SALAU,	Died August 19, 1725. Buried August 20, 1725. Aged 18 months.
ASSELIN, Jacques	Died August 20, 1725. Buried August 21, 1725. Son of Thomas ASSELIN and Jeanne GUBERT. Aged 12 months.
BIGEON, Pierre	Died August 21, 1725. Buried August 22, 1725. Son of Remy BIGEON and Marie MILARD. Aged 3 1/2 months.
BERNARD, Jean	Died and buried August 11, 1725. Native of Calais. Recorder on the ship BELONNE. Aged about 35 years.
PERUS, Vincent	Died and Buried August 20, 1725. Master carpenter on the ELEPHANT.
DES BROSSES. Claude Janneau	Died and buried August 23, 1725. Clerk of supplies on the ELEPHANT.
ALAIZE, Jacques	Died and buried August 24, 1725. Native of Lorient. Sailor and pilot on the ship ELEPHANT.

Name	Date of Death or Burial and Comments
LALAILLE, Jacques	Buried August 27, 1725. Son of Simon LALAILLE and Magdelaine MARIE. Aged 2 years.
VIGNE, Jean	Buried August 27, 1725. Son of Etienne VIGNE and Catherine HUBERT. Aged 7 months.
GIRAULT, Catherine	Died August 31, 1725. Buried September 7, 1725. Child of Estienne GIRAULT AND Catherine HEMERYS. Aged 4 years.
EMARD	Died the last of August, 1725. Buried September 7, 1725. Child belonging to Sieur EMARD, a baker.
CABACIER, Michel	Died September 3, 1725. Buried September 4, 1725 Native of Montrail, Bishopric of Quebec. Resident of New Orleans. Aged 44 years.
VALERAN, Jacques	Buried September 7, 1725. Son of Jacques VALLERAN and MARTE BUREL, resident of New Orleans. Aged 2 months.
DELAITRE, Marie Geneviève	Died and buried August 8, 1725. Daughter of Louis DELAITRE and Marie Geneviève CARON, residents of New Orleans. Aged one year.
ESCON, Guillaume	Died September 6, 1725. Buried September 7, 1725. Son of ESCON and Jeanne VRELIER. Aged 11 1/2 years.
DUBOIS, François	Died September 12, 1725. Buried September 13, 1725. Native of Anbord, near Rochefort. Master cooper. Aged 62 years.
PREHIN, Anne	Died September 13, 1725. Buried September 14, 1725. Wife of Laurent QUEL (KELLE), brick-maker for the Company of the Indies. Aged 37 years.
COLLIGNON, Marie Anne	Died September 13, 1725. Buried September 14, 1725 Wife of Joseph CATOIRE, resident of New Orleans Aged 30 years.
CARON, Marie Anne	Died September 17, 1725. Buried September 18, 1725 Child of Antoine Michel PATRON (CARON?) who works for the Company of the Indies, and Marie DODIN. Aged about 11 months.
MANSEAU, Louis	Died September 20, 1725. Buried September 21, 1725. Son of François MANSEAU and Marie Magdelaine SALOT. Aged 9 months.

Name	Date of Death or Burial and Comments
VALIN, Jeanne	Died September 21, 1725. Buried September 22, 1725. Native of Grez in Compte. Wife of Jean Louis LE BORD, called MONTEAUBAN, soldier in Le Blanc's company. Aged 39 years.
DEMAIN, Marianne Elizabeth	Died September 23, 1725. Buried September 24, 1725. Daughter of Pierre DEMAIN and Mariane ELEURY.
LA BOURRE, Jean Pierre	Died September 25, 1725. Buried September 26, 1725. Son of Jean LA BOURRE and Perrette LE ROY. Aged 11 years.
PIERRE	Died September 25, 1725. Buried September 26, 1725. Negro belonging to M. de Chavanne, secretary of the Superior Council of Louisiana.
DUPLECHIN, Angelique	Died and Buried September 26, 1725. Daughter of Joseph DUPLECHIN and Anne Marie TAVERNE, residents of Oumas. Aged about 9 months.
AMOND, Anne	Died September 28, 1725. Buried September 29, 1725. Native of Marchelpau, Bishopric of Peronne. Wife of Claude BAGUEROIS, resident of New Orleans. Aged 29 years.
HOUVEZ, Anne	Died October 1, 1725. Buried October 2, 1725. Wife of Jean FUMAS, resident of New Orleans. Aged about 40 years.
DEBAS, Marie Magdelaine	Died October 4, 1725. Buried October 5, 1725. Native of Paris, parish of St. Eustache. Wife of Mathieu GOTS, called LA VIOLETTE. Aged 27 years.
MARCHAND	Died October 6, 1725. Buried October 7, 1725 Child of Nicolas MARCHAND and Marie GUILLET.
LEBON, Toussaint	Died and buried October 2, 1725. Son of Julien LEBON, native of Plumenier in Brittany. Aged about 29 years.
LANGLOIS, Pierre Martin	Died October 7, 1725. Buried October 8, 1725. Aged 43 years.
PECQUERY, Pierre	Died October 6, 1725. Buried October 7, 1725 Son of Pierre PICQUERY and Jeanne FADEE. Aged 17 months.
BRIDON, Louise	Died October 7, 1725. Buried October 8, 1725. Native of St. Mars, Bishopric of Tours in Touraine. Wife of Jean NAVERS, resident of New Orleans.

Name	Date of Death or Burial and Comments
VIGER, Pierre Louis	Died October 14, 1725. Buried October 15, 1725. Son of Sieur Louis VIGER, resident on the Mississippi.
FUMANT, Jean François	Buried October 14, 1725. Son of Jean FUMANT and the late Anne TRUBATTE. Aged about 6 months.
GRATTE, Didier	Died and buried October 15, 1725. Called DUPRE. Engagé of M. de Verteuil. Native of Plaussat, Bishoptic of Lyon. Died at the hospital. Aged 23 years.
CHEVET, Jeanne	Died October 20, 1725. Buried October 21, 1725. Native of Paris, parish of St. Victor. Wife of Mathieu LAVIGNON, called PROVENCAL, soldier. Aged 22 years.
HENRY, Marie Françoise	Died October 21, 1725. Buried October 22, 1725. Daughter of Nicolas HENRY and Elizabeth HAMARD. Aged 7 days.
LAFONS, Louis	Died October 25, 1725. Buried October 26, 1725. Native of La Vauffrance, diocese of Limoges. Aged 44 years.
PITACHE, Jeann Catherine	Died October 20, 1725. Buried October 21, 1725. Aged 3 1/2 years.
ADAM, Louis	Died November 5, 1725. Buried November 6, 1725. Native of La Vannes Bourg, near Vitry. Aged 23 years.
VIEILLE VIGNE, François	On the deposition of the Sieur DREUX, I, Frère Hyacinte de Verdun, Capucin missionary, certify that François VIEILLE VIGNE, resident of Gentilly, was buried in the cemetery of that place. Native of Ortex in Languedoc.
COLLET, Henry	Buried November 10, 1725. Born October 9, 1725 to _______________ and Susanne SERCLET.
KUNIC, Barthelemic	Buried November 3, 1725. Native of Nalchaulsen, canton of Lusernes in Switzerland. Cooper. Soldier in Merveilleux's company. Aged 40 years.
BENTEYER, Margueritte	Buried November 13, 1725. Native of Hunbaque. Daughter of Cristiane BENTLIJER and Dame FOCY. Wife of Jean UNIK, a Swiss. Aged 48 years.

Name	Date of Death or Burial and Comments
BOUILLAUX, Jean	Died November 10, 1725. Buried November 11, 1725 Soldier in Dartaguette's Company. Native of the parish of Chasseneuil, diocese of Poitiers. Aged 50 years.
GETS, Michel	Died November 20, 1725. Buried November 21, 1725 Son of Laurent GETHZ and Elizabeth BALLY, resident on the Mississippi. Aged about 15 days.
DELAISTRE, Jean Louis	Died November 4, 1725. Buried November 5, 1725. Native of Paris. Son of ___________DELESTRE.
BAYER, Pierre	Buried November 26, 1725. Resident of this parish. Aged about 24 years. Native of Brussels in Germany. Witnesses: Nicolas DE HIMET and Jean FUCLES both of whom have made their mark.
LOUFFINARD	Died November 25, 1725. Buried November 27, 1725. Native of Dauphiné.
GUERET, Justin	Died December 1, 1725. Buried December 2, 1725. Native of Orléans on the Loire. Bailiff of the Superior Council of Louisiana.
FOULON, Marie	Died November 27, 1725. Buried December 2, 1725. Died at the hospital.
MARCHAND, Mathurine	Died June 8, 1725. Buried June 9, 1725 Wife of Pierre CLERAUX, Native of the parish of Nef, Bishopric of Vannes. Aged 32 years. Died at the hospital.
LAGRANDEUR	Buried September 7, 1725. Sargeant in the marine regiment. Aged 48 years. Died at the hospital.
RADOUX, André	Buried September 9, 1725. Worker on the Dumanoir concession. Native of St. Malo. Aged 31 years.
RENEUX	Buried September 19, 1725. Cadet in the naval regiment. Native of Paris, parish of St. Paul Died at the hospital.
LAMBERT	Died October 25, 1725. Buried October 26, 1725. Native of Paris, St. Jacques Street, parish of St. Paul. Aged 23 years. Died at the hospital.
RICHARD	Died October 6, 1725. Buried October 7, 1725. Sailor. Native of Brest in Brittany. Aged 45 years.

Name	Date of Death or Burial and Comments
HEUX, Claude	Died October 15, 1725. Buried October 16, 1725. Master of the ship ELEPHANT. Native of Havre de Grace in Normandy. Aged 45 years. Died at the hospital.
DUGUAY, Françoise	Buried October 10, 1725. Aged 17 years. Died at the hospital.
EUE	Died December 8, 1725. Buried December 9, 1725. A German. Died at the hospital.
PERIER, Marie Bastienne	Buried December 16, 1725. Daughter of Guillaume PERIER and Marie BAUCHE.
MAJOR, Françoise	Buried November 15, 1725. Daughter of Bastient MAJOR. Wife of Claude GOUET.
CLERO, Jeanne Marie	January 4, 1725. Daughter of Pierre CLERO and Mathurinne MARCHAND. Aged 4 years.

(This list was compiled by Frère Mathias de Sedan, Capucin missionary, and by Frère Hyacinte de Verdun, Capucin missionary.)

1726

LIST OF THOSE PERSONS WHOSE DEATH WAS RECORDED FROM JANUARY 8, 1726 to JANUARY 10, 1727.

Name	Date of Death or Burial and Comments
DUROCHER. Jean	Died January 8, 1726. Native of Lorient. Worked on the DUMANOIR Concession as a cook. Died at the hospital. Aged about 34 years.
SEIGNE, François	Died January 9, 1726. Son of Jacques SEIGNE and Isabelle SUCE. Aged about 3 months.
BLANCHARD, Marie	Died January 25, 1726. Native of Lanevoix, Bishopric of La Rochelle. Wife of Hillaire CHENEAU, master gunner in this city.
DESNOYER, Pierre	Died January 31, 1726. Son of Laurent DESNOYER, former sargeant in the Naval Regiment, and Marie Angelique CHARTRAN. Aged about 12 days.
SILVESTRE, Charlotte	Died February 15, 1726. Daughter of Madame SILVESTRE. Aged, 6 months and 4 days.
BANQUIORES, Michel	Died February 14, 1726. Native of Blaye. Son of Jacques BANQUIORES and Marie Anne DURANT. Died at the hospital. Aged about 23.
VALLERAN, Jacques François	Died February 18, 1726. Aged 4 1/2 months.
GILLIN, Marie Jeanne	Died February 22, 1726. Native of Paris. Wife of François BOURDON, carpenter. Aged, 30 years.
PERON, Anne	Died February 26, 1726. Aged 1 year.
HANNEQUIN, Sebastien	Died February 26, 1726. Native of Donchéry near Sedan, diocese of Rheims. Embarked on the <u>ELEPHANT</u> at Lorient, in August, 1721. <u>Engagé</u> on M. Daffel's concession. Aged about 50 years.
GRANDIN, Michel	Died February 26, 1726. Called LA FORGE. Soldier in Dartaguette's Company. Died at the hospital. Aged 26 years.

Name	Date of Death or Burial and Comments
PIERRE	Died March 1, 1726. Baptised Indian belonging to M. de Bienville.
TRANSAGUE, Louis Antoine	Died March 7, 1726. Native of Orléans. Son of Jacques TRANSAGUE and Marie Geneviève JIQUE of the parish of Ste. Catherine. Soldier in Le Blanc's Company. Died at the hospital.
FONTAINE, Georges Joseph de	Died February 11, 1726. Director of M. Le Blanc's Concession. Native of Sedan, Bishopric of Rhins. Aged 42 years.
JACQUES (Indian)	Died March 23, 1726. Belonged to M. de Boisbriant.
DUVALLET	Died March 25, 1726. Overseer of the Company's Negroes.
CHERAS, Jean François	Died March 27, 1726. Native of Malozein, Comté of Avignon. Aged 45 years. Came to Louisiana on the vessel MARIE in order to work on M. Law's concession. Died at the hospital.
FROGER. Philibert	Died March 28, 1726. Native of Sinay. Came to Louisiana on the vessel LE TILLEUL, aged 30 years.
A negro	Died March 28, 1726. Belonged to the Company.
DURANTE, Coësard	Died April 2, 1726. Son of Sieur DURANTE, sargeant. Aged about 3 1/2 years.
BOURDON, Antoine	Died March 8, 1726. Son of François BOURDON, master carpenter. Aged about 2 1/2 months.
WEBER, Anne Catherine	Died April 17, 1726. Daughter of Jean WEBER and Marie STADELER. Aged about 3 weeks.
FONTAINES, Jean Dominique de	Buried April 25, 1726. Aged about 3 1/2 months.
COUCHER, Joseph	Died April 26, 1726. Son of Pierre COUCHER, edged-tool maker. Aged 8 or 9 days.

Name	Date of Death or Burial and Comments
BONNAVENTURE, Louis de	Died May 4, 1726 and buried the same day. Naval guard, resident of New Orleans. Aged about 32 years.
NAVER, Joseph	Died May 8, 1726. Aged 7 months.
BUY, Antoine	Died May 17, 1726. Sawyer. Native of Clermont in Auvergne. Son of François DENIS and Marianne PRALLES. Came from M. Le Blanc's concession. Aged 45 years.
MULQUAIN, Jean	Died May 18, 1726. Native of Beaumont, country of Haynant. Engagé on the Ste. Reyne concession.
SAMSON, Jeanne Gabrielle	Died May 21, 1726. Aged 3 1/2 years.
VAUDRIN, Yves	Died June 7, 1726. Native of Henubon. Came to the colony as a gunsmith on the Law concession. Died at the hospital. Aged 55 years.
ELIZABETHE	Died June 8, 1726. A German. No one knows her surname. Died at the hospital. Aged about 15 years.
PAUGER, Adrien de	Died June 10, 1726. Chevalier of the order of St. Louis. Engineer-in-chief of this province. Buried the same day.
PIERRE	Died June 26, 1726. A negro belonging to M. Delery, resident of Chapitoulas.
CEARD, Pierre	Died June 24, 1726. Director of the Ste. Reyne Concession.
PIERRE	Died July 3, 1726. Mulatto belonging to M. DELORME, former director of the Company. Aged about 4 years.
XAVIER, Charles	Died July 4, 1726. Child of Marie ACQUERIE. Aged about 4 months.
CHARASSE, Jean Scipion	Died February 26, 1726. Native of Malaverne, Diocese of Traison in the Compté of Avignon. Died at the hospital. Aged 25 years.

Name	Date of Death or Burial and Comments
GLENIS, François	Died June 12, 1726. A German. Native of Mayence. Died at the hospital. Aged about 35 years.
JOHAN, Barbe	Died July 5, 1726. Aged 3 years, 4 months.
GAUJOUX, Jean	Died July 5, 1726. Son of François GOUJOUX and Charlotte BOURBAUD. Native of the parish of St. George du Vigean. Aged 53 years.
JASON, Nicolas	Died July 7, 1726. Negro belonging to Sieur DUVAL, auditor.
DINAN, Françoise	Died July 8, 1726. Native of Paris. Wife of Sieur BROUET, master wheelwright, resident of New Orleans.
LAFOND, Jean Baptiste	Died July 6, 1726. Son of Louis LAFOND. Aged 5 years.
JARDELA, Marie	Died July 12, 1726. Daughter of Allin JARDELA and Marie QUERIQUE. Aged 4 years.
THIBAULAUT, Françoise	Died July 11, 1726. Aged 2 1/2 years.
FABIEN, Jeanne	Died July 13, 1726. Daughter of the late Jean FABIEN. Aged 3 1/2 years.
LE NOBLE, Jeanne	Died July 14, 1726. Native of Paris, parish of Ste. Margueritte. Wife of René TOUCHE, called DUPONT, a soldier. Aged 22 years.
COPIN, Joseph	Buried July 15, 1726. Soldier. Son of Jean Baptiste COPIN, apothicary, and Marie FERDINAND. Native of Tournay, in Flanders, parish of St. Jean.
BRODIEST, Guillaume	Died July 16, 1726. Called LA MONTAGNE. Native of Quimper. Came to Louisiana on the vessel UNION. Died at the hospital. Aged 40 years.
LA CRUNE, Jeanne	Died July 25, 1726. Native of Rochefort. Wife of Antoine Micou CALFAT, carpenter for the Company. Aged about 63 years.
PIED, Catherine	Died July 23, 1726. Wife of Sieur PITACHE. Aged about 23 years.

Name	Date of Death or Burial and Comments
RILTS, Marie Anne	Died July 25, 1726. Widow of Christianne Pol and wife of Pierre CESARD. Aged about 45 years.
TRIBOT, Yves	Died July 11, 1726. Native of Brest. Son of Charles TRIBOT, sailor on the LOIRE. Died at the hospital. Aged 25 years.
CAMBRAY, Jacques	Died July 25, 1726. Sailor on the LOIRE. Son of Alain CAMBRAY. Native of Rignes. Died aboard ship.
NEVER, Jacques le	Died August 2, 1726. Native of Lorient. Caulker on the LOIRE. Son of Jacques LE NEVER. Died at the hospital. Aged 24 years.
D'AUVILLE, Geneviève	Died August 3, 1726. Aged 1 year.
PAQUET, Pierre	Buried August 5, 1726. Resident of Mobile. Native of Angers. Aged 46 years.
MARTIN, Rodolphe	Died August 7, 1726. Native of Bern, Switzerland. Aged about 34 years.
KREISNAVE, Jean George	Died August 11, 1726. Resident on the lower Mississippi. Aged 50 years.
LE VEUVE, Urbin	Died August 14, 1726. Son of Antoine LE VEUVE and Jeanne DAMAS. Aged about 1 month.
CESARD, François	Died August 15, 1726. Son of Pierre CESARD, resident of the German Coast. Aged 2 1/2 years.
LE PORTIER, Jacques	Died August 18, 1726. Native of Cherbourg in Normandy. Son of Jacques PORTIER. Died at the hospital. Aged about 32 or 33 years.
A Child	Buried July 15, 1726. Aged about 1 year. Died at the home of Sieur CARITON, the tailor. Cariton refused to give the child's name.
DRILLANT. Marie Françoise Thérèse	Buried August 19, 1726. Aged about 15 months.
LA RUE, Marie	Died August 24, 1726. Native of Danaud in Normandy. Wife of Nicolas Gaumy de LA RIVIERE, master carpenter. Aged about 35 years.

Name	Date of Death or Burial and Comments
MINELESCHUVI (?), Marie Jacobé	Died August 24, 1726. Daughter of Antoine D'IESCHVOIS and Anne MARIE. Aged 3 months.
BRILIAN, Halin	Died August 24, 1726. Soldier in La Marque's Company. Native of Ponsecord, Bishopric of Vanne. Died at the hospital. Aged 31 years.
ESTIENNE, Gilles	Died August 26, 1726. Son of Louis ESTIENNE and Marie RICULIN. Farmer from Baudmois. Baptized at St. Mars, Bishopic of Cornuailles in Brittany. Came to Louisiana to work on the Ste. Reyne concession. Died at the hospital. Aged 30 years.
LA LANCETTE, Charles	Buried Sept. 5, 1726. Aged 3 years. The father and mother are unknown.
CHENOT, Hilaire	Died September 8, 1726. Son of Hilaire CHENOT, master gunner of this city. Aged 4 years.
BOURSILLIER, Toussaint	Buried September 12, 1726. Aged about 1 year. Son of Toussaint BOURSELLIER and Vincente CORTE.
LABRE, Marie	Buried September 17, 1726. Native of Kerme in Alsace, Bishopic of Landriau. Aged 19 years.
BAUDIN, Antoine	Died September 17, 1726. Son of Louis BAUDIN and Adrienne AUMORS.
NICOLAS	Buried Sept. 25, 1726. Negro, aged 2 years.
DURAND , François	Died September 20, 1726. Called FRAPE DABORD. Tailor. Soldier in La Tour's Company. Native of Tour in Tourenne. Died at the hospital Aged about 30 years.
BENARTIER, Roch	Buried Sept. 19, 1726. Native of Sables d'Aulonne. First pilot of the ship LOIRE. Died at the hospital.
PLOUIN, Pierre	Died Sept. 24, 1726. Native of Briaucois, Bishopric of Euvreas. Came to the colony to work on the Diron Concession as a farmer. Died at the hospital.

Name	Date of Death or Burial and Comments
VILDEGER, François	Buried Sept. 25, 1726. Native of the parish of Brillac de Poitiers, Bishopric of Poitiers, province of Poitou. Son of Joly VILDEGER and Marie JOLY. Died at the hospital.
GLANDU, Joseph François	Died September 27, 1726. Aged 5 days.
SERING, Marie Salomée	Died September 28, 1726. Daughter of Michel SERING, master carpenter in New Orleans. Aged 18 years.
MARQUEMBOULE, François	Died Sept. 29, 1726. Native of Vaudeuve in Champagne. Metal worker. Soldier in Mandeville's company.
PITACHE, François	Died October 1, 1726. Son of François PITACHE, Company employee. Aged 20 months.
BERTRAND, Barbe	Buried October 4, 1726. Native of Elbrant. Daughter of Jean Michel BERTRAND. Her father died at Lorient. Died at the hospital. Aged about 19 years.
CHRISTINE	Died October 10, 1726, at the hospital. A German.
LA FRANCE	Died October 12, 1726. Soldier in Renaud's Company which is at the Yazoo Post. Native of Mezières, Archbishopric of Rheims. Died at the hospital.
FONTAINE, Maximilien	Died at the hospital October 18, 1726. Native of the upper city of Charleroy, bishopric of Namur.
FAUCHE, Marie Anne	Died October 11, 1726. Wife of Sieur DURANTE, sargeant. Native of Nantes, parish of St. Nicolas.
IZABOT	Died October 19, 1726, at the hospital. Native of Ennebont, bishopric of Vannes in Brittany.
MEINTER, François	Died October 20, 1726, at the hospital Son of Louis MEINTER and Marguerite CHAUSSARD. Native of Morlaix, bishopric of St. Meleine.

Name	Date of Death or Burial and Comments
DESPLACE, François Pierre	Died October, 1720 at the old fort (Biloxi?) and buried by the Reverend Père Paulin. He came to the colony in 1719 as a vagabond aboard the MERCURE. Called LA PLACE.
GODEBERT, Margueritte	Died October 24, 1726. Wife of Sieur Jean François CHARAS, native of Malaulinne of the County of Avignon, bishopric of Vison. Brought to this colony for the Law Concession.
METIVEE, Jean Baptiste	Died October 25, 1726. Son of Alexandre METIVIER and Cerinne VALLIER. Aged 12 months.
A child	Buried October 26, 1726. In the care of Claude GRISON. The father is unknown.
SIVIE, Henry	Buried September 13, 1726. Worker on the Le Blanc Concession. Native of the vicinity of Bordeaux.
NANTY, Gabriel Thérèse	Died November 1, 1726. Aged 7 days.
MASSON, Pierre	Buried November 1, 1726. Called CHEVALLIER. Soldier of the Naval Regiment of this city. Son of Jean MASSON and Jeanne DE HIC. Native of Mans, bishopric of Mans in Champagne. Came to the colony as a "homme de force."
VELSEDOR, Gertrude	Died October 29, 1726. Daughter of François VELSEDOR and Fuille MIDIADONGUE. Native of La Haye in Holland. Wife of Gabriel Hyacinte GUILLAUME, soldier in MANDEVILLE'S Company.
DRILLANT, Margueritte	Died November 2, 1726. Daughter of the late Pierre DRILLANT and Marie Therese LEGRAND. Aged about 3 years.
SPELLE, Ursulle	Died November 1, 1726. Wife of Michel SERINGUE, master carpenter of this city.
HABERT, Jean	Arrived in the colony in 1720 aboard the ship AURORE. In July of this year he was buried at the Old Fort (Biloxi?) according the death certificate of M. Davion.

Name	Date of Death or Burial and Comments
VANDOEUVRE, Marie Christinne	Died November 4, 1726. Daughter of François VANDOEUVRE and Marie ENSUCRE. Native of Dunkirk.
MOROPAYS, Etienne	Died November 5, 1726. Soldier in Du Tisné's Company. Father: _______?_______ and Catherine VULUAY, mother.
DUVAL, Guillaume Chevreuil	Died November 7, 1726. Goldsmith. Resident of this city.
CHASSIGNON, Louis Pierre	Died November 8, 1726. Soldier in Dartaguette's company. Son of Jean CHASSIGNON and Marie MANSAR. Died at the hospital. Called FOELIX
PARISIEN, Sion (Simon?)	Arrived at Natchez December 8, 1721. Native of Paris, parish of St. Luc. He died in Natchez according to the certificate of Father Hyacinte, Capucin missionary.
LANTIER, Thérèse	Died November 12, 1726. Native of Arras. Wife of Martin NAUTIER, master carpenter of this city.
BALTAZER, André	Died November 14, 1726. Aged about 1 year.
CHARLA, Claude	Buried November 20, 1726. Native of the parish of St. Marcellin in Dauphiné. Came to Louisiana to work on the Dubuisson Concession as a gardener.
HABITANT, Antoine	Died November 20, 1726. Native of Valentienne. Voyageur.
SAVIGNON, François	Died November 20, 1726. Soldier in Du Tisné's Company. Native of Brichée in Dauphiné, parish of St. Pierre. Died at the hospital.
LEONNARD, Anne	Died November 21, 1726. Native of Calais. Wife of Jean VALIER (VATIER?), tiler, resident of this city.
BIDIER, Jeanne	Buried November 23, 1726. Daughter of Pierre BIDIER and Marie LOUISE. Died at the hospital.
ALBERT, Charles	Died November 22, 1726. Native of Bruse in Flanders, parish of Varene.

Name	Date of Death or Burial and Comments
ANDRIN, Yvon	Died November 24, 1726, at the hospital. Native of Corlaix, bishopric of Cornuaille in Brittany. Son of Jacques Yvon and Marianne AIMERI.
FRISSOT, Jean Baptiste	Died November 28, 1726. Called GENET. Son of Trensele FRISSOT. Husband of LA CROIX. Phiffer in the army.
GILES, Pierre	Died December 2, 1726. Sailor. Native of Pleveson, diocese of St. Brieue. Died on board the ST. ANDRE.
COURTAY, François	Died December 6, 1726, at the hospital. Soldier in Du Tisné's Company. Son of Pierre COURTAY and Margueritte SANTAU. Native of Loche, bishopric of Langre.
VELLY, Jeanne	Died December 15, 1726. Married for the second time to Joseph DESCHAMP. Native of the parish of Drigue, bishopric of Corneville.
BARAT, André	Died December 15, 1726. Called GENTILHOMME. Aged about 18 months.
RIGET, Jean Adam	Buried December 10, 1726. He had been buried on his farm about 5 miles from New Orleans, but his body was removed and he was buried again in the New Orleans cemetery.
DURANTE, Marie	Died December 18, 1726. Aged about 2 years.
PERE, René	Died December 25, 1726. Marshal. Son of René PERE and Louise BODINRANT. Native of Port Louis, bishopric of Vannes.
CHARPENTIER, Antoine	Died December 27, 1726. Sailor on the ST. ANDRE. Native of Crosou but lived at Lorient, bishopric of Vannes. Died aboard the ST. ANDRE.
FONTENELLE, Louise	Died December 22, 1726. Native of Rouen.
KESSENAVE, Jean Baptiste	Died December 27, 1726. Aged 15 months.
SIMONET, Jean	Died January 1, 1727. *Voyageur*. Native of Bourbonnois, parish of L'eglise, bishopric of Gona.

Name	Date of Death or Burial and Comments
MARIE	Died January 2, 1727. Negro belonging to Sieur LE DUC.
ITALICE, Michel Pierre	January 3, 1727 (died.). Master gunner in the service of the Company.
HULE, Charlotte	Died January 6, 1727. Wife of François VITREQUIN, resident of New Orleans.
BERKEMAIRE, Marie Libet	Died January 5, 1727. Wife of Jean Joseph DAUPHIN, resident of Cannes Brulées. Died in New Orleans.
LOYER, Antoine	Died January 10, 1727. Called LA BONTE. Soldier in Du Tisné's Company.

(Signed by Father Raphaël, Capucin missionary)

1727-1728

LIST OF THOSE PERSONS WHOSE DEATH WAS RECORDED AT NEW ORLEANS BETWEEN JANUARY 6, 1727 and FEBRUARY 11, 1728

Name	Date of Death or Burial and Comments
LETTRIER, Marie Anne de	Died January 6, 1727. Wife of M. de GAUVRIT, Captain of this garrison. Aged 33 years.
DUFLOT, Marie Thérèse	Died January 4, 1727. Aged about 5 years.
JOLY, Jacques	Died February 25, 1727. Native of Chimiz, diocese of Liège. Came to this colony to work on the CHAUMONT concession as a cook. Aged about 49 years.
LA LANCETTE, Jeanne	Died February 5, 1727. Native of Dunkirk. Aged 26 or 27 years.
MARIE ANNE	Died February 17, 1727. Indian belonging to M. de PAUGER.
BONNAUD, Laurent	Died April 6, 1727. Son of Laurent BONNAUD and Margueritte VOLTEILLE. Native of Voix in Ansenis, bishpric of La Rochelle. Came to this colony to work on the VALDE-TERRE concession. Died at the hospital.
ST. QUENTIN, Edmé de	Died April 1, 1727. Bookkeeper for the Company. Native of Paris.
PAUL	Died April 18, 1727. Baptized Negro belonging to M. PELLERIN, Head Storekeeper for Louisiana.
GRAVOUILLE, Marie	Buried April 29, 1727. Wife of Blaise REGOT. Native of Bernard in Poitou, diocese of Luçon. Daughter of François GRAVOILLE and Margueritte GOUTONNE. Lived on the DIRON concession.
DAMARON, Jean Charles	Buried April 30, 1727. Son of M. DAMARON, apothicary of this city.
A Negro	Buried May 6, 1727. Belonged to M. FAZENDE.

Name	Date of Death or Burial and Comments
CARON, Anne Manette	Buried May 2, 1727. Daughter of Jean CARON and Anne MONIE.
CRISTINA, The child of	Buried May 10, 1727. The child of the woman called CRISTINA.
FLOTTE, Joseph	Died May 21, 1727. Son of the late Guillaume FLOTTE and Gillette GAUTIER. Aged about 4 years. He drowned in the Mississippi River near Cannes Brulées.
SAUCON, Michel	Buried May 27, 1727. Native of Abbeville in Picardy, parish of St. Gilles and resident of Chantilly (Gentilly?)
JOSEPH	Buried May 3(?), 1727. Belonged to M. BIGOT of this parish.
A Negro	Died June 8, 1727. Belonged to M. ST. MARTIN former Head Storekeeper.
CADOT, Paulin	Buried June 16, 1727. Son of François CADOT and Marie BAUDOUIN. Native of Paris, parish of St. Eustache. Came to this colony as a prisoner.
ROBILLARD, Baptiste	Buried June 17, 1727. Son of François ROBILLARD. He mother is an Indian.
LA HAYE, Margueritte	Buried June 18, 1727. Wife of BARBIER. Daughter of Joseph LA HAYE and Marianne BASTIEN. Native of Sogny, country of Haynault, archdiocese of Cambray. Lived on the MEZIERES concession.
VIEIL, The child of	Buried July 7, 1727. The child of Jean VIEIL, a sailor for the Company. The child was born in the colony.
DUMONT, Henry	Buried July 8, 1727. Native of Liège. Wife at Lorient. A cooper. Former storekeeper on the Company's ship the BALAINE.
ROSEAUD, Bernard	Buried June 27, 1727. Native of Bezars in Languedoc. Came to this colony to perform the functions of storekeeper.
RICHAUME, Pierre ✓	Buried June 28, 1727. From Canada, parish of Arpentiny.

Name	Date of Death or Burial and Comments
DESARBOIS, François	Buried July 19, 1727. Native of Brittany.
DUPRE. Marie Françoise	Buried August 21, 1727. Daughter of Jacques DUPRE and Magdelaine MEZIERES. Aged about 11 months.
GUILLAIN, Robert	Died July 19, 1727. From Cambray, master shoemaker of this city. Aged about 34 years.
CHAMPION, Guillaume	Burial date, June 27, 1727. Sailor. Native of St. Malo. Died at the hospital.
COUTOIS, A child of	Died July 27, 1727
HUMBERT, Margueritte	Buried July 27, 1727. Aged 18 months. Daughter of Nicolas HUMBERT and Victoire VERLANT.
JARIN, Grégoire	Died August 1, 1727. Son of Claude JARIN. No one knows the mother's name. Native of Moulin in Bourbonnois, bishopric of Autun. Died at the hospital and buried the same day.
BOUDINET, Marie	Buried August 14, 1727. Wife of François LE MOINE. Daughter of Jean BOUDINET and Anne LE BRUN. Native of Paris, parish of St. Germain.
LOEIL, Joseph	Buried August 24, 1727. Son of Jean LOEIL and Marie Catherine DUPRE. Native of Vieux Brequin, country of Haynault, bishopric of Arras. Died at the hospital.
RIVIERE, Child of	Buried July 19, 1727. The son of Antoine LA RIVIERE. Died at COUTOIS' house.
LE DAIN, Louis	Buried August 23, 1727. Son of Jean LE DAIN and Jeanne MARQUETTE. Native of Brittany Lives on M. MARIE's concession.
BETZ, Jean Georges	Died August 24, 1727. "Prevot" of the Germans. Aged about 35 years.
FRANCOIS, Jean	Buried August 30, 1727. A Negro. Son of Gom and Marie, negroes belonging to the Company. Aged 1 day.

Name	Date of Death or Burial and Comments
FASCIAN (PHASCIAN)	Buried August 30, 1727. Son of Philippes PHASCIAN and Elizabeth ALGRAIN. Native of Siply, bishopric of Combran. Aged about 35 years. Lived on the Kolly concession.
LE VASSEUR, Marie	Buried August 30, 1727. Wife of ST JEAN. Daughter of Jean LE VASSEUR and Marie PELIVROSNE. Native of Tour in Touraine.
DIDIER, Charlotte	Buried September 12, 1727. Daughter of Gaspard DIDIER and Françoise ROBERT. Aged 15 months.
CACHELET, Marie	Buried September 13, 1727. Wife of BOURDON, a carpenter. Daughter of Nicolas MONTRECHAT and Anne Marie CACHELET. Native of Fort Louis on the Rhine, archdiocese of Strasbour. Came to this colony with ___?___.
GRENIER, Geneviève	Buried September 16, 1727 Daughter of Pierre GRENIER and Marie GRENIER. Native of Paris, parish of St. Honnoré. Came to this colony as a prisoner.
AMONT, Catherine	Buried September 23, 1727. Wife of Nicolas BAUCHE, resident of Yazoo. Daughter of François AMOND and Françoise LE GRESLE. Native of Quimper, bishopric of Cornuaille. Volunteered to come to this colony.
GENEST, Thienette	Buried September 23, 1727. Wife of LA CROIX, fifer. Daughter of Antoine GENEST and Jeanne FRESSON. Native of Sers in Burgundy. Came to this colony as a prisoner.
PITRE, Pierre	Died September 26, 1727. A German. Son of Michel ROSE and Marianne ROSE. Native of St. Angile. Came to this colony with M. de RESBOURG.
LE FEVRE DE PONTARLY	Buried September 24, 1727. Soldier in Dartaguiette's Company. Son of Jean Jacques FEVRE. Native of Fribourg. Came to this colony with the Swiss.
MEIN, Marie Anne	Died September 30, 1727. Widow of Sieur LANTEAU, pilot of the king's ships at Dunkirk. Born at St. Omer, parish of Ste. Aldegonde, aged 44 years.

Name	Date of Death or Burial and Comments
TANGUY, Nanette	Buried October 1, 1727. Wife of Claude FLEURIE. Daughter of François TANGUY and Fanchon COULE. Native of Pleumur, diocese of Vannes in Brittany. Brought to this colony by the Company.
MANNE, Thérèse	Buried September 3, 1727. Daughter of François MANNE and ISABO. Native of Provençe. Brought to the colony as a worker on the Law concession.
DORE, Charles	Buried August 30, 1727. Fifer. Son of Jean Baptiste DORE and Françoise CHARTIER. Native of Port Louis, diocese of Orientel.
PAUMIER, Louis	Died __________30, 1727. Son of Jacques PAUMIER and Anne BAUMONT. Native of Deure in Boulonnois, diocese of Boulogne. Brought to the colony as a worker for the Company.
GREFFIER, The child of	Died 1727. The child of Vincent GREFFIER.
SEL, Antoine	Buried September 6, 1727. Soldier in Du Tisné's Company. Son of Jacob SEL. Native of Vil Rouge, diocese of Strasbourg. Brought to the colony by M. Le Blanc
DAMAS, Jeanne	Buried September 2, 1727. Wife of Sieur Antoine LE VEUF, saloonkeeper of this city. Native of St. Omer.
GOTARDE, Barbe	Buried October 7, 1727. Wife of BALTAZARD. Daughter of GOTARDE and Anne GOTARDE. Native of Worms. Came to this colony with the Germans.
BESSON, The child of	Buried October 9, 1727. Born in this colony.
MONTE, Baltazar	Died October 22, 1727. Aged about 40 years. Native of Silesia in Germany. Died after having received the sacraments.
BAGUETTE, Jean Bastien de	Buried October 10, 1727. Drummer in Renault D'Hautrive's Company. Son of François Guillaume BASTIEN and Catherine BASTIEN. Native of Marenne in Aunix, diocese of Senitte. Volunteered as a soldier for the colony.

Name	Date of Death or Burial and Comments
THOMAS	Buried October 14, 1727. Son of François THOMAS and Suzanne MASSERON. Native of Long Labaye, diocese of Dumant. On the Dumanoir concession.
GRENIER, Geneviève	Buried October 14, 1727. Daugher of Geneviève GRENIER and foster-child of LA FORGE.
AUFRESCHE, Jean	Buried October 29, 1727. Called LA RIVIERE. Son of Nicolas AUFRESCHE and LEONNARTINE. Native of Partemine, diocese of Dal. Brought to this colony for the Law concession.
PERIER, Marie Blanche	Buried October 30, 1727. Wife of Guillaume PERIER, resident of this city. Native of Grenoble.
PROUE, Nicolas	Buried November 1, 1727. Son of Nicolas PROUE and Jeanne CHAURAUX. Native of the parish of Grevache, diocese of Luçon. Brought to the colony for the Danseny concession.
CHENEAU, René	Buried November 4, 1727. Resident ot this parish. Native of Angers in Anjou.
PELLEGRIN, Marie Anne	Buried October 22, 1727. Aged about 6 years. Daughter of the late Henry PELLEGRIN and Jeanne FOUCARD.
MAROTTE, Descendre	Buried September 9, 1727. Called LANDREDY. Soldier in Du Tisné's Company. Son of Girard de SANDRE and Marie Gerard DU CHATEAU. Native of Landrecy, archdiocese of Cambray. Brought to this colony as a prisoner.
BRUSLE, Antoine Arnault	Buried November 9, 1727. Son of Antoine BRUSLE and Marthe FREMOND. Churchwarden of this parish.
GENETEL, Jacques	Buried November 13, 1727. Son of Jean GENETEL and Margueritte FROU. Native of Martisset in Poitou, diocese of Poitiers. Brought to this colony as a prisoner.
LE GRAND, Michel	Buried November 14, 1727. Son of Jean LE GRAND and Jeanne LE FEVRE. Native of Quimper Corentin, diocese of Cornuaille. Came to this colony as a sailor for the Company.

Name	Date of Death or Burial and Comments
AUFRERE, Paul Antoine	Buried November 17, 1727. Son of Antoine AUFRERE and Mathurine GUILMOT of this parish.
CADOU, Olivier	Buried November 17, 1727. Called LA FRAMBOISE. Soldier in Du Tisné's Company. Son of Guillaume CADOU and Anne HIDOU. Native of Pontivy, diocese of Vannes. Came to this colony from Canada.
LARIEUX, Marie	Died at 9:00 p.m., November 7, 1727. Wife of M. RAGUET, attorney general. Buried at 5:00 p.m. November 8, 1727.
BAUNE, Guillaume	Buried November 9, 1727. Son of M. BAUNE and Catherine BASILE of this parish.
LE VEUF, Catherine	Buried November 22, 1727. Daughter of Antoine LE VEUF and Jeanne DAMAS (see entry for September 2, 1727, above), resident of this city.
JANVIER	Buried November 23, 1727. Called CARPENTRAS. Carpenter of this city serving the Company. From near Maure in Poitou. Aged 60 years.
ST. AMANT, Jacques	Died November 24, 1727. Son of Jean François de ST. AMANT and Marie Françoise DUBUISSON of this parish.
GASTON, Guillaume	Died and was buried at Old Fort Biloxi in April, 1721 during the course of an epidemic. His name was not entered upon the death register at that time because the priests had all they could do taking care of the sick. He was a native of Ireland.
MEDY, Jean	Drowned in the Mississippi River in 1722. A sailor employed by the Company of the Indies. He was a native of Waterfort in Ireland. No one remembers the month or day that he drowned.
MOISSAN, Pierre	Drowned in 1722. A sailor for the Company.
ALENIER, Gilbert	Buried November 30, 1727. Son of Antoine ALENIER and Claudine DURANT. Native of Bois en Forêt, diocese of Lyon. Died at the hospital.

Name	Date of Death or Burial and Comments
MARIE FRANCOISE	Buried December 1, 1727. Indian belonging to M. RAGUET.
LA FOSSE, Jeanne de	Buried December 12, 1727. From Jullet in the diocese of Orange. Wife of Pierre Comet de St. Martin de LANDEL, carpenter.
A Negro	Died December 4, 1727. A negro belonging to M. MORANT, inspector of workers.
BRETONNE, Françoise	Died December 16, 1727. Son of BRETONNE
MANTEAU	Died December 18, 1727. Called Michel MORIN. Soldier in Renaut's Company. Son of François LE MANTEAU and Anne RIVAL. Native of La Rochelle, parish of Limeau. Was a volunteer.
DEVILLE, Marie	Buried November 25, 1727. Wife of François d'ORGOT. Native of Henault, diocese of Namur.
VISSE, Jean	Buried December 1, 1727. Native of Valerin, Canton of Bern.
DUCHAISNE	Buried November 2, 1727. From Angers.
NOISEL, Gérard	Buried November 26, 1727. Son of Nicolas NOISEL and Catherine Bärbe of this parish.
HERAULT, Pierre	Buried December 27, 1727. Son of Charlot HERAULT and Margueritte REONION. Native of Renesé, diocese of Poitier. Came to the colony as a prisoner. Called POITEVIN.
ROY, Etienne	Buried December 3, 1727. Resident along the Mississippi. Aged about 36 years. He died at his home on November 29 and was brought to New Orleans for burial by Sieurs BELLOIR, JARY, VILLEUR, MENARD and AUFRERE.
BAUCHE, Jean Louis	Buried January 17, 1728. Son of Nicolas BAUCHE and Catherine HAMON.
COQUELIN, Jacques	Buried January 18, 1728. Son of Etienne COQUELIN and Marie de la ________. Native of Vitry in Brittany, diocese of Rennes. Was a volunteer soldier. Called LA FORME.

Name	Date of Death or Burial and Comments
DANEL, Claude	Buried February 3, 1728. Son of Louis DANEL and Catherine. Soldier in the colonial army.
POLIDIENNE, Yves	Buried February 11, 1728. Tanner. Son of Jean POLIDIENNE and Anne CRESME. Native of Lavence, diocese of St. Paul de Léon. Brought to this colony to work on the concession of M. de la Harpe.

1728

LIST OF CHILDREN BAPTIZED IN THE PARISH OF NEW ORLEANS DURING THE YEAR 1728.

Name	Date	Comments
ANDRE, Louis	Jan. 9, 1728	
EDELMEYER, Marie Christine	11	
DONE, François	15	
FISSEAU, Marie Françoise	16	
ROUSSEAU, Marie Anne	Feb. 2	
FIOU, François	8	
DARGARE, Michel Jacques	12	
PERIER, Antoine Louis de	Mar. 1	Son of M. PERIER, Governor
GATHES, Jean	8	
CARRIERE, Louis François	15	
BONO, Catherine Elizabeth	27	
BARSON, Jean Baptiste	30	
CARETON, Jean François	Apr. 4	
FOUDELY, Jean François	7	
COSSINE, Marie	10	
BAQUET, Marie Catherine	May 2	
STRIMPH, Anne Barbe	9	
CENTON, François	17	
DIDIER, Marie Louise	June 7	
CARON, Michel Georges	11	
MAHON, Anne Margueritte	20	
ROMMEL, Jean	20	
MICHEL, Jean Louis	25	
DAUBLIN, Pierre Jean	29	
BARON, Pierre	July 4	
LAMBERT, Marie Anne	11	
KINTREE (?), Marie Françoise	15	
FORTIER, François	15	
SABANIER, Margueritte	18	
FAZENDE, Gabriel Jean	Aug. 8	
BIGNARD, François	9	
SERINGHES, Michel Jacques	16	
LA CLEF, Nicolas	16	
LANGLOIS, Estienne	20	
LE CLERC, Marie Jeanne	21	
BOISSIERE, Marie Jeanne	30	
GUILLAUTELLE, Joseph	31	Twin
GUILLAUTELLE, Marie Gilles	31	Twin
DUCHATEAU, Marie Magdelaine	31	
DU VERNET, François	Sep. 4	
BAREE, Marie Jeanne	11	
BUQUOY, Joseph	12	Twin
BUQUOY, Marie	12	Twin
DAMARON, Marie Louise Catherine	13	

Name	Date	Comments
BAPTISMS (cont.)		
LE VITTE, Marie Françoise	Sep. 14, 1728	
PERON, Nicolas	16	
SONGY, Pierre	19	
LOUISE Marie	20	
DABOUS, Agriant Claude	22	
BERRARD, Charles Pierre	28	
DU CREY, Helaine Perine	Oct. 2	
VICH, Jean	3	
LARCHEVESQUE, Louis Jacques	10	
PETIT, Charles Louis	11	Sieur de Levilliers
DORMOIS, Marie Louise	15	
VIEN, Michel	19	
BAULNE, Jean Louis de	Nov. 6	
LECHE, Marie Margueritte	16	
BRUSLE, Jacques	16	Son of M. Bruslé, Councilor
BORDESON, François	21	
TREBOULOT, Marie Jeanne	26	
DE LILLE, Pierre Joseph	28	
BROUILLON, Marie Therese	28	
MARCHAND, Marie Catherine	29	
PIQUERIE, Jeanne Marie	Dec. 1	
BAPTISTE, Jean	9	
LANGLOIS, Marie Joseph	10	
FONTAINE, Nicolas	11	
PICART, Marianne	28	
AUFRERE, Marie Therese	29	

Signed by Father Raphaël

1728

LIST OF THOSE WHOSE DEATH WAS REGISTERED AT NEW ORLEANS DURING THE YEAR 1728

Name	Date of Death or Burial and Comments
HAUTEBARD, Jean François	Buried January 14, 1728. Son of Pierre Hautebard and Marie LE BEE. Native of Lille in Flanders, diocese of Tournay. Brought to this colony to work on the Le Blanc concession.
Jean Louis	Buried January 17, 1728. Said to be the son of Nicolas BAUCHE and Catherine HAMON.
COQUELIN, Jacques	Buried January 18, 1728. Called LA FORME. Son of Estienne COQUELIN (called LA FORME) and Marie DELAS. Native of Vitry in Brittany, diocese of Rennes. Came to the colony as a volunteer soldier.
DANEL, Claude	Buried February 3, 1728. Son of Louis DANEL and Catherine, wife of Pamel, soldier in the army of this colony.
POLIDIENNE, Yves	Buried February 11, 1728. Son of Jean POLIDIENNE and Anne LE CRESME. Native of Lavence, diocese of St. Paul de Léon. Came to colony to work of La Harpe's concession.
François (Negro)	Buried February 28, 1728. Negro belonging to Gaspart Didier, carpenter of New Orleans.
CARDINAL, Bertrand	Buried March 1, 1728. Native of Montreal in Canada, diocese of Quebec. Resident of New Orleans. Aged about 35 years.
RAYMOND, Georges	Buried July 3, 1728. Son of Pierre RAYMOND and Marie CORSON. Native of Coyeux in Saintonge, diocese of Sainte. Came to this colony as a volunteer.
RONDON, Jean	Buried April 4, 1728. Son of Jean Rondon and Benoitte BELIN. Native of Berlin (?) diocese of Viennes en Bauphiné. Brought to this colony as a prisoner.

Name	Date of Death or Burial and Comments
DAHOUX, Catherine	Buried April 4, 1728. Wife of Ponsel GONZALOT, a soldier. Daughter of Claude DAHOUX and Margueritte VILLEMIN. Native of Belançon in Franche Comté. Brought to this colony as a prisoner.
Pierrot	Buried April 14, 1728. A negro belonging to M. Fleuriau.
LARTAUT , Marie Louise	Buried April 17, 1728. Daughter of Pierre LARTAUT, master tailor, and Louise BENEDIC.
Marie	Buried May 18, 1728. A negro belonging to M. de Noyan.
Catherine	Buried June 6, 1728. A negro belonging to the Company.
MANTIER, Jean	Buried June 11, 1728. Native of the diocese of Mahin, Paon de la Compagnie. Aged about 28 years.
DAVID, Daniel	Buried June 18, 1728. Native of Ireland. Soldier in Du Tisné's company. Died at the hospital. Aged about 40 years. (Husband?) of Margueritte ESSE, a native of Ireland.
BENADIQUE, Louise (LE FEL)	Buried June 26, 1728. Native of Versailles. Daughter of Mathieu LE FEL. Wife of Pierre LARTAUT, tailor.
BAJORY, Michel	Buried July 15, 1728. Called DUCLOS. A carpenter. Native of Rennes in Brittany. Aged about 45 years. He was killed accidently when he fell from a tree on the lands of Sieur de Chavannes.
MOUGIN, Jean	Buried July 17, 1728. Mason. Native of Eloye, diocese of Angers. Son of Didier MOUGIN and Jeanne DUPONT.
GAUBERT, François	Buried July 21, 1728. Son of Nicolas GAUBERT. Native of Dieppe, archdiocese of Rouen. Soldier. Died at the hospital. Came to this colony to work on the Diron concession.

Name	Date of Death or Burial and Comments
MAUBERT, Jean Petit	Buried July 24, 1728. Former soldier at Mobile. Son of Jean Petit MAUBERT and Marie Margueritte MOGUON. Native of Crepit en Valois, diocese of Seulis. Brought to this colony as a prisoner. Died at the hospital.
POUYADON DE LA TOUR, François	Buried August 13, 1728. Surgeon major of the city. Native of ____________. Aged about 35 years. Died the same day.
Charlotte	Buried August 22, 1728. A negro belonging to M. de Noyan.
UZELLE, Marie Barbe	Buried August 22, 1728. Daughter of Antoine UZELLE and Marie LANDRIN. Aged about 7 years.
BIGNARD, François	Buried September 2, 1728. Aged about 1 month.
DION, Julien	Buried September 4, 1728. Called FRAPE DABORD. Soldier. Native of St. Michel Dubois, diocese of Angers. Died September 3.
GUILLOTEL, Joseph	Buried August 4, 1728. Aged about 6 days.
BOURDON, François	Buried September 2, 1729. Master carpenter. Died Sept. 1, 1728.
BOISSIER, Jeanne	Buried September 5, 1728. Aged 6 days.
KINDLER, Margueritte	Buried September 6, 1728. Wife of Jacob KINDLER. A German. Native of Grombach in Phalh.
LE FEVRE, Jacques	Buried September 7, 1728. Sailor. Native of Hermonville, diocese of Bayeux.
BONPAYS, Michel (DE LA RAMEE)	Buried September 9, 1728. Soldier. Native of the town and diocese of Rennes.
FONDELIK, François	Buried September 9, 1728. Aged 5 months.
ROBIDOU, Sebastien	Buried September 13, 1728. Master carpenter.
BOURDON, Therese	Buried September 3, 1728. Aged 4 years.

Name	Date of Death or Burial and Comments
RAGUET, Louis	Buried September 12, 1728. Aged about 2 years.
Louise	Buried September 13, 1728. An Indian belonging to M. Caron.
Marie Anne	Buried September 13, 1728. An Indian belonging to BUNEL, a hunger.
BAILLY, Vivien	Buried September 20, 1728. Sail-maker for the Company. Native of the parish of St. Jean d'Angely, diocese of Sainte. Aged about 38 years.
REE, Jean	Buried September 15, 1728. Sailor on the FLORE. Native of Boumeuf, diocese of Nantes. Died at the hospital.
HERISSE, Jean François	Buried September 20, 1728. Called RINGAL. Soldier in Du Tisné's company. Native of Chambelly, diocese of Beauvais. Died at the hospital.
MAMELIN, Jeanne	Buried September 23, 1728. Wife of Nicolas JARDINIER, a soldier. Native of Auxere. Died at the hospital.
RAUCHE, Bernard	Died September 24, 1728. Resident of the German parish where he was buried. Aged about 50 years.
Marie Anne	Buried September 23, 1728. An Indian belonging to Sieur POUPART, carpenter of New Orleans.
Catherine	Buried September 24, 1728. An Indian belonging to Sieur COMPTOIS, a hunter.
MOREGAU, Joseph	Buried September 24, 1728. Native of the province of Vieille in England. Died at the hospital.
BRIE, Louis de	Buried September 28, 1728. Called ST. AMOUR. Soldier in Dartaguette's company. Native of Villeroy, dioeese of Meaux in Brie. Died at the hospital.
BOURQUIN, Georges	Buried October 3, 1728. Called DUBOIS. Soldier in Gauvrit's Company. Native of Bâles, diocese of Polantru. Died at the hospital.

Name	Date of Death or Burial and Comments
CHENIES, Jacques	Buried October 4, 1728. Aged 21 months.
FUCRET, Helaine Perisse	Buried October 4, 1728. Called BELHUMEUR. Aged about 8 days.
Marie	Buried October 5, 1728. Indian belonging to M. LAGOUBLAYE.
MADRE, Barthelemy	Buried October 5, 1728. Died at the hospital the previous day. Aged about 18 months.
LA CLEF, Nicolas	Buried October 5, 1728. Aged 7 months.
CONONQUE, Marie Magdelaine	Buried September 23, 1728. Aged about 6 months.
PETIT, Jean	Buried October 7, 1728. Aged about 2 years.
REMBAULT, Laurent	Buried October 8, 1728. Called ST. LAURENT. Soldier in Dartaguiette's company. Native of Perigné, diocese of Besançon in Franche Comté. Died at the hospital.
LE COMPTE, Gillette Therese	Buried October 2, 1728. Wife of ST. LAURENT. Native of Paris, parish of St. Nicolas Deschamps. Died at the hospital.
HEUX, Claude	Buried October 3, 1728. Master coppersmith. Native of Amiens. Died at the hospital.
FISSEAU, Anne Marie	Buried October 16, 1728. Aged 3 years.
BACHER, Pierre Jean	Buried October 17, 1728. Aged 17 years.
ST. LAURENT	Buried October 12, 1728. Native of this parish. Died at the hospital.
LE ROY, Mathieu	Buried October 10, 1728. Master locksmith. Native of the parish of Toulet in Picardy.
DIDIER, Gaspart	Buried October 18, 1728. Master carpenter. Native of St. Donat, diocese of Vienne. Aged about 36 years.
VALENTIN, Marie Louise	Buried October 17, 1728. Aged about 6 days.
MICHEL, Jean Louis	Buried October 20, 1728. Son of Roch MICHEL, employed by the Company, and Louise PHILIPPE.

Name	Date of Death or Burial and Comments
GUILLIN, Joseph	Buried October 20, 1728. Aged about 3 years.
D'AMOUR, Hierome	Buried October 21, 1728. Native of Pontrivy, diocese of Noailles in Brittany. Died at the hospital.
AMELIN, Antoine	Buried October 22, 1728. Native of Lisieux, diocese of the same name. Died at the hospital.
BONPAYS, Catherine	Buried October 28, 1728. Died October 22. Aged about 9 months.
CHEVALIER, Marie Jeanne	Buried October 22, 1728. Wife of Joseph PETIT, tiler.
JOUAU, Louis	Buried October 24, 1728. Native of Quimper, diocese of Vannes.
MARTINOT, Marie Anne	Buried October 28, 1728. Aged 29 months.
Simon	Buried October 28, 1728. Negro belonging to the Company. Aged about 3 years.
RODOLPHE, Jeanne Margueritte	Buried November 2, 1728. Aged about 3 years.
Louis	Buried November 2, 1728. Negro belonging to M. de Chamilly. Aged about 3 years.
COURT, François	Buried October 31, 1728. Employed in the Company's store. Native of La Clusse, diocese of Geneva in Savoy.
LAMBERT, Simon	Buried November 1, 1728. Soldier in Gauvrit's Company. Native of Philipsburg, bishopric of Spire. Died at the hospital.
HUETTE, Perine	Buried November 4, 1728. Wife of Sieur Durant, called BELHUMEUR. Native of St. Jean, diocese of St. Malo.
WALERAN, Jeanne	Buried November 4, 1728. Aged 13 months.
FORTIER, François	Buried November 5, 1728. Aged about 8 months.
PERON, Nicolas	Buried November 4, 1728. Aged about 3 weeks.
HUBERT, Jean Pierre	Buried November 8, 1728. Native of Quimper, diocese of Cornoailles.

Name	Date of Death or Burial and Comments
MANDEVILLE, François de	Buried November 4, 1728. Chevalier de St. Louis. Major-General in the colonial army. Pallbearers included M. Perier, Commandant General of the Province; members of the Superior Council; and officers of the local garrison.
FOUGERE, Pierre	Buried November 12, 1728. Called LA CROIX. Fifer. Native of Ste. Croix, near Etampes, diocese of Sauze in Burgundy. Died at the hospital.
LAUZE (LOSE), Henry	Buried November 12, 1728. Native of Dinan, diocese of Dol in Brittany. Died at the hospital.
Jeanne	Buried November 12. Died on the Company farm.
LE ROY, Wife of	Buried November 13, 1728. Wife of the Sieur LE ROY who died at her residence on the river above New Orleans.
POUPART, Marie Therese	Buried November 14, 1728. Aged 4 years.
Gabriel, Called BONAVENTURE	Buried November 14, 1728. Aged 3 years.
VIGOUREUX, Louis	Buried November 15, 1728. Carpenter.
KERNE, Marie Elizabeth	Buried November 16, 1728. Wife of David MEUNIER.
PHILIPPE, Germain	Buried November 19, 1728. Soldier in Renault's Company. Native of Laon .
TRAVERS, Jean	Buried November 21, 1728. Called BRUNO. Soldier. Native of the parish of Lion, diocese of Mans, province of Perche. Died at the Ursuline Convent. Aged 37 years.
BERTON DE LA PERIERE, Etienne	Buried November 22, 1728. Native of Jimelle sur Bart, near Troyes. Resident of New Orleans.
DORMOIS, Claude	Buried November 27, 1728. Called COUTOIS. Aged about 30 years. Master carpenter.
BAUDOUIN, Jeanne	Buried November 29, 1728. Wife of GRATIEN, employee of the Company.

Name	Date of Death or Burial and Comments
CLAIREFONTAINE, Pierre Morel	Buried December 6, 1728. Employed as a bookkeeper for the Company.
LA SALLE, Pierre de	Buried December 9, 1728. Native of Carcasonne. Storekeeper at Biloxi. Aged about 56 years.
A Negro	Buried December 16, 1728. A negro belonging to M. Rinart.
PIQUERIE, Marie Jeanne	Buried December 20, 1728. Aged about 2 years.
BLANVILLAIN	Buried December 18, 1728.

Signed by Father Raphaël

1729

LIST OF THOSE CHILDREN WHO WERE BAPTIZED IN THE PARISH OF NEW ORLEANS BETWEEN FEBRUARY 6, 1729 AND DECEMBER 29, 1729

Name	Date	Comments
Marie Françoise	Feb. 6, 1729	Negro belonging to M. ST. MARTIN.
Marie	8	Negro belonging to M. ST. MARTIN.
Jacques	6	Negro belonging to M. BRULE
DUPRE, Marie Jeanne	11	Daughter of DUPRE and Anne Marie BIENVENU.
DUPRE, Louise Marie	14	Daughter of DUPRE and Anne Marie BIENVENU.
DUPUY, Marie	14	Daughter of Sieur DUPUY and Françoise RICHARD.
DUPUY, François	14	Son of Sieur DUPUY AND Françoise RICHARD.
Pierre	14	Negro belonging to M. VOISIN.
CORBIN, Pierre Claude	15	Son of Jean CORBIN and Judith Anne HARDY.
LAMBERT, François	22	Son of François LAMBERT and Marie Catherine.
Françoise	26	Indian belonging to M. RAGUET.
Nicolas	Mar. 20	Negro belonging to M. BIENVILLE
MARTINOT, Pierre Louis	24	Son of Pierre MARTINOT and Marie JOLY.
BLOYE, Susanne	24	Daughter of Nicolas BLOYE and Susanne de DIVALLE.
Marie Françoise	25	Negro belonging to M. COUSTILLIAS.
Pierre François	27	Negro belonging to the Company.
Jacques	27	Negro belonging to M. DAUSSEVILLE.
Margueritte	Apr. 2	Negro belonging to M. FLURIAU.
Marie	3	Negro belonging to M. DREUX.
Jean Baptiste	4	Negro belonging to the Caphchins.
MANSSIAU, Pierre Phillipe	7	Son of François MANSSIAU.
Jacques Louis Alexandre	16	Negro belonging to M. PERIER.
Claude Alexis	16	Negro belonging to Abbé Berthelon.
Louis	16	Negro belonging to M. DE LA CHAISE
Jean François	16	Negro belonging to M. ROSSARD.
Jacques and Françoise	16	Negroes belonging to M. PERIER.
Elisabethe	16	Negro
Jeanne Marie	16	Negro belonging to M. ST. MARTIN.
CARRIERE, Margueritte	18	Daughter of Joseph CARRIERE and Margueritte ENPASSIER.
Françoise	18	Negro belonging to M. Joseph CARRIERE.

Name	Date	Comments
BRELY, Marie Françoise	Apr. 20, 1729	Daughter of Jean Baptiste BRELY and Marie Françoise AJETTE.
Anne	24	Negro belonging to M. PERIER.
Marie	24	Negro belonging to M. PERIER.
Magdelaine	29	Negro belonging to M. MANADE.
Jeanne	May 1	Negro belonging to Dr. PRAT.
LABROT, François	5	Son of Jean LABROT and Jeanne GILBERT.
Jean Thomas	18	Negro belonging to M. de NOYAN.
PHILIPE, Marie	16	Daughter of Jean PHILLIPE and Magdelaine DUTEIN.
RAGUET, Jean Bapt. Claude	21	Son of Claude RAGUET and Janne Anne BACHEMIN.
Jean Baptiste Antoine	21	Negro belonging to M. RAGUET.
François	22	Negro belonging to M. FLEURIAU.
François	22	Negro belonging to M. PERIER.
Michel	22	Negro belonging to the Company.
Jeanne	26	Negro belonging to M. COUSTILLIAS.
Marie Therese	30	Negro belonging to M. TRUDEAU.
Jacques	(May) 4	Negro belonging to M. FLEURIAU.
Jacques Phillipe	4	Negro belonging to M. DAUPHIN.
Charlotte	4	Negro belonging to M. D'HAUTRIVE.
Magdelaine	4	Negro belonging to M. CHAPAR.
DUPRE, Antoine François	June 4	Son of Sieur Jacques DUPRE.
Charles	4	Negro belonging to M. TISSERANT.
Catherine	12	Negro belonging to M. Adrien CHARPENTIER.
Jean Baptiste	27	Indian belonging to M. DE VILLENVILLE.
Marie	26	Negro belonging to M. BONNAUD.
Jacques	26	Negro belonging to M. BONNAUD.
VOISIN, Catherine	28	Daughter of Sieur Pierre VOISIN.
Paul	July 4	Negro belonging to M. BRULE.
Marie Claude	4	Negro belonging to Antoine HALARD, Called POSTILLON.
Marie Françoise	16	Negro
BESSON, Pierre François	21	Son of Jean Baptiste BESSON and Marie Jeanne LE GRAND.
Anne	24	Negro belonging to the Company.
Ignace	27	Negro belonging to DE LA CHAISE.
Toinette	31	Negro belonging to M. de NOYAN
Jacques	Aug. 5	Negro belonging to PIQUERY.
VALERAN, Pierre Thomas	6	Son of Jacques Thomas VALERAN, and Jeanne LANDRON.
AUBERT, François	11	Son of Françoise AUBERT and Marie Margueritte ROCH.
Laurent	11	Negro belonging to M. DURANTE.

Name	Date	Comments
LEMESLE, Jacques	Aug. 14, 1729	Son of François LEMESLE and Marie Louise MARIETTE.
François	16	Negro belonging to M. TRUDEAU.
Marie Louise	20	Negro belonging to M. PROVANCHER.
Philippe	21	Negro belonging to the Company.
MEUNIER, François	19	Son of David MEUNIER and Anne Marie VERLES.
JOSEPH, Jeanne Cecille	24	Daughter of Claude JOSEPH and Marie Anne LE BLANC.
Françoise	24	Negro belonging to Augustin LANGLOIS.
Marie	Sep. 4	Negro belonging to M. BIENVILLE.
Françoise	4	Negro belonging to Jean Louis MATTET
Anne	10	Negro belonging to the Company.
FORTIER, Jeanne	12	Daughter of François FORTIER, master gunsmith, and Gabrielle MOREAU.
Gillette	18	Negro belonging to Sieur SENET.
Antoine Joseph	21	Negro belonging to M. ALEXANDRE
Louis	25	Negro belonging to M. PERIER.
Louis	28	Negro belonging to Louis BRASSILLES.
Elisabethe	29	Negro belonging to the Company.
LANGLOIS, Antoine François	Oct. 12	Son of Estienne LANGLOIS and Marie Catherine BAUDROT.
LARCHEVEQUE, Marie Jeanne	Oct. 4	Daughter of Jacques LARCHEVEQUE and Marie LEMOINE.
PETIT, Roch	Oct. 16	Son of Joseph PETIT and Françoise LEFEBVRE.
Marie Anne	16	Negro belonging to Madame SAUCRE.
Marie Jeanne Françoise	16	Negro belonging to DE CHAVANNES.
GERANT, Louis André	21	Son of Estienne GERANT and Catherine HULCOIS.
BAREE, Rose	26	Daughter of Gilbert BAREE and Marie Jeanne GAUDEFROY.
DEGAUORY, Jeanne Catherinne	25	Daughter of Joachin DEGAUORY and Catherine PIERRE.
LE VIGIER. Joseph	26	Son of Louis LE VIGIER and Marie Anne GIRAUDON.
Therese	Nov. 3	Negro belonging to M. BROUTIN.
DEGLE, François	6	Son of Estienne DEGLE and Marie Anne DESPEROUX.
Pierre	6	Negro belonging to M. DEGLE.
Agnes Joseph	12	Negro belonging to M. KOLY.
Julie	15	Negro belonging to Jean Louis CHANTRE.
BOUSSEILLER, Guillaume	20	Son of Toussaint BOUSSEILLIER and Vincente CHARLET.

Name	Date	Comments
VIEN, Magdeleine	Nov. 27, 1729	Daughter of Michel VIEN and Françoise LEVEST.
Gabrielle	27	Negro belonging to the Company.
DUCRET, Nicolas Philippe	27	Son of Nicolas DUCRET and Marie Louise CATEAU.
LECHE, Marie	28	Daughter of Thomas LECHE and Marianne CHELANDETRE.
Jean Christophe	30	Negro belonging to Sieur MICHEL
JARRY, Roch	Dec. 2	Son of Louis JARRY and Anne SOUILLET.
Marie Jeanne	2	Negro belonging to DE LA CHAISE.
MENU, Hugue	4	Son of Catherine MENU.
ROBIN, Joseph	8	Son of Jean ROBIN and Marie ROSE.
LANNE, Joseph François	13	Son of Antoine LANNE.
BISSOTTON, Marguerite Cath-erine	14	Daughter of Sieur BISSOTTON and Dame Margueritte DE LA CHAISE.
LEMAIRE, Jacques	14	Son of Jacques LEMAIRE, a sol-dier, and Marie Françoise GRENIER.
George	14	Negro belonging to M. MICHEL.
Jean	16	Negro belonging to M. DAUVILLE.
Marie Joseph	18	Negro belonging to M. KOLY.
Marie Anne	18	Negro belonging to M. D'HAUTRIVE.
POCH. Marie Françoise	20	Daughter of Jean POCH and Catherine HISTINGER.
LAVERGNE, Françoise	25	Daughter of Louis LAVERGNE and Elisabeth TOMLIN.
BOISSIER, Heleine	27	Daughter of Laurent BOISSIER and Renée HUET.
DALCOUR, Etienne	29	Son of Sieur Etienne DALCOUR and Marie Joseph TRUDEAU.
CARITTON, Marie Angelique	Sep. 1, 1729	Daughter of Jean CARITTON, mas-ter tailor, and Anne DINAN.

There follows the names of approximately 15 negroes baptized by Father Raphaël during the course of 1729.

Signed by Father Raphaël

1729

LIST OF THOSE WHOSE DEATH WAS RECORDED IN NEW ORLEANS DURING THE YEAR 1729

Name	Date of Death or Burial and Comments
Marie	Buried February 17, 1729. Negro belonging to M. BRULE. Aged 5 days.
Pierre	Buried February 18, 1729. Negro belonging to M. BONNAUD. Aged 7 years.
RIVARD, Antoine	Died February 11, 1729. Resident of Bayou St. Jean.
Perinne	Buried February 20, 1729. Negro belonging to M. VOISIN. Aged 6 days.
Antoine.	Buried February 21, 1729. Negro belonging to M. DESELEVAL.
CONGLEMENT, Marie	Died February 26, 1729 at the hospital.
BRIET, Jean Baptiste	Died March 4, 1729. Aged about 2 years.
LA FONTAINE, Nicolas	Buried March 1, 1729. Aged about 3 months.
DUVAL, François	Died February 24 and was buried February 25, 1729. Treasurer of the colony and warden of parish.
MAISONEUVE, Jacquette	Died March 11, 1729. Wife of Nicolas PROUET. Native of Brest, diocese of Léon. Died at the hospital.
BLOYE, Marie Susanne	Died and was buried March 25, 1729. Aged 2 day
LABORDE, Daniel	Died April 3, 1729. Sailor on the GALATEE. Native of Bayonne. Died at the hospital.
BACHEMIN, Anne	Died April 4, 1729. Aged 3 years.
JEANROT (JAUROT?), Claude	Died at the hospital April 4, 1729. Native of Bourguinon, diocese of Langres.
LE BAS, Mathurin	Died April 11, 1729. Master carpenter. Native of Leroux Boitreaux, diocese of Nantes.
Pierre	Buried April 14, 1729. Negro belonging to the Jesuit fathers.

Name	Date of Death or Burial and Comments
Jeanne	Buried April 20, 1729. Negro belonging to M. BACHEMIN, resident of the area below New Orleans.
ASSELIN, Jacques	Buried April 23, 1729. Aged about 3 years.
POTEVIN, Jeanne	Died May 20, 1729. Aged about 4 years.
DUVERNAY, Joseph	Buried May 23, 1729. Called DAUPHINE. Native of Baye in Vivarest.
HENRY, Nicolas	Died June 9, 1729. Native of the diocese of St. Loireine.
CHERVILLIER, Marie Rose	Died June 20, 1729. Aged about 7 years.
Jacques	Buried June 30, 1729. Negro belonging to M. BONNAUD.
Pierrot	Buried July 7, 1729. Negro belonging to the Company.
HAUROT, Gilles	Died August 10, 1729. Native of Foussagé, diocese of Liège.
BESSON, Francois and Jean Louis (Twins)	Buried July 24, 1729. Born July 21, 1729.
AUBERT, François	Buried August 18, 1729. Aged about 10 days.
DARGARCY, François	Buried August 20, 1729. Aged about 4 years
SOYER, François	Buried August 20, 1729. Native of Sery, archdiocese of Paris.
RIVAL, Claude	Buried August 29, 1729. Native of Port Louis, diocese of Cornouailles. Died at the hospital.
LELAUNEY, Charles	Buried September 5, 1729. Soldier in M. Renaut's Company. Native of Paris. Died at the hospital.
BABASSE, Claude	Buried September 12, 1729. Son of Claude (?) BABASSE and Catherine BILLIER.
PIQUEUR, Marie	Buried September 14, 1729. Aged 7 years.
ROGER, Michel	Buried September 16, 1729. Native of Rion in Auvergne.

Name	Date of Death or Burial and Comments
CARITON, Marie Angelique	Buried September 17, 1729. Aged about 16 days.
KERLI, Marie Françoise	Buried September 18, 1729. Aged about 4 months.
MARTIN, Marie Simon	Buried October 11, 1729. Wife of CAILLOU. Native of Paris.
LE ROY, François Antoine	Buried October 15, 1729. Aged about 6 months.
LE KENE, Rose	Buried October 16, 1729. Wife of COURSAN, resident of New Orleans. Native of Favoille, diocese of Cornouailles.
PICARD, Marianne	Died October 22, 1729. Aged about 8 months.
LAVILLE, Henry.	Buried October 25, 1729. Corporal in Gauvrit's Company. Native of Azé Le Rideau, diocese of Tours. Died at the hospital the previous day.
VOISIN, Marie Françoise	Died November 1, 1729. Aged 6 years.
ROGER, Charles	Died November 7, 1729. Native of Paris. Former storekeeper for the Company.
KERLIDOU, Martin	Died November 18, 1729. Caulker for the Company. Native of Lorient, diocese of Vannes.
DELONAY, Elisabeth	Died December 3, 1729. Wife of MONTAUBAN, a soldier.
DROMONT, ?	Died December 19, 1729. Passenger on the ALEXANDRE.
BIDEAU, Jean	Died December 20 and buried December 23, 1729. Baker on the ALEXANDRE. Native of Cape, diocese of Bayeux.
BRONIER, Jean François	Died December 20 at the hospital and was buried December 26, 1729. Native of Boubonne les Beses, diocese of Besançon.
BOISSIER, Heleine	Buried December 28,1729. Aged 1 day.
JOUTEUR, Etienne	Buried December 16, 1729. Aged 3 years.
LANNE, Joseph François	Died December 30, 1729. Aged about 6 days.

Signed by Father Raphaël

NOVEMBER 1, 1729 - AUGUST 1, 1730

LIST OF THOSE WHO DIED "IN THE TIMES OF THE MASSACRE BEGUN BY THE NATCHEZ INDIANS ON NOVEMBER 1, 1729 AND LASTING TO AUGUST 1, 1730."

Name	Comments
AT THE NATCHEZ POST	
DECHEPART	A Basque. Commander of the post.
DU CODER	Native of St. Simphorien. Commander of the Yazoo post.
POISSON, Father	Missionary at the Yazoo post.
BAILLY PICARD	Chief Clerk
DE LA LOIRE DES URSINS	From St. Germain En Laye
MASSE	Lieutenant. Also killed: wife and niece.
DE NOYERS	Ensign "expectative" functioning as aide-major and director of the Terre Blanche Concession. His wife is living and married to Sieur JOYE, called ROUJOT.
DUGES	Called LA SONDE. Surgeon. His widow is still living.
DELONGRAIS	Director of the Ste. Catherine Concession.
DE KOLLY	Father and son.
RENEPER	Notary.
VILLE NEUVE	From Gascony. Also killed: wife & 1 child.
MIRAULT, Louis	Called ST. LOUIS. Tailor. Also killed: son. Wife is living and married to a man called PLAISANT, a fisherman.
LE TORTILLIER, Louis	Called LA MARCHE. Came to the colony as a prisoner. Also killed: wife and child.
LIVERNAI	Worked on the concession of M.W. Also killed: wife and child.

Name	Comments
GAVIGNON, Antoine	Called FRAPE. Wife is living and married to a man called JUDICE.
BOURGUIGNON, Jullien Chartier	Worked on the Kolly Concession. Also kill wife and child.
DISPASSE, Jean	Called BEAU SEJOUR. Came to the colony as soldier. Also killed: a child.
DUBIE, François	Native of Paris, parish of St. Sulpice. H wife is living.
LE MAIRE, Jean Charles	Called CAMBRELOT. Native of CAMBRE. Came to the colony as a soldier-worker on M. Le Blanc's concession. Also killed: His German wife.
HENRY, Louis	Called LE PETIT ST. LOUIS. Also killed: wife and 2 children.
DABEVILLE, Picard	Also killed: wife and son-in-law.
LEONARD	A Gascon. Came to the colony to work on the Law concession.
CHARENTE	Also killed: wife, 2 children and a slave
BRISE BOIS	A Canadian.
MESPLET	Native of Peau in Bearn.
ST. AMAND	His wife is living and married to a man named MEVILLON.
CARON	Native of Paris
PASCAL	Native of Provençe. Boat owner. His wife is living and married to a sailor named AUBERGISTE.
SABANIER	Native of Bayonne. Also killed: wife.
LANGLOIS	Native of Paris. Came to the colony as a cadet.
HURLOT, Laurent	Called LA SONDE. Surgeon. Also killed: wi and daughter.
JOUARD, Antoine	Called MOULON. Native of Savoy. Came to t colony as a soldier.

Name	Comments
SCUT, Jean George	Called L'ALEMAND. His wife is living and married to a man called NICOLAS.
ROUSIN, Jean	
BILLY, Pierre	Called LA JEUNESSE. A Gascon.
DU CROC, Joseph	Native of Provençe. Cooper for the Company.
DOVIDO, Pierre	Called LE BLEU. A Gascon. Came to the colony to work on the Law concession.
LA FOREST	Came to the colony as a prisoner. Also killed: wife.
LA PLANIE, Grimaud	Also killed: wife, child and a niece.
LE CHOUX	Clerk and interpreter. Also killed: child and niece. His wife is living and married to a man called CANTREL.
FOUCAULT, Anselme	Called LA FLEUR. Parisien shoemaker. Came to the colony as a soldier.
SENTIR, François	A German.
DILLON, Jean	Also killed: a child.
CERTAIN, François	Also killed: 2 children and brother-in-law.
POULIN, Gabriel	Native of Paris. His wife is living and married to a man named VANDOME.
L'EVESQUE	Native of La Rochelle. Also killed: a Gascon.
LAMBREMONT, Pierre	Worked on M. Siar's concession. Also killed: one child.
DUPIN, Jean Louis	Came to the colony as a soldier.
FLANDRIN, Jean	Native of Mont Dragon. Also killed: wife, 2 children.
PICARDE, Françoise Fresson	Wife of Michel BEAU.
PAPIN	Also killed: wife and 2 children.
LONGUEVILLE, Louis	Worked on the Kolly concession.

Name	Comments
LA FERTE	A Canadian
REINE, Etienne	A Flemming. His wife is living and married to a man named ROY who works on the concession of M. Scard.
LARTEAU	A tailor from La Rochelle.
BIDEAU	Son of a wheelwright of Paris. Came to the colony as a soldier. Also killed: wife and an unborn child.
PONCONNET	Also killed: wife and 2 children.
MAUDET	
LE DRUSSEAU	Also killed: wife.
BARBIER	
MASSIOT	
PICARDE, Cantrel	Wife of. Mid-wife by profession.
GUERIN	Also killed: wife and 1 child.
FONDERE, Wife of	Daughter of the wife of SOUBANIER, and sister of the wife of ROUSSEAU.
ROBINET, Simon	Native of Burgundy. His wife is living and married to a man named LA COSTE.
DU CHENE	Worked on the Kolly concession.
QUIDOR	Native of Burgundy who came to the colony as a prisoner. Also killed; Pierre, Quidor's <u>engagé</u>.
FOULIAUX	Worker on the Kolly concession. Also killed: wife and 1 child.
LE CLERC	Also killed: wife and 2 children.
LONGRAIS, Nephew of	
MADAME	Worked on the Kolly concession.
VALIN, Poy	Worked on the Le Blanc concession. Also killed: wife and 1 child.

Name	Comments
ROBECHON	Also killed: wife and 1 child.
AUBERLUS	Also killed: wife and 1 child.
SELSEMITTE, Pierre	Also killed: wife, 1 child, and brother.
TILLY, Gaspard	Also killed: brother, wife, and 2 children.
ROSSORT	Also killed: wife and 1 child
LA DOUCEUR	Came to the colony as a soldier-worker on Dartaguet's concession
LA COUR, Nicolas	Child of
MASSON	Called LE GRAND. Native of La Rochelle. Also killed: wife and 2 children.
SANS SOUCY	Domestic of M. GUYOT.
ESTIENNE	Founder on M. LONGRAIS' place.
MIRLY, Wife of	Also killed: 1 child. Worked on the Le Blanc concession.
DU COUROY	Cooper from La Rochelle.
PASCAL	Cooper from La Rochelle.
LA LANDE	Also killed: wife.
GOREPIL	
BONNAVENTURE	
JOLY	A carpenter. Also killed: wife. Both from Paris.
LE COEUR	Carpenter from Paris.
LE GERE	Carpenter from Paris. Came to the colony as a soldier-worker on M. Reveillon's concession.
ISBU	Carpenter from Paris. Came to the colony as a soldier.
BAPTISTE	Carpenter from Paris. Came to the colony as a soldier.

Name	Comments
JOUAN, Jean	Native of Paris. His wife is living and married to a man named ST. LOUIS.
RIBERT	Native of Paris. Came to the colony as a soldier.
PICARD	Native of Paris. Came to the colony as a soldier.
MONTHUY	Native of Picardy. Also killed: wife and son.
CHARLOT	M. Kolly's servant.
BOURBEAUX	Was killed while descending the river. He was a native of Poitou.
TOUDON, Pierre	Also killed: wife and child.
BEAUSOLEIL	Sabanier's engagé.
CORNERAY	Cooper from Nantes. Also killed: wife.
RICHARD, Widow of	Also killed: one child.
LA RENAUDAIS	Native of Rennes. Storekeeper on the Terre Blanche concession.
LITANT, Pierre	Soldier.
Benichere	
ST. PIERRE	Worker for M. BOURBEAUX. Came to the colony to work on the REVEILLON concession.
BADAUD	
LE MAIRE	Cooper from La Rochelle. Worked for the Company.
DAUPHINE	Also killed: wife and adopted daughter.
MONTAUBAN	
DU GUAY, Pierre Alain	Called LE PETIT MACON. Native of Renne in Brittany. His wife is living and married to a man named LA PRADE.
AUBRELAY	Also killed: wife and 1 child.

Name	Comments
A German	Also killed: a son. No one knew their name.
BOURGUIGNON	Tailor. Came from Du Manoir's concession.
BRUNET, Louis	Called LA GIBERNE. Native of Paris. Came to the colony as a soldier.
BERONSONIS	Native of Provençe. Came to the colony as a soldier.
DOYER, François	
BACANAL	Native of Burgundy. Drummer in Le Blanc's Company.
BOURY, Wife of	Also killed: her daughter.
CASLAHOUET	Native of Picardy. A sailor. Came to the colony as a prisoner.
CAILLON	Native of Douai in Flanders. Also killed: wife and daughter. He came to the colony as a prisoner.
COLLIN	Also killed: wife. Worked on the LE BLANC concession.
CAPPE	Also killed: wife and brother-in-law.
CHEVALIER	Native of Lonnin (?) A soldier-worker. Maker of chain on the Diron concession.
Two children	Presently at the convent. No one knows their family name.
DE VIENGE	Officer for the Company.
DE BOURG	Native of Brittany. A soldier.
FELIX	A corporal.
FRATTIN, François	Also killed: brother-in-law. Worked on the Le (Blanc?) concession.
FLAMAND	Also killed: wife.
FUMA	Native of Provençe. Came to the colony to work on the Law concession.
SOYOUX	

Name	Comments
FONTAINE, Jean Baptiste	Native of Artois. A soldier.
A child	A boy of about 7 years who died at Chaouachas. No one knows his name.
GRALIEN	Called PRANTIN (?) from Pays d'Arcour. Worked on the LE BLANC concession.
GOUPY	
HERMUSSAU	Native of Artois.
D'HOLLANDE, Jean	Native of Holland. Also killed: wife. Came to the colony as a prisoner.
LOUIS, Jean	A soldier
LE PRINCE	Corporal. Domestic for the Count de VREUX. Worked on the LE BLANC concession.
LA JEUNESSE	A soldier-worker. Worked on the LE BLANC concession.
LA HOUSSAYE	His wife is living and is married to the gardener for the Jesuits.
LAUCHUNE (LAUCHUME?)	A soldier
LORRAIN	A soldier
LE BOITEUX	Also killed: wife and 1 child.
LA SERTE	Native of Burgundy. Worked on the KOLLY concession.
LOTTIEZ, Jacques	
LA FRANCE	A soldier
LIONNAIS	Soldier on the LE BLANC concession.
LA LAZARETTE	Worked on the Terre Blanche concession
LAROZE	
LA CROIX	Native of Paris. His father is Clerk of __________. A soldier on the LE BLANC concession.

Name	Comments
LA GIBARDIERE	
LA FORTUNE	A corporal on the LE BLANC concession.
SANS CHAGRIN	Native of Auvergne. Also on the LE BLANC concession.
PARISIEN	
PIERRE	Also killed: wife.
Two children	Probably the children of Sieur LE SAGE DU PRAT.
POULIN	
PETIT JEAN	
POSTILLON	Native of Abbeville. Soldier. His wife is living and married to a man named AUBERGISTE, from Avignon.
PICHON, Charles	Called LA RAMEE. Also killed: wife and 1 child.
QUIMPERT	Native of Brittany. Officer on the Siaud concession.
Three children	At the house of RAIMOND. One was his, but no one knows the names of the other two.
A man	At ROUSSEAU's house. No one knows his name.
A Child	At ROCANCOURT's house. No one knows the child's name.
RABIER	Native of Gascony. Worked on the Law concession.
ST. DENIS	Called LA LANCETTE. Came to the colony as a soldier. His wife is living and married to a man named FERRAND, the innkeeper.
SALOMON, Paul	Native of Brest. Worked on the ST. HOUE concession.
ST. FRANCOIS	His wife is living and married to a man named MONPIERRE

Name	Comments
ST. JEAN	A soldier
ST. SIMON	A soldier. Native of Lisle in Flanders.
TRIANON	A cadet. Native of Brittany.
VISSE BRAS	A Breton. Worked on the DUMANOIR concession.
VA DE BON COEUR	A Breton. Worked on the LE BLANC concession.
AT THE YAZOO POST	
DES ROCHES, Chevalier	Commander of the post.
SOUEL, Father	Also killed: his negro servant.
POUPART	Son of a Paris butcher.
FRUSOL	Native of Provençe
GEORGE, André	Native of Orléans, aged 29 years. His family is at the home of M. DE VILLEROY in Paris.
COSSARD	Surgeon. Native of Paris.
CASTOR	Worked on the Law concession.
AUBRY	Came to the colony as a soldier on DARTAGNAN's concession. Also killed: an Englishman, his associate.
DE LANGLICHE	
ADRIEN	Builder from St. Malo

NOVEMBER 28, 1729

LIST OF PERSONS AT OR NEAR THE NATCHEZ POST WHO WERE KILLED BY THE NEIGHBORING INDIANS IN THE MASSACRE OF NOVEMBER 28, 1729.

Name	Comments
DE DECHEPART	Commander of the post.
MASSE	Lieutenant. His wife and niece.
DESNOYERS	Sub-lieutenant. Director of the Terre Blanche concession.
The garrison	Composed of 24 men of whom only one, BELAIR, escaped with his life.
BAILLY	Director
LA SONDE	Surgeon major
HURLOT, Laurent	Assistant surgeon
KNEPER	Notary
DUBIER, François	Sacristan
DES LONGRAIS	Director of the Ste. Catherine concession.
LA RENAUDAIS	Storekeeper on the Terre Blanche concession.
PASCAL	Boat owner. He arrived two days before the massacre.
CARON	Boat owner. He arrived two days before the massacre.
LA LOERE DES URSINS	Ex-councilor
SABANIER	Wife and one of his children also killed.
VILLENEUVE	Wife and one of his children also killed.
MIRAULT, Louis	Tailor. One child also killed.
LE TORTILLIER, Louis	Called LA MARCHE. His wife and one child also killed.
LIVERNAIS	His wife and one of his children also killed.
GARVIGNON, Antoine	Called FRAPE DU BORD. Also killed:2 of his children.
CHARTIER, Julien	
DESPACE, Jean	And one child.
LE MAIRE, Jean Charles	Native of CAMBRELOT.
HENRY, Louis	Called LE PETIT ST. LOUIS, and 2 children.
CHAUDRONIER, Picard	His wife and his son-in-law, LEONARD.
CHARANTE	And his four children.
JOUARD, Antoine	Called MOUTON.
SCHUTZ, Jean George	Called JEAN L'ALLEMAND
ROUSSIN, Jean	And one child.
BILLY, Pierre	Called LA JEUNESSE
DUCROCQ, Joseph	Cooper for the Company
DAUVIDO, Pierre	Called LE BLEU.
LA FORE	And his wife.
LA PLAINE, Grimault	His wife, a child, and his niece.

Name	Comments
LE HOUX	His child and a niece. Ex-storekeeper at the Arkansas post.
FOUCAULT, Anseline	Called LA FLEUR.
CENSIER, François	
DILON, Jean	And one child.
FERTIN, François	Two children and his brother-in-law.
POULIN, Gabriel	
L'EVESQUE	And one child.
LAMBREMONT, Pierre	And one child.
DUPIN, Jean Louis	
FLANDRIN, Jean	His wife and two children
BEAU, Wife of Michel	
PAPIN	Interpreter. His wife and 2 children.
LONGUEVILLE, Louis	
FERTE, La	
EVRARD, Jean	Native of Bohemia.
STROUP	Native of Bohemia. His wife and 1 child.
RENE, Etienne	
LARTAULT	Tailor
BIDEAU	His wife and one child.
PONCONET	His wife and two children.
MODESTE	Brewer. And his wife.
BARBIER	
MASSIOT	
CANTERELLE, Wife of	The mid-wife.
GUERIN	His wife and two children
FONDER, Wife of	And 1 child.
ROBINET, Simon	
DUCHESNE (DES INVALIDES)	
QUIDOR	And Pierre, his domestic.
FOULIAU	His wife and 1 child.
LE CLERC	and his wife.
DE LONGRAIS, Nephew of	
MADAME	Overseer on the Terre Blanche concession.
PONVALIN	His wife and 1 child
ROBICHON	His wife and one child.
TUBERLET	His wife and 1 child.
SCHMIT, Pierre	His wife, a child, and his brother-in-law.
TILLY, Gaspard	His wife and 2 children and his brother.
LA COUR, Child of Nicolas	
LE GRAND MASSON	His wife and 2 children.
SANSSOUCY	Domestic for M. GUYOT
Etienne	Founder on the LONGRAIS place.
MIRLY, Wife of	And 1 child
LE BLANC, Pierre	
DUCORROIR	Cooper
PASCAL	Cooper
LA LANDE	
GOUPIL	
BONAVENTURE	

Name	Comments
LA VIEILLE CHEVALIER	A native of Bohemia.
LA MUETTE	And three children.
JOLY	Carpenter and his wife.
LE COEUR	Carpenter
LEGER	Carpenter
ISBRA	Carpenter
BAPTISTE	Carpenter
JOUAN, Jean	Carpenter
RIBERT	Carpenter
PICARD	Carpenter
MONTHUY	His wife and one child.
TONDON, Pierre	His wife and one child.
BEAUSOLEIL	SABANIER's domestic.
CORMURET	Cooper
RICHARD, Widow	and 1 child.
LITANT, Pierre	
BENICHOU	
BADEAU	
LE MAIRE	Cooper
DAUPHINE, Wife of	
MONTAUBAN, Wife of	and two children.
DUGUAY, Alain	Called LE PETIT MACON
HYACINTHE, François	
JOSSIAU, Gilles	
LA PIERRE	Called CHATELAIN

PERSONS WHO HAD ARRIVED AT NATCHEZ ONLY A FEW DAYS BEFORE

DUCODERE	Commander of the Yazoo Post.
POISSON, Father	A Jesuit missionary at the Arkansas post.
KOLLY	And his son from New Orleans
LANGLOIS	Kolly's clerk
VERLUG, Charlot	A boy from Chapitoulas
BOURBEAU	Resident of New Orleans
ST. PIERRE	Bourbeau's employee
POUPAR	From Yazoo
BOURGUIGNON	From Yazoo
MESPLET	Burned to death
MARTY AND DOMINIQUE	Scalped
ST. AMANT	Died in combat
BRISEBOIS and NAVARRE	

Signed by Father Philibert, Capuchin missionary at Natchez, on board the DUC DE BOURBON, June 9, 1730.

1730

LIST OF THOSE PERSONS WHO WERE BAPTIZED
IN THE PARISH OF NEW ORLEANS.

Name	Date	Comments
DRONILLON, Marie Anne	Jan. 1, 1730	Daughter of Louis DRONILLON and Françoise HERO.
PELLERIN, Louis Gérard	2	Son of Sieur Gérard Pellerin an Françoise RUGLAN
FAUCHE, François	4	Son of Guillaume FAUCHE and Marie Jeanne QUESNEL
KINDELER, Marie Joseph	6	Daughter of Jacques KINDELER an Marie
ROLAND, Nicolas	15	Son of Anne ROLAND.
ASSELIN, Jeanne Catherine	16	Daughter of Thomas ASSELIN and Jeanne HUBERT.
Jacquemine	17	Negro belonging to M. LABEE.
Marie Anne	22	Negro belonging to M. BLANPIN.
GUIDOU, Charles	23	Son of Nicolas GUIDOU and Gennevieve MAURES.
CARRIERE, Henry	25	Son of Joseph CARRIER and Mar-gueritte TREPANIER.
BROUET, Louis	Feb. 2	Son of Louis BROUET and Marie KRIEMER.
LAMOUREUX, Anne Marie	3	Daughter of Jean Baptiste LAMOUREUX and Catherine (SAUVAG
Jeanne	4	Negro belonging to M. BRULE.
FAUCHE, Susanne	4	Daughter of François FAUCHE and Marie Anne GIRARD.
LEMOINE. Jean Baptiste	5	Son of Charles François LEMOINE and Marie MERCIER.
KREISMAN, Marie	5	Daughter of Jacques KREISMAN an Catherine.
François & Pierre (Twins)	5	Negroes belonging to M. DREUX.
BROUETTE, Catherine	6	Daughter of Pierre BROUETTE and Margueritte NERCINE.
MOUTART, Jean Baptiste	8	Son of Jean Baptiste Moutart an Louise LEMIRE.
PRAT, Jacques Louis	9	Son of M. PRAT, councillor, and Marie Louise DE LA CHAISE.
Catherine	9	Negro belonging to M. BROUTIN.
Marie	12	Negro belonging to François du Bayoux.
BUISSON, Marie Anne	13	Daughter of Sieur BUISSON and Marie Anne BERTIN.
Marie	13	Negro belonging to M. DAUSSEVIL
Jean Baptiste	14	Negro belonging to M. FLURIEAU.

Name	Date	Comments
PHILIPE, Nicolas	Feb. 23, 1730	Son of Jean PHILIPE, called LA PIERRE, and Marie Jeanne BAPTISTE.
LABBEE, Jean Baptiste	27	Son of Jean Baptiste LABBEE and Christine HALARD.
DEVAUBERCY, Nicolas Hector	Mar. 1	Son of Hector DEVAUBERCY and Genevieve TREPANIER.
DEVAUBERCY, Joseph Hermand	1	Son of Hector DEVAUBERCY and Genevieve TREPANIER.
VIEL, Alexandre Antoine	1	Son of Sieur Bernard Alexandre VIEL and Servane Perine LAMOUREUX.
Françoise	3	Negro belonging to ST. JULIEN.
PATTIN, George	6	Son of Antoine PATTIN.
PIQUERY, Françoise	6	Daughter of Pierre PIQUERY and Jeanne FADES.
Françoise	8	Negro belonging to M. DE STE. THERESE.
Pelagie	8	Negro belonging to M. DE STE. THERESE.
François	8	Negro belonging to M. MORAN
Marie Anne	25	Negro belonging to M. COUSTILLIAS
Marie Louise	25	Negro belonging to the Widow DUGE.
MICHEL, Jeanne Catherine	26	Daughter of Sieur Roch MICHEL and Louise PHILIPEAU.
François Antoine	Apr. 4	Son of the Tunica chief and Marie.
Rose Angélique	4	Daughter of an Tunica warrior and Marie.
RAGUET, Jeanne Françoise	6	Daughter of Sieur François RAGUET And Jeanne BACHEMIN.
Jean Baptiste	16	Negro belonging to Joseph GIRARDY.
DE MOUY, Charlotte	9	Daughter of François DE MOUY and Charlotte DUVAL.
CHAUVIN, François	9	Son of Nicolas CHAUVIN and Marguerite LE SEURS.
Marie	9	Negro belonging to M. SAUCIER.
SAUCIER, Michel	14	Son of François SAUCIER and Magdeleine BAPTISTE.
BARA, Anne	16	Daughter of Jean BARA and Anne PLEINE.
Marie Francoise	16	Negro belonging to the Company.
Joseph	18	Negro belonging to Sieur PROVANCHE.
Pierre	20	Negro belonging to Michel CHARPENTIER.
Marie Anne	23	Negro belonging to François HEGUET.
Jean Baptiste	23	Negro belonging to Etienne LANGLOIS.
Marie	23	Negro belonging to LANGLOIS.

Name	Date	Comments
OZANNE, Julie	Apr. 30, 1730	Daughter of Jacques OZANNE and Charlotte Julie MOREAUX.
BERTEAU, Julie	30	Daughter of André BERTEAU and Marie PODEVINE.
Pierre	May 1	Negro belonging to Jean François DAUPHIN.
Théodore	3	Negro belonging to M. BRULE
FION, François Louis	5	Son of François FION and Marie Louise LE ROY.
LAMERS (?), Louis	16	Son of Catherine LAMERS (?).
Gabrielle	16	Negro belonging to M. SENET
CHAPERON, Joseph	16	Son of Joseph CHAPERON and Louise COUQ.
Antoine	16	Negro belonging to M. CHAPERON.
PERON, François	16	Son of Louis PERON and Marie BOQUEAN.
François	21	Negro belonging to DE LA CHAISE.
FLEURIAU, Charles Jean Baptiste	23	Son of François FLEURIAU and Dame PELAGIE.
Joseph	27	Negro belonging to M. PRAT.
Louis	27	Negro belonging to M. MONDRELAY.
Louis	27	Negro belonging to M. DAUSSEVILLE
Nicolas	27	Negro belonging to Sieur DAUPHIN
Margueritte	27	Negro belonging to Sieur Joseph DAUPHIN.
Angelique	27	Negro belonging to OZANNES.
Catherine	27	Negro belonging to MATHIEU
Jeanne	27	Negro belonging to LAU.
François Raphaël Hyacinthe Jacques Dominique	27	This person and the following four were baptised on May 27, 1730. They belonged tø the Capuchin missionaries.
Louis	Apr. 8	Negro belonging to Poupar, master carpenter.
Jacques	May 28	Negro belonging to M. DE ST. JULIEN
Françoise	30	Negro belonging to M. TRUDEAU
DELATE, Louis	June 3	Son of Joseph DELATE and Margueritte LEJEUNE.
DRAPEAU, Marie Anne	2	Daughter of Zacherie DRAPEAU and Marie Anne PRIS.
Heleine	4	Indian belonging to M. DE BELISLE.
MERAN, Claude	5	Son of Claude MERAN AND Marie Jeanne HONNORE.
Augustin	7	Negro belonging to M. PELLERIN
A negro	8	Negro belonging to M. PAQUIER.

Name	Date	Comments
Marie	June 8, 1730	Negro belonging to Sieur PAQUIER.
Françoise	8	Negro belonging to Sieur DREUX
FONLEICK, Marie	24	Daughter of Albert FONLEICK and Genevieve TEREAU.
DELERY, Laurence	25	Daughter of Sieur Joseph CHAUVIN DELERY and Françoise Laurence LE BLANC.
ELOY, François	26	Son of Marie ELOY (ELECQUE?)

Signed by Father Raphaël

1730

LIST OF PERSONS WHOSE DEATH WAS RECORDED IN THE PARISH OF NEW ORLEANS.

Name	Date of Death or Burial and Comments
Negro	Buried January 12, 1730. Belonged to M. DE LA CHAISE
GIRARD, Paul	Buried January 12, 1730. Called DOMINGUE Interpreter for the Company.
PICARD, Jean	Died at the hospital, January 12, 1730. Sailor on the ALEXANDRE. Native of St. Servant, diocese of St. Malo.
FONCK, Nicolas	Died January 13, 1730. Aged about 6 years.
VOSSOLLE, Tiennette	Died January 21, 1730. Wife of Etienne POUSSARD. Native of Rennes in Brittany.
BERNARD, Pierre	Died January 29, 1730. Native of Cusson in Poitou. Resident of New Orleans.
LARCHEVEQUE, François	Buried February 3, 1730. Resident on the river above New Orleans.
ROLAND, Nicolas	Buried February 5, 1730. Aged about 15 days.
DE GAUVRY, Jacques	Died February 5, 1730. Aged 6 years.
DE LA CHAISE, Jacques	Died February 6, 1730. Commissary (Ordonnateur) and First Councillor of the Superior Council. Aged about 55 years.
MARTIN, François	Died February 11, 1730. Native of La Ferte on the Morne, diocese of Langres.
LAVALLEE, Etienne	Died at the hospital, February 14, 1730. Soldier in Renaud's Company. Native of Liese.
LEDIZIERS, François	Buried February 19, 1730. Master barber. Native of Marseille.
VIDAL, André	Died February 25, 1730. Barber. Native of Paris, parish of St. Laurent.

Name	Date of Death or Burial and Comments
DALEINE, Louis	Buried March 12, 1730. Native of _________ in Picardy.
LEPINE, Marie	Died at the hospital, March 10, 1730. Wife of the late Chevallier. Native of Amsterdam.
Catherine	Buried March 12, 1730. Negro belonging to Madame RIVARD.
CHANLIN, Jacques	Buried March 24, 1730. Native of Chassy, diocese of Sens.
GRAVELLE, Anne	Buried March 29, 1730. Wife of Nicolas ROUSSEAUX. Native ofIsle de Ré, diocese of La Rochelle.
FROMA (FUMA?), Jeanne	Buried April 3, 1730. Wife of LA PIERRE. Native of Vienne in Dauphiné.
PILVAIN, Gabriel	Died April 5, 1730. Sailor on the BALEINE.
BRIQUE, Yves	Buried April 20, 1730. Called LA FLEUR. Native of Quimper Corantin.
BARA, Anne	Died April 21, 1730. Aged about 15 days.
TURPIN, Marie Madeleine	Buried May 20, 1730. Wife of SANS REGRET, resident of New Orleans. Native of La Rochelle.
CHAPERON, Joseph	Died May 19, 1730. Aged about 8 days.
LENORMAND, Alexandre	Died May 26, 1730. Sailor on the BALEINE.
JARRY, Louis	Died June 2, 1730. Native of Paris.
BERANGER, Jean	Died at 5:30 a.m., June 18, 1730. Buried the same day. Captain of the GIRONDE.

Signed by Father Raphaël

FEBRUARY, 1721

LIST OF GERMANS WHO CAME ASHORE FROM THE GARONNE BECAUSE OF ILLNESS AND WHO ARE AT BREST AND LANNION WITH A LIST OF THOSE THAT SUBSEQUENTLY DIED.

Name	Date of Death	Comments
ORCHE	Feb. 10, 1721	Wife of Adam STEEMAIR
ANNE MARIE	Feb. 13, 1721	Wife of Magnous de BOUQU MANE
QUELLER, Joseph	Feb. 18, 1721	
BRACQUINE, Lisbette	Feb. 18, 1721	
HERSINE, Marie Orchel	Feb. 19, 1721	
MARIE MAGDELAINE	Feb. 20, 1721	Daughter of Natieusse HAISLAIR
MILAIR, Dilbolde	Feb. 20, 1721	
RONCLE, Anne Marie	Feb. 22, 1721	
LERRINNE, Agnes	Feb. 23, 1721	
HAISLAIR, Joseph	Feb. 24, 1721	
LERRINNE, Eva	Feb. 24, 1721	
CHEZNAIDRE, Jacob	Feb. 24, 1721	
LESTERINE, Catherine	Feb. 25, 1721	
STEEMAIR, Adam	Feb. 26, 1721	
FOURY, Anna Barbe	Feb. 26, 1721	
CHAUFF, Hans Felte	Feb. 27, 1721	

NAMES OF THOSE GERMANS WHO ARE ACTUALLY AT LANNION AS OF THE 25th OF FEBRUARY, 1721

Those at M. LESPION's place

AISMANE, Simon	
ORCHE, Marie	Wife of Simon AISMANE
AISMANE, Hans	Son of Simon AISMANE
HIL, Hermane	
CHAUFF, Hans Petre	
LISBILDINE, Marie	Wife of Hans Petre CHAUF
CHAUFF, Hans Felte	Son of Hans Petre CHAUFF
CHAUFF, Marguerite	Daughter of Hans Petre C
DESTE, Hans Ernst	
PITCINE, Loutsay	Wife of Hans Ernst DESTE
VIGNERINE, Orchelle	
RONCLE, Michel	
BRAQUINE, Anna	Wife of Michel RONCLE

Name	Comments
MERLINE, Lisbet	
QUELLER, Joseph	
QUELERINE, Marie Magdelaine	
STEEMAIR, Adam	
STEEMAIR, Jean	
LITENER, Martin	
STRIN, Anna Erbe	Wife of Martin LITENER
LITENER, Antoine	
LITENER, Joseph	
LITENER, Anna Marie	
LITENER, Magdelaine	
RIQUIER, Petre	
COULBE, Barbe	
FIX, Cristianne	
CRAIDY, Michel	
CHAUFF, Jacob	
ANNE MARIE	Wife of Jacob CHAUFF
CHAUFF, Antoine	
CHAUFF, Ansiacop	
CHAUFF, Anna Marguerite	
CHAUFF, Catherine	
STEEMAIR, Marie Catherine	
RIQUIER, Joseph	
STEEMERINE, Catherine	
CAPPE, Thomas	
BROUST, Catherine Barbe	
BLOUME, Vilhelme	
CAUFMANE, Orchelle	
MAYER, Laurans	
MAYER, Magdelaine	

<u>Those at M. Morrel's Place</u>

Name	Comments
MILAIR, Hans Dibolde	
SILLERINE, Anna Grede	
PROUERE, Connerat	
PROUERE, Catherine	

Name	Comments

Those Germans at M. Morrel's Place (cont.)

GUISINGRE, Joseph
FRAY, Lisbet
GUISINGRE, Marie Lisbet
GUISINGRE, Marie Magdelaine
COUSTRE, Mathieu
SIFFRE, Marie
JANNE, Margueritte
LERINNE, Anna Marie

FICHINE, Catherine

HAISLAIR, Natieuse

CHAUFF, Anna Marie

HAS, Frome
HAS, Susanne
HAS, Agatte
VERLAY, Tourt
VERLAY, Hans André
VERLAY, Catherine
VERLAY, Barbe
PERRINE, Torotay

CREVINE, Anna Marie
EBRECLE, Joseph
EBRECLE, Eva
EBRECLE, Daniel

CHEZNAIDRE, Hans Venard
VAGUERINE, Anna
CHEZNAIDRE, Catherine

MANCE, André
VAISLERINE, Marie Margueritte

OCTOBER 30, 1726

LIST OF PERSONS SUPPOSEDLY RESIDING IN LOUISIANA ABOUT WHOM INQUIRY IS BEING MADE IN FRANCE.

Name	Comments
SAVARY, Gabrielle	This woman is known in New Orleans by the name Madame SAUCIER.
CHABERT, Jean	
BIDAULT, Jean Baptiste	
TEXIER	This item mentions Mandeville.
TRIBAULT, François	This item mentions Luc THIBAULT.
BOISPINEL, Sieur	This item mentions BEAUCHAMPS and PAUGER.
SINACEST, Jacques	
BOISSEAU	
DESPLACES	
SION, Jean	This item mentions François LIGUEREUX, a sailor.
CAME	
FALICE	This item mentions a TIXERRANT
√ LAMBERT, Claude	
LA CROIX, Jacques Antoine de	This item mention Thomas LA CROIX.
LA COMTE	

1731

LIST OF ORPHAN GIRLS WHO ARE LIVING AT THE URSULINE CONVENT IN NEW ORLEANS

Name	Age
GOUMY, René	12
CLAUSE, Jeanne	9
DRIAN, Marianne Thérèse	11
CHINQUE, Margueritte	9
SIMPEL, Margueritte	7
CHEMITE, Catherine Pitre	6
ST. DENIS, Marie	7
Agnes	11
MELIQUE, Françoise	10
BERNARD, Margueritte	10
CLERMONT, Marie Joseph	8
CLERMONT, Françoise	3
HENRY, Catherine	8
DENET, Marie Jeanne	3
MARCHAND, Suzanne	11
ST. ESTEF, Marie Jeanne	9
REINE, Marie Jeanne	7
GRIMON, Marianne	10
VIEUX, Marianne	12
BIC, Marie du	8
BOYER, Anne Madelaine	12
FLANDRIN, Marie	4
BREDA, Marianne	3
DRAPAU, Catherine	12
LAROSE, Isabelle	5
CHALANTE, Louise	4
TARRARE, Anne	5
DRAPAU, Marie	8
CAILLON, Françoise	7
LE GRIS, Marie Barbe	9
The two sons of Boubant who was killed at Natchez	2
The son of LA VAUVRET	1

GENERAL ROLL
OF
LOUISIANA TROOPS
1720 - 1770

Editor's Note. In order to avoid having to print repetitious statements concerning many of the individuals listed below, the following code will be used where applicable

(A) Discharged September 15, 1763. His name appears on the roll of soldiers dated January 1, 1763, folio _.

(B) His name appears on the roll of soldiers dated January 1, 1763, folio _.

(C) The decision regarding the amount of half-pay was made April 4, 1764. Notification of the decision was received at the Bureau des Invalides the following day, April 5, 1764.

(H) Died at the hospital in New Orleans.

(P) Drowned in the shipwreck of the Père de Famille, February 17, 1770, while returning to France.

A

Auvray, Jacques	(H), December 25, 1755. Macarty's Company
Abriel, Pierre	
Alliot, Jacques	Discharged August 10, 1754 on half-pay of 6 livres. Decision of October 10, 1764. Sent the same day to the Bureau des Invalides.
Amon, Jean	
Albin, Nicolas	On half-pay of 6 livres. Decision of May 16, 1764. Sent the same day to the Bureau des Invalides
Aubert, Joseph	
Augeron, Joseph	
Anselin, Pierre	Discharged May 1, 1750

Arnal, Jacques Marie	Discharged May 1, 1750
Aupert, Jacques	
Andrieux, Jean	
Alorge, Pierre	Sergeant. Died November 19, 1757. Du Telles Company.
André, Jean Baptiste	
Albert, Pelageou Petail	
Agé, Louis	
Alain, Guillaume	Died October 28, 1745. LeBlanc's Company
Arnoult, Pierre	Died August 3, 1720.
Auger, Louis	Deserted February 5, 1739.
Antheaume, Louis	Died January 17, 1750.
Arbelat, Pierre	Died September 25, 1750.
Allemand, Claude	Died October 23, 1751.
Argillier, Etienne	Shot September 6, 1751.
Arcis, Jean Ollivier	Died September 30, 1751.
Allemande, Joseph	Died October 3, 1751.
André, Nicolas	Died August 25, 1751.
André, Pierre	
Aurique, Antoine	
Arbus, Pierre	
Audran, François	Died at Natchez, July 7, 1756. Grandpré's Company.
Aussart, Jacques	Dismissed September 10, 1756.
Abert, Jean	(H), January 3, 1754. Gramont's Company
Aubertin, François	Drowned in the river while going to Pointe Coupée, March 5, 1754. Murat's Company.
André, Jacques	Deserted June 15, 1756.
Arnaud, Hugues	Deserted July 4, 1756.
Amblard, Claude	Deserted in 1750
Andry, Louis Antoine	Discharged July 1, 1756.
Ancelin, François	Died August 27, 1755. Mazan's Company.
Artaud, Pierre	Deserted September 3, 1757. Condemned, <u>in absentia</u>, July 24, 1758, to be shot. See the roll of June 1, 1760, folio 12.
Ancart, Pierre Joseph	(A), folio 21.
Aguillé, Antoine	Discharged March 31, 1761. See the roll of the same year, folio 3.
Aulard, François	
Antoine, François	(A), folio 2.
Ardilly, Louis	(A), folio 23.
Assassin, Pierre Joseph	Died in June, 1758. See the roll of June 1, 1760, folio 4.
Audin, François	(A), folio 10.
Audin, Jean	(H), July 2, 1759. See the roll of June 1, 1760, folio 9.

Arlot, Jean	Departed for France on the Samson, October 1, 1769. (B), folio 44.
Andoue, Claude	(A), folio 1.
Albot, Pierre	(A), folio 13
Arbre, Michel	
Aupin, Charles	(A), folio 18.
Argadan, Pierre Joseph	Discharged September 15, 1763. On half-pay of 6 livres. (C).
Alliaume, Joseph	(P)
Alexandre, Louis	Discharged August 1, 1761. See the roll of the same year, folio, 32
Armand, François	Discharged March 1, 1765. (B), folio 32.
Auvray, Nicolas	
Anox, Claude	Departed for France on the Thëtis, April 14, 1770.
Arias, Jean	(A), folio 2.
Anjours, Jacques Antoine	
Arbonne, Antoine	
Airault, René	Cadet soldat. Departed for France on the King's ship Fortune, January 1, 1759. See the roll of June 1, 1760, folio 1.
Aulard, François	(A), folio 20.
Amandox, Pierre Alexis	Died at New Orleans, August 27, 1768. (B), folio 35.
Anjoura, Jacques Antoine	Sergeant. Discharged in Louisiana, July 28, 1762. On half-pay of 12 livres per month, payable at Arles. Decision of September 22, 1763, sent to the Bureau des Invalides October 12, 1763.
Arlay, Jean Baptiste	On half-pay of 6 livres. Decision of March 22, 1765. Sent to the Bureau des Invalides.
Auvray, Nicolas	Corporal. Discharged February 6, 1770. On half-pay of 6 livres per month. Decision of April 28, 1770.
Arbre or Arber, Michel	Discharged February 6, 1770. On half-pay of 4 livres 10 sol per month. Decision of April 28, 1770. Increased to 9 livres. Decision of November 1, 1771.
Avigny, François	Discharged February 6, 1770. Vaugine's Company

Arnoux, Claude	Fusilier. Discharged August 20, 1770. On half-pay of 4 livres 10 sol. Decision of October 17, 1770
Angenoil, Denis	(A), folio 1.
Aumont, René	(A), folio 22.

B

Beat, Jean	
Brisset, Simon	
Boileau, Nicolas Joseph	
Bonne, Michel	Discharged August 1, 1750.
Borin, Jean Baptiste	
Belin, Joseph Alexis	
Bonneau, Jacques	(H), March 21, 1757, Gourdon's Company.
Bouginot, Nicolas	
Bouture, Jean Baptiste	(H), November 7, 1756. Reggio's Company.
Bonnefond, Jean	Discharged September 15, 1763. On half-pay of 6 livres. (C).
Bridel, Pierre	
Blanchard, Jacques	Departed for France on the Samson, October 1, 1769.
Berger, Jean	
Bonan, Charles	Discharged May 1, 1751.
Baton, Jean Cristophe	Died at Natchitoches May 31, 1755. Hazeur's Company.
Boudard, Louis François	Died September 3, 1746. LeBlanc's Company
Bongas, Jean	
Borne, Jean Louis	Discharged February 1, 1751.
Barbay, Louis	
Bouteille, Jerosme	Drummer.
Bideau, Julien François	
Bourdet, Jean	
Bourgeois, André	Discharged May 1, 1751. Settled in the colony.
Barbotin, Mathurin	
Bienfait, Jean Baptiste	Died December 20, 1745. Benoist's Company.
Brazier, Pierre	Died June 30, 1751.
Bideau, Pierre	
Bidaux, Jean Baptiste	Discharged May 1, 1750.
Belluque, Claude	Discharged May 1, 1750.
Bouté, Claude	Discharged May 1, 1750.
Bodin, Antoine	
Bonin, Antoine	
Bertrand, Claude	Sergeant. Died October 29, 1756. Benoist's Company.

Bibo, Jean Baptiste	Deserted August 1, 1758. See the roll of June 1, 1760, folio 6.
Bernardin, Pierre	
Butteux, Louis	
Barbet, François	Discharged May 1, 1750.
Boulanger, Louis	(A), folio 7. On half-pay of 9 livres. Decision of June 11, 1764, sent to the Bureau des Invalides on the 12th.
Bergerot, Jean Laurent	Captain. (A), folio 8.
Bouton, Mathieu Denis	Shot April 15, 1763. (B), folio 10.
Baudin, Mathieu Denis	
Baron, Antoine	
Belette, Anselme	
Beré, Pierre	Died at New Orleans November 10, 1757. Chavoye's Company.
Benetot, Claude	Died November 11, 1751.
Biorin, Jacques	Corporal. (A), folio 6. On half-pay of 9 livres. (C).
Baudet, Yves	
Buteaux, Louis	Died in Illinois August 1, 1756. Dutillet's Company.
Bourdel, Nicolas Paul	(H), August 20, 1759. See the roll of June 11, 1760, folio 2.
Bertrand, Maximilien	
Blancloeil, Clément	
Baudyer, Yves	
Binche Bins, Martin	Discharged November 30, 1769.
Bureau, Noël Philipes	Deserted. Sentenced, <u>in absentia</u>, to be shot. See the proceedings of May 15, 1753.
Bony, Jean	Died while serving in Grandpré's Company. The date of his death is not on the roll sent to France in 1746.
Blin, François	Discharged October 1, 1750
Bontems, François	Deserted to the Spanish, March, 1757. See the roll of June 1, 1760, folio 11.
Butteaux, Jean	Discharged August 10, 1754.
Berthole, Barthelemy	Discharged August 1, 1750.
Boulet, Jean	(A), folio 13.
Baudemont, Louis	Discharged March 1, 1751
Bideau, Antoine	Discharged May 1, 1751.
Brunot, Pierre	
Böete, Nicolas	
Benaye, André	Deserted at Balize November 10, 1745. Le Verrier's Company
Berceau, Claude	Discharged August 18, 1751.

Baudemont, Pierre	Died while serving in Le Verrier's Company. The date of his death is not on the roll that was sent to France.
Baudry, Pierre	
Bellerose, ?	Died March 8, 1744. Macarty's Company
Brande, Dominique	Shot July 14, 1745 for sedition. Gauvrit's Company.
Brouillard, Jean Baptiste	Discharged August 1, 1750.
Brette, Sebastien	Died October 3, 1736.
Bessand, Jacques	Died September 21, 1734.
Boullanger, François Le	Died June 26, 1736.
Benous, Prospère	Died June 30, 1738.
Bernard, Joseph	Died October 26, 1737.
Bourée, Jean François	Died September 26, 1737.
Bidot, François	Died October 25, 1737.
Bosset, Jean	Died November 20, 1737.
Blemure, Louis	Died December 8, 1737.
Bodichon, Nicolas	Died June 3, 1742.
Barbier, Pierre	Died April 6, 1734.
Bourgeois, Pierre	Drowned October 22, 1738 while on convoy to Illinois.
Basle, Nicolas	Deserted February 5, 1739.
Bigois, Jean	
Boudard, Louis François	Died in 1746.
Brasier, Pierre	See Brazier, Pierre, above.
Bodion, Hudinet	
Brignac, Jacques Simon	Died in Alabama, August 10, 1754. Gourdon's Company.
Brangé, Etienne	Died October 18, 1750.
Bergerot, Guillaume	Discharged April 1, 1750.
Bion, Joseph	Died November 1, 1750.
Brouillard, Jean Baptiste	Discharged August 1, 1750.
Bonnefoy, Jean	Deserted at the end of September, 1750.
Boidet, Pierre	Drowned June 24, 1750.
Blanché, Pierre	Deserted July 1, 1750.
Broc, Antoine	Died August 28, 1751.
Baudouin, Charles	Discharged October 16, 1751.
Bertranche, Etienne	Died October 28, 1751.
Bauderel, Jacques Laurent	Discharged June 1, 1751.
Blin, Jean	Died July 22, 1751.
Bridel, Jacques	Died December 20, 1751.
Bernard, Jean	Shot February 27, 1751.
Bruneau, Joseph	Discharged May 1, 1751.
Broche, Jean	Died August 29, 1751.
Bouriliac, Jean	Shot May 6, 1751.
Bonnefond, Leonard	Died October 28, 1751.
Bercau, Michel	Died March 16, 1751.
Boutonnet, Nicolas	Died November 30, 1751.

Baudin, Pierre Joseph	Died October 4, 1751.
Bance, Pierre	Died October 16, 1751.
Besson, Vincent	Discharged May 15, 1751.
Billaud, Jacques	
Bondic, Philippe	
Barthélemy, Antoine	
Bonnarme, Étienne	Discharged September 30, 1769. (B), folio 38.
Bertin, Pierre	
Bellard, Louis Lucien	Died December 27, 1767. (B), folio 35.
Boisdor, Louis	Sergeant. Killed by Indians, August 1, 1754. Dorgon's Company.
Boisquet, Charles	Died September 28, 1755. Dorgon's Company.
Bénard, Etienne Louis	Discharged April 11, 1756. Dorgon's Company
Bouville, Masson	Died October 4, 1754. Derneville's Company.
Barre, Pierre	Died August 18, 1755. Derneville's Company
Bertrand, Nicolas	(H), November 1, 1756. Latour's Company.
Beaugrand, Jean	Deserted June 15, 1756.
Bonnac, Jean	Condemned to the galleys for life, February 9, 1756. Montchervaux's Company.
Bretton, Michel	(H), November 19, 1754. Bonnille's Company.
Barou, André	Deserted in October, 1754.
Bertrand, Jean	(H), December 25, 1754. Pontalba's Company.
Bisquet, Jean Marie	Discharged April 18, 1756 and returned to France.
Bellegarde, Jean Baptiste	Discharged April 18, 1756 and returned to France.
Bonnefond, Joseph	Drowned in the river while going to Pointe Coupée, March 4, 1764. Pontalba's Company.
Billochon, Jean	(H), July 15, 1755. de La Houssaye's Company.
Bufetaud, Joachim	Discharged July 10, 1756 and returned to France.
Boyer, Charles	Deserted April 1, 1754.
Bruno, Jean	(H), October 29, 1754. Villemont's Company.
Billet, Pierre	Shot August 1, 1754. Villemont's Company.
Berthelot, Louis Urbain	Discharged January 1, 1754.
Bonvalet, Antoine	Died at Balize January 1, 1755. Gautraye's Company.

Brulé, Barthelemy	(H), August 10, 1756. Desmazellieres' Company.
Barry, Charles	Deserted November 20, 1756.
Bouillot, Pierre	(H), October 1, 1755. Gamont's Company.
Blare, François	Died at the Arkansas Post, October 19, 1756. Reggio's Company.
Bouton, Nicolas	Died in Illinois February 23, 1755. Reggio's Company.
Brunet, Joseph	Deserted June 15, 1756.
Bigarne, Jacques	Discharged April 18, 1756 and returned to France.
Baudouin, Jean	(H), January 6, 1756. Neyon's Company.
Blazeau, Alexandre	Deserted April 9, 1754.
Brie, Le Chavelier de	Cadet a l'aiguillette. Died at Fort Chartres December 26, 1756.
Bercle, Adam	Deserted July 4, 1755.
Bouilly, Vincent	Discharged August 27, 1756.
Beaudevin, François	Deserted July 4, 1755.
Beaudrap, Philibert	Died in November 1755. Varenne's Company.
Balle, Jean	Deserted June 19, 1755.
Busigny, Bernard	Drowned at Balize January 10, 1754.
Boulanger, Jean	Deserted in April, 1754.
Barbier, Claude Antoine	Drowned while going down river from Natchez, October 2, 1754. Macarty's Company.
Blanc, Antoine	Deserted July 17, 1755.
Bernard, Jacques	Deserted July 17, 1755.
Blaise, Jean Baptiste	Discharged March 1, 1756.
Blanchard, Jean	Deserted June 8, 1755.
Boucard, André	Deserted August 10, 1754.
Blanchet, Antoine	Died at New Orleans, October 15, 1757. Grandchamp's Company.
Bonnefoy, Isaac	Drowned in the river, July 9, 1757. Desmazellieres' Company.
Blanc, Jean	Died at Fort Chartres, October 4, 1757. Montchervaux's Company.
Bailly, Joseph	On half-pay of 6 livres. (C).
Bezieres, Claude	Died at English Turn, January 13, 1757. D'Aubry's Company.
Beignot, Pierre	Deserted October 20, 1757.
Bazille, Joseph François	Broken on the wheel for having assassinated his commanding officer. Executed June 7, 1757. Trant's Company. On the roll of June 1, 1760 he is listed under the name of Joseph François Barille.

Blanchard, Guy	Discharged January 11, 1752. D'Artaud's Company. Settled in the colony.
Broyard, Etienne	Discharged January 13, 1753. Settled in the colony.
Bonnard, Jean Clement	Drum major of Benoist's Company. Discharged October 1, 1766. On half-pay of 10 livres per month. See the decision of April 15, 1767.
Bredat, Antoine	
Blaize, Pierre	Discharged September 30, 1769. (B), folio 49.
Bourgeonneau, Jean	On half-pay of 6 livres. (C).
Boyaux, Pierre	On half-pay of 6 livres per month.
Bandé, Jean	Discharged August 1, 1764. (B), folio 27.
Bessé, Pierre	(A), folio 20.
Bastien, François	Discharged March 31, 1761. See the roll of detached French companies, folio 3. Died at Pointe Coupée June 5, 1767. (B), folio 35.
Bastien, Antoine	On half-pay of 6 livres. (C).
Bragance, Felican Albert	(A), folio 20.
Bauby, Claude Cyprien	On half-pay of 15 livres. (C).
Bourbon, Jean	(A), folio 19.
Boursin, François	Discharged September 1, 1764. (B), folio 30.
Boucherie, Jean	(A), folio 4.
Baudin, Antoine Robert	(A), folio 6.
Bou, Pierre Elie	
Baptiste, François	(H), June 25, 1758. See the roll of June 1, 1750, folio 3.
Bouquet, Jacques	
Brolliard, Simon	
Battelier, François	On half-pay of 6 livres. (C).
Bosquet, Pierre	On half-pay of 9 livres, payable at Rodez in Rouergue. (C). Corporal. Discharged September 15, 1763.
Brignac, Jacques	
Brisset, Gabriel	
Bedagres or Bedagues, Jean	(A), folio 6.
Boulifay, Jean	(A), folio 6.
Bourgeois, Paul	On half-pay of 6 livres. (C).
Berranger, Jean	
Blin, Louis	Drowned February 27, 1764. (B).

Brosseau, Jean Baptiste	Deserted August 30, 1761. See the roll of that year, folio 16.
Bourdon, Jacques	
Boulard, Louis	(A), folio 8.
Boulanger, Pierre	(A), folio 8.
Bouteselle, Charles	Discharged October 8, 1769. (B), folio 43.
Bonneau, Jean Pierre	
Blanchard, Gabriel	
Bernard, Jean Baptiste	
Bruneau, Louis Pierre	
Bourier, Nicolas	(A), folio 9.
Boissinot, François	On half-pay of 9 livres. Decision of June 11, 1764. Sent to the Bureau des Invalides June 12, 1764. (A), folio 9.
Brignac, Pierre Simon	(A), folio 11. On half-pay of four livres ten sol. Decision of June 11, 1764, sent to the Bureau des Invalides.
Barutel, Blaize	Discharged at Havre. See the
Boutté, Jean	general roll of February 22, 1761, folio 7, sent to that port. The King ordered on July 10, 1761 that he be given a copy of his discharge which was stolen from him on rue Madelaine in Paris.
Bourgeois, François	On half-pay of 6 livres. Decision of March 12, 1764, sent to the Bureau des Invalides the same day.
Bonneau, Jacques	(H), March 21, 1757. See the roll of June 1, 1760, folio 8.
Bruxelles, Etienne	Returned to France on the ship Orphie, March 17, 1769. (B), folio 41.
Brouet, Pierre	
Beauverlet, Lambert	
Brignac, Michel	(A), folio 23.
Brion, René	
Berry, Antoine	(A), folio 24.
Beschet, Jean	
Bailly, Louis	Died October 10, 1764. (B), folio 29.
Bachart or Bachat, Nicolas	
Bravet, Claude François	Died in Illinois February 28, 1763. (B), folio 22.
Braillard, Antoine	Discharged and returned to France on the King's ship Fortune, January 1, 1759. See the roll of June 1, 1760, folio 6.

Brisson, Louis	
Basque, Pierre	Died November 21, 1769 at New Orleans. See the copy of a list by M. Daubenton concerning the shipwreck of the Pere de Famille. Also see the roll of January 1, 1763, folio 34.
Billard, Jacques	(H), March 12, 1758. See the roll of June 1, 1760, folio 6.
Butor, François	
Bouquet, Antoine Dauja	(A), folio 11.
Brunot, Jean Augustin	(A), folio 12.
Bonnardel, François	
Boulanne, Jean	
Baillot, Pierre	
Beau, Etienne	
Bache, Claude	
Barbier, André Joseph	(A), folio 2.
Beauchesne, Laurent	Discharged February 1, 1768. (B), folio ?
Baudoux, Jean	Discharged September 15, 1763. On half-pay of 6 livres. (C).
Bragnard, Nicolas	Discharged November 30, 1764. (B), folio 47.
Barthe, Antoine	Died at the house of M. Marault on April 12, 1768. (B), folio 36.
Bordat, Antoine	
Beaudet, François	(A), folio 4.
Bernard, Jean Baptiste	Drowned at Mobile March 19, 1761. See the roll of the same year, folio 36.
Baillot, Simon	
Bertrand, Jean	
Bourgeois, Jean Gabriel	
Beauvais, Aubin	
Bertrand, Mathieu	Settled in Arkansas December 31, 1769. (B), folio 51.
Bruneau, Marin	
Bidallier, Joseph	On half-pay of 6 livres per month. Decision of October 25, 1769.
Barbier, Louis Antoine	
Bedouet, François	(H), September 16, 1769. (B), folio 48.
Bouillon, André	(A), folio 16.
Bailly, Jean	
Battin, François	(A), folio 23.
Biguer, Joseph	
Bezançon, Pierre Joseph	(A), folio 2.

Bernard, Guillaume	Died in France in the hospital at La Rochelle, March 27, 1770. The death certificate, attached to a letter from M. Le Moyne, has been placed in the carton of the Isle de Ré for the month of July, 1770.
Brignac, Mathieu or Jacques	(A), folio 10. On half-pay of 4livres 10 sol. Decision of June 11, 1764, sent to the Bureau des Invalides on the 12th.
Bessiere, Jean	
Bremontier, Pierre	Died at Mobile December 6, 1759. See the roll of June 1, 1760, folio 11.
Bessé, Pierre	
Bouty, Pierre Antoine Simon	Discharged July 1, 1764. On half-pay of 6 livres. Decision of March 12, 1764 and sent to the Bureau the same day.
Beaufin, Henry	(A), folio 19.
Bec, Clement	
Baule, Antoine	(A), folio 1.
Broutin, Narcis	
Brunet, Pierre	
Battelier, François	
Baudoin, Nicolas	Discharged September 15, 1763. On half-pay of 4 livres 10 sol. (C).
Bornarme, Etienne	"est porté en 1752."
Bouteille, Jerome	(A), folio 7
Boulard, Laurent	Discharged September 30, 1769. (B), folio 42.
Berard, Antoine	Discharged October 1, 1769. (B), folio 37.
Bonin, Antoine	(A), folio 9. On half-pay of 9 livres. Decision of June 11, 1764, sent to the Bureau on the 12th.
Buraux, Jean	Discharged April 1, 1764. (B), folio 29.
Bardon, Jean	(A), folio 13.
Bachat, Nicolas	Died at Balize December 13, 1766. (B), folio 33.
Brunet, Jacques	
Bunel, Jacques	Discharged November 30, 1769. (B), folio 42.
Berger, Jean Baptiste	Discharged. See the roll dated at Calais, May 2, 1763.

Boiret, Sebastien	Discharged. See the roll dated at Calais, May 2, 1763.
Bedague, Jean	Sergeant. Arrived at Bordeaux on February 22, 1770. On half-pay of 9 livres. (C).
Billy, Mathias	On half-pay of 6 livres. (C).
Baudron, François Simon	Discharged February 6, 1770. Duplessis' Company.
Boutrou, Pierre	Sergeant. On half-pay of 20 livres. (C).
Bourcier, Pierre	On half-pay of 6 livres. Decision of May 21, 1765, sent to the Bureau on the 22nd.
Beauregard, Jean	Drummer. On half-pay of 6 livres. (C).
Boyaux, Pierre	Native of Lyons, has served 17 years. Discharged in Louisiana on November 30, 1768. Presented his discharge at the Bureau as a half-pay soldier at 6 livres per month. Decision of June 18, 1769 and sent to the Bureau
Bergerot, Laurent	Sergeant. 30 years service. Half-pay of 12 livres per month Decision of October 25, 1769, sent to the Bureau on the 27th.
Boisroger, Jean Baptiste	Sergeant. (P).
Boutteselle, Charles	Drummer. (P).
Bernard, Jean Baptiste	(P).
Bernard, Jacques	(P).
Beaulieu, Etienne	(P).
Baptiste (Negro slave)	M. Destour's servant. (P).
Beranger, Jean	Corporal. Discharged February 6, 1770. On half-pay of 9 livres per month. Decision of April 28, 1770.
Blanchard, Gabriel	Corporal. Discharged February 6, 1770. On half-pay of 6 livres per month. Decision of April 28, 1770.
Bouquet, Jacques	Discharged February 6, 1770. On half-pay of 6 livres per month. Decision of April 28, 1770.
Bourgeois, Jean Gabriel	Discharged February 6, 1770. On half-pay of 4 livres 10 sol per month. Decision of April 28, 1770.
Beauori, Antoine	Discharged February 6, 1770. Desmazilliere's Company.

Berard, Antoine	Discharged February 6, 1770. Desmazilliere's Company.
Billaud, Jacques	Discharged February 6, 1770. Desmazilliere's Company.
Buisson, Louis	Discharged February 6, 1770. Vaugine's Company.
Bourdon. Jacques	Discharged February 6, 1770. On half-pay of 6 livres per month from the date of his discharge. Decision of August 21, 1770.
Bessé, Pierre	Discharged February 6, 1770. Villier's Company.
Brouyard, Simon	Discharged August 20, 1770. On half-pay of 6 livres per month. Decision of October 17, 1770.
Bernard, Jean	Discharged August 20, 1770.
Beauchesne, Laurent	Discharged August 20, 1770.
Bosquet, Pierre	On half-pay of 4 livres per month. Decision of September 8, 1770.
Boudron, Pierre	Discharged September 15, 1763. (B), folio 1.
Baffé, Claude	Departed for Santo Domingo on the frigate <u>Aigrette</u>, July 22, 1763. (B), folio 3.
Bauvais, Claude Ciprien	(A), folio 19.
Boulé, Julien	(A), folio 22.
Boissinot, Louis	(A), folio 25.
Bonnard, Jean Clément	(A), folio 32.
Bourdelais, Jean Louis	(H), September 13, 1767. (B), folio 34.
Baudet, Yves	Wounded. Returned to France on the <u>Samson</u>, October 1, 1769. (B), folio 37.
Bouvry, François	Departed for France on the <u>Caméléon</u>, October 1, 1764.
Bourguignon, Joseph	Discharged October 31, 1769. (B), folio 36.
Barriere, Jean	Banished July 23, 1769. (B), folio 36
Brouillard, Nicolas	Discharged November 30, 1769. (B), folio 48.
Bessé, Pierre	Returned to France on the <u>Samson</u>, October 1, 1769. (B), folio 49.
Bernard, Louis	Discharged October 8, 1769. (B), folio 55.
Bourcin, François	Entered service May 1, 1769. Discharged October 8, 1769. (B), folio 55.

C

Caussin, Jean Baptiste Marc	
Chevel or Chenel, François	Discharged July 1, 1750.
Cabat, Nicolas	
Chavanne, Louis de	
Cochard, Guillaume	
Cresson, Etienne	Discharged August 10, 1754.
Cajot, Pierre	Discharged November 1, 1751.
Chevalier, Cristophe	
Clavet, Michel Gerard	Killed or taken by the Cherokee or Chickasaw Indians, November 9, 1757. Grandpré's Company.
Certain, François	
Carpinet, Honoré	Died November 7, 1750.
Chapart, Arnoult	Discharged June 1, 1750.
Cordonnier, Etienne	
Chardon, Jacques	
Chapelin, Martin	
Chaperon, Etienne	On half-pay of 15 livres. (C). Sergeant. (A).
Chenel, François	
Champagne, Jean Baptiste	
Caillé, Joseph	Discharged June 1, 1751.
Colette, Louis	(A), folio 7.
Caillé, Jean	Discharged May 1, 1751.
Chevalier, Nicolas	(H), September 2, 1767. (B), folio 34.
Cirier, Joseph	Discharged June 17, 1751.
Caunoir, Pierre	
Cristal, Antoine Ange Auguste	
Charvet, François	
Cantel, Pierre	(A), folio 5.
Cherel, Robert	
Chatellier, François	Discharged September 15, 1763. On half-pay of 4 livres 10 sol. (C).
Cortesy, Louis	Discharged September 15, 1763. On half-pay of 4 livres 10 sol. (C).
Chauoin, Pierre	Sergeant. On half-pay of 15 livres. Decision of November 28, 1764. Sent to the Bureau.
Copin or Coupin, Jean	Died September 3, 1756. Bonnille's Company.
Colin, François	Discharged May 1, 1750.
Cheoert, Guillaume	(A), folio 4.
Court, Joseph	
Chemin, Gilles	
Couvrechef, Adrien	

Cassou, Antoine	Discharged August 10, 1754.
Chevrety, Laurent	Discharged May 1, 1751.
Caffin, Paul	Died in Marest's (Latour?) Company. The date of his death is not on the roll sent to France.
√Chelatre, Michel	Discharged July 1, 1751.
Caloé, Julien	
Clignot, Jean Baptiste	Discharged June 1, 1751.
Chesnau, Philippes François	
Chapuy, François	Discharged March 9, 1764. (B), folio 27.
Chassot, Joseph	
Cardinal or Chardinel, Jean Baptiste	
Couturier, Jean	
Champagne, Jean	Died September 30, 1750.
Cheval, Michel	
Colin, Louis	(A), folio 14.
Chevalier, Pierre	
Collet, Jean Baptiste	Died August 15, 1745. Macarty's Company.
Coroni, François	Died January 28, 1738.
Cholts, Ignace	Died August 28, 1738.
Chaumonneau, François	Died October 12, 1737.
Courcelle, Jean	Died October 7, 1737.
Clavel, Claude	Died October 21, 1736.
Champré, Jean	Died August 19, 1735.
Crépin, Honoré	Died August 14, 1734
Clonier, Pierre Joseph	Deserted February 5, 1739.
Cligny, Nicolas	Corporal. Deserted February 5, 1739.
Chire, Charles	Shot June 3, 1750.
Chevalier, Jacques	Deserted at the end of August, 1750.
Collu, Marin	Died September 3, 1750.
Combesseuze, François	Died October 22, 1750.
Ceringe, Nicolas	Discharged May 1, 1750.
Couvert, Antoine	Died November 5, 1751.
Chasse, Antoine	Discharged July 1, 1751.
Chuistre, Chrisostome	Died September 3, 1751.
Carabé, Dominique	Discharged May 1, 1751.
Cheverry, Dominique	Died November 7, 1751.
Chevallier, Claude	Shot June 16, 1751.
Chenestre, Frédéric	Died September 1, 1751.
Chambrié, François	Died October 10, 1751.
Clement, Jean Joseph	Died November 15, 1751.
Chapelle, Jean	Died October 27, 1751.
Cousin, Guillaume Joseph	Shot April 6, 1757. Villermont's Company.
Cochard, Nicolas	Died October 15, 1751.
Chantre, Pierre	Died October 26, 1751.
Craber, Pierre	Died November 2, 1751.

Croisy, Pierre	Deserted October 31, 1751.
Canelle, Le Sieur	Cadet à l'auguillette. Died August 18, 1746.
Coudhere, Jacques	
Casade, Louis	
Chalin, Michel	Died at the Arkansas Post, June 22, 1766. (B), folio 33.
Calandreau, Claude François	(A), folio 16.
Contresty, Pierre	
Confeniac, Pierre	
Comparios, Jean	(A), folio 28.
Cavallier, Jean	Discharged July 10, 1756, and returned to France on the *Rhinocéros*.
Chapsal, Antoine	
Capron, François	
Calbarins, Jean	(A), folio 12.
Celenix, François	Deserted January 29, 1763. (B), folio 24.
Castagnet, Laurent	Deserted June 3, 1757, from Fort Chartres. See the roll of June 1, 1760, folio 11.
Condamin, Jean	Discharged April 18, 1756 and returned to France on the *Messager*.
Changeux, Etienne	(H), June 21, 1756. Chavois' Company.
Caumet, Mathieu	Drowned in the river. Hazeur's Company. The roll of December 24, 1758 does not mention the year in which he drowned.
Cofiniaque, Pierre	Deserted July 19, 1755 and condemned to the galleys on the 29th of that month.
Cremont, Jean	Deserted July 19, 1755 and condemned, *in absentia*, to be hanged.
Chabeau, Jean Charles François	Deserted March 4, 1754.
Cochin, Jean	Died at Kaskaskia October 6, 1756. Favrot's Company.
Cussor, Antoine	Died in Illinois September 22, 1755. Favrot's Company.
Court, Joseph	Died at Mobile December 21, 1754. Favrot's Company.
Castille, Salvador	Drowned in the river while going down river from Natchez, October 2, 1754. Pontalba's Company.
Carelard, Michel	Deserted September 1, 1754.
Chambon, Jean	Discharged September 15, 1756.
Chabert, Joseph	Died in Illinois November 22, 1754. de la Houssaye's Company.

Chervieux, Jean Claude	(H), October 9, 1756. Grandchamp's Company.
Chauves, François Firmin	(H), November 4, 1756. Grandchamp's Company.
Couturier, Jean	Died at Fort Chartres March 9, 1756. Gautraye's Company.
Cheveux, Laurent	Died at Mobile August 27, 1754. Gautraye's Company.
Chevrey, Simon	Discharged April 1, 1756.
Chenel, Louis Jacques	Discharged August 10, 1754.
Cochois, Pierre	Discharged May 29, 1754 and returned to France.
Caré, Dominique	Deserted June 15, 1756.
Cailleux, Nicolas	Discharged April 1, 1756.
Colin, Jean Baptiste	Died July 4, 1755. D'Artaud's Company.
Cordier, Blaise	(H), February 17, 1756. Populus' Company.
Cerizier, Michel	Discharged July 10, 1756, and returned to France.
Chop, Jean Tobie	Deserted July 17, 1755.
Charpentier, Pierre	Discharged July 5, 1756.
Cadron, Jean	Cashiered and condemned to the galleys for life.
Cordonnier, Jean Baptiste	(H), October 9, 1757. Grandchamp's Company.
Cailleaux or Cailleux, Jean	Deserted June 3, 1757. Montberault's Company. See the roll of June 1, 1760, folio 6, where he is listed under the name of Cailleux.
Casbergue, Mathieu	
Colasse, Jean Claude	(H), March 30, 1757. Neyon's Company.
Charpentier, Joseph	(H), December 30, 1757. Desvarennes' Company.
Cheron, Pierre	Deserted at Vera Cruz, July 11, 1757. See the roll of June 1, 1760, folio 10.
Caillaux, François	Sergeant. Deserted August 30, 1761. See the roll for that same year, folio 23.
Chausseligne, Guillaume	(H), November 13, 1757. Murat's Company. See the roll of June 1, 1760, folio 12, where he is is listed as Chausselegue.
Cochet, Etienne	Discharged September 15, 1763. On half-pay of 6 livres. (C).
Cousin, Louis	
Chambon, Etienne	Discharged May 1, 1765. (B), folio 33.

Cirque, Jean	(A), folio 20.
Cardeur, Claude	
Coursin or Coussin, Fourcy	(H), September 27, 1751. See roll of the same year, folio 4.
Cerf, François	Deserted February 1, 1759. See the roll of June 1, 1760, folio 12.
Cannoir, Paul	
Clairet, Charles	(A), folio 5.
Charemberg, Guillaume	Discharged October 30, 1769. (B), folio 52.
Claudon, Antoine	(A), folio 25.
Charmier, Jean Francois	
Cartoir or Catoir, Antoine	
Calasson, Francois	
Courdeau, Jean Louis	Discharged October 21, 1759, being unworthy to serve, and returned to France on the *Union*.
Coday or Cauday, Charles	(A), folio 6.
Corsonnet, Charles Francois	
Carré, Charles	
Couzin, Guillaume Joseph	Deserted February 15, 1757, and shot April 6, 1757. Villermont's Company.
Chelingre, Joseph	
Creté, Michel Jerosme	Deserted September 29, 1768. (B), folio 36.
Couvert, Blaize	Discharged June 1, 1765. (B), folio 31.
Cresson, Hubert François	
Cavars, Claude	
Charey, Michel	
Carlin, Dominique	
Chaloche, Antoine	(A), folio 7. On half-pay of 6 livres. (C).
Cabannes, Martin	Died November 6, 1761. See the roll for that year, folio 17.
Clairet, Jean	(A), folio 8.
Carlier, Jean Pierre	(A), folio 24.
Crochet, Jean	Discharged November 30, 1769. (B), folio 43.
Coquillard, Nicolas	Discharged and settled in Arkansas, December 31, 1769. (B), folio 50.
Castelain, Pierre	
Colomb, Philippes	
Colomb, Thierry Joseph	
Caillet, Pierre	
Coquet, Jacques	(A), folio 13.

Charembeau, Jean	Discharged November 15, 1769. (B), folio 50.
Chevalier, Louis	Discharged September 15, 1763. On half-pay of 6 livres. (C).
Coutant, François	
Connant, Louis	Discharged March 31, 1761. See roll of the same year, folio 21. Half-pay of 6 livres. (C).
Calmes, Etienne	Discharged September 1, 1764. On half-pay of 6 livres per month. Decision of December 10, 1765. Sent to the Bureau on the 13th.
Colin, Nicolas	Discharged and returned to France on the <u>Fortune</u>, January 1, 1759. See the roll of June 1, 1760.
Colette, Gilles	
Chirvet, Benoist	
Cauvin, Antoine	Discharged July 1, 1765. Roll of January 1, 1763, folio 32.
Collet, André	
Carron, François	Drowned in Bayou St. John, February 10, 1766. (B), 32.
Cavier, Nicolas	On half-pay of 9 livres per month payable at Amiens. Decision of September 8, 1770. Sent to the Bureau on the 14th.
Chiron, Paul	Died in Missouri May 15, 1763. Roll of January 1, 1760, folio 11.
Cassaigne, Joseph	Discharged September 1, 1761. See the roll for the same year, folio 27.
Chop, Joseph	Discharged September 30, 1769. (B), folio 46.
Chimenne, Antoine	
Chambray, François	Discharged July 1, 1764. (B), folio 29.
Carré, Etienne	
Croisset, Antoine	(A), folio 14.
Charpentier, Michel Denis	
Chaussade, François	
Charroye, Claude	Deserted March 29, 1758 and condemned, <u>in absentia</u>, to be hanged. Decision of July 24, 1758. See the roll of June 1, 1760, folio 10.
Chauvet, Jean Baptiste	
Coquelin, Jacques	
Cervraize, Claude	
Cholet, Damien	

Cloquet, Bernard	(A), folio 16.
Corne, Gabriel	Died November 15, 1764. (B), folio 27.
Caux, Raymond	On half-pay of 6 livres. (C).
Ceraize, Joseph	
Cochu, Charles Leger	Discharged at Havre. See the general roll of February 22, 1761, sent to that port.
Castel, Alain	(P).
Cavallier, André	(A), folio 18.
Clozeaux, François	
Caillou, Etienne	Discharged December 30, 1763, after having served since 1752. Villiers' Company.
Caron, François	
Carlier, Jean Pierre	
Charlier, Remy	
Cherly, Pierre	Deserted August 1, 1758. See the roll of June 1, 1760, folio 6.
Castetin, Pierre	
Colain, Jean Baptiste	Deserted August 30, 1761. See the roll of the same year, folio 33. He arrived in Louisiana in 1757.
Carré, François	Discharged September 30, 1769. (B), folio 48.
Casbergue, Mathurin	(A), folio 25.
Connard, Pierre	
Cervraize, Claude	
Comble, Pierre	
Chaux, Pierre	Recruit who went to Louisiana on the ship <u>St. Claude</u> in 1756. He disembarked at Boulogne May 1, 1763, and was present at the Bureau on May 17 with a passport dated May 1, countersigned for his discharge.
Cousin, Antoine Joseph	Arrived in the colony in 1750. Discharged June 1, 1751.
Cenant, Louis	Discharged September 15, 1763. On half-pay of 9 livres. (C).
Cavalier, Claude	Sergeant. On half-pay of 12 livres. Decision of June 11, 1764, sent to the Bureau the same day.
Cousin, Louis	(P).
Cresson, Hubert François	(P).
Calasson, François	(P).
Caunoir, Pierre	Sergeant. Discharged February6, 1770. On half-pay of 12 livres per month. Decision of April 28, 1770.

Cassade, Louis	Discharged February 6, 1770. On half-pay of 4 livres 10 sol per month. Decision of April 28, 1770.
Charlier, Remy	Discharged February 6, 1770. On half-pay of 4 livres 10 sol per month. Decision of April 28, 1770.
Comble, Pierre	Discharged February 6, 1770. Duplessis' Company.
Chaulet, Damien	Discharged February 6, 1770. Villiers' Company.
Cardeur, Claude	Drummer. Discharged February 6, 1770. On half-pay of 6 livres per month, computed from July 1, 1770. Decision of October 1, 1770. Trudeau's Company.
Charpentier, Michel Denis	Discharged February 6, 1770. Trudeau's Company.
Chauvet, Jean Baptiste	Discharged February 6, 1770. Trudeau's Company.
Chassey, Michel	Fusilier. Discharged August 20, 1770. On half-pay of 6 livres per month. Decision of October 17, 1770.
Caillet, Pierre	Discharged February 6, 1770. On half-pay of 6 livres per month. Decision of October 17, 1770.
Cardeur, Claude	Discharged February 6, 1770. Listed above. On half-pay soldier of 6 livres per month.
Colomb, Joseph	(A), folio 2.
Carnier, Laurent	(A), folio 25.
Collmare, Jean	(A), folio 26.
Chauvin, Pierre	Discharged July 14, 1764. (B), folio 27.
Chausse, David	Drowned August 28, 1767. (B), folio 35.
Chevert, Benoit	Discharged September 30, 1769. (B), folio 38.
Cadet, Léonard	Discharged September 30, 1769. (B), folio 42.
Coquier, Julien	Discharged October 31, 1769. (B), folio 42.
Carlin, Joseph	Discharged August 8, 1769. (B), folio 47.
Camus, Jean	Discharged September 30, 1769. (B), folio 48.

Chatelin, Pierre	Discharged and settled in Arkansas, December 1, 1769. (B), folio 50.
Coutty, Jean	Discharged November 30, 1769. (B), folio 51.
Casmann, Marc	Departed for France on the <u>Samson</u>, October 1, 1769. (B), folio 51.

D

Didier, Claude Petit	
Durand, Joseph	
Desormeaux, Jean Baptiste	Discharged due to injuries.
Du Chesne, Antoine François	Discharged May 16, 1754.
Doniot, Alexis	
Daguerre, Charles François	(H), September 11, 1758. See roll of June 1, 1760, folio 2.
Dumesnil, François	Died September 12, 1757. D'Hauterive's Company.
Dodé, François	
Drien, Philippe	Discharged May 1, 1755.
David, Claude	Discharged September 15, 1763. On half-pay of 9 livres. Decision of of June 11, 1764.
Desmaisons, Sylvain	
Demante, Nicolas Marin	
Digoix, Jean Nicolas Romain	Discharged June 1, 1751.
Dupuy, François	
Diard, Nicolas	
Dlené, Nicolas	
Dumot, Joseph	
Deschamps, Charles	
Dubois, Jean Baptiste	Discharged May 1, 1751.
Delpeche, Louis	
Dubois, Henry	Discharged November 30, 1769. (B), folio 46.
Duchemin, Sébastien	Died at Natchez, March 29, 1759. Dorgon's Company.
Deduy, Charles Nicolas	Died April 30, 1755. Dorgon's Company.
Dupart, Claude	Died at Mobile, November 30, 1755. Marintin's Company.
Du Croz, Joseph	Discharged March 1, 1751.
Duvert, Jean	
Devers, Jean	(A), folio 15.
Dubois, Pierre	
Dumanche, Pierre	
Duc, Joseph	Discharged February 1, 1751.
Doré, Pierre	
Davion, Jean Baptiste	Discharged April 1, 1750.
Doucet, François	(A), folio 21.

Dardenne, Charles	Discharged November 1, 1750.
Davion, Julien	Died March 5, 1750.
Dubut, Jacques	(H), September 16, 1764. (B), folio 28.
Donne à Dieu, Marc Antoine	Died December 23, 1750.
Desnots, Jean Baptiste François	Died March 31, 1755. Villiers' Company.
Desprieux, Gabriel	
Drouin, André	Discharged October 15, 1751.
Doué, Claude	
Desholliers, Louis	
Desbordes, Claude	Discharged December 1, 1759. See roll of June 1, 1760, folio 11.
Duman, Jean	
Dégout, Etienne	Discharged July 1, 1764. (B), folio 30.
Diot, Jacques	Died July 18, 1745. Ganory's Company.
Dubois, Jacques	Died August 7, 1744. LeBlanc's Company.
De Dieu, Chrétien	Deserted August 20, 1746. Gavorit's Company.
De Bau, Nicolas	Died October 19, 1737.
Duval, Jean Francois	Died February 19, 1720.
DuMas, Jean	Died August 4, 1738.
Doublon, Nicolas	Died October 6, 1738.
Damiens, Guillaume	Died January 29, 1734.
Denis, Etienne	
Doucet, Simon Pierre	(A), folio 18.
Devost, Claude	Demoted July 2, 1756.
Du Meche, Etienne	Died January 9, 1750.
Dutisne, Pierre	Cadet. Died October 8, 1750.
DuBois, René de la Chambre	Died March 6, 1750.
Du Soulier, Antoine	Discharged June 1, 1751.
Denizmendy, Alexandre	Discharged August 7, 1751.
Dupuy, Bernard	Deserted in June, 1751.
Dodane, Claude	Died November 4, 1751.
Deliot François	Died October 25, 1751.
David, Joseph	Died September 11, 1751.
Druet, Joseph	Died July 11, 1751.
Du Breüil, Jean	Deserted August 20, 1751.
Du Buisson, Joseph	Died August 5, 1751.
Ducros, Jean	Discharged June 26, 1751.
D'Angoulême, Jean Louis	Died December 7, 1751.
Delpux, Jean	Deserted at Cap Français, September 7, 1750.
Duhard, Martin	Died December 7, 1751.
Dantonin, Nicolas	Discharged June 1, 1751.

Delong, Joseph	
Dubras, Pierre	(A), folio 13
Dufort, Jean	
Desturbé, Jacques	Condemened to the galleys for life, February 9, 1756.
Ducuire, Laurent	(A), folio 24.
Dezert or Dessert, Guy	(A), folio 31.
Desmoulins, Nicolas	
Dumant, Pierre	
Dunant, Jean Baptiste	
Daix, Gilles	
Dalmasse, Jean	Deserted August 30, 1761. See roll of the same year, folio 33.
Dapognet, Jacques	Discharged May 24, 1756. Benoist's Company.
Donjon, Jean Baptiste	(H), August 10, 1756. Chavoye's Company.
Dufour, Jacques Augustin	Discharged and returned to France on the *Messager*.
Dassigny, Jean	Died at Kaskaskia, May 16, 1755. De Sommes' Company.
Destreval, Francois	Discharged March 1, 1756. Latour's Company.
Dupuis, Charles	Died November 13, 1756. Latour's Company.
Doré, Antoine	Condemned to the galleys, July 24, 1755. Hazeur's Company.
Ducousseau, Joseph	Died in Arkansas, December 21, 1754. Hazeur's Company.
Daumean, Alexis	Discharged August 10, 1754.
Débarbier, Etienne	Died in Illinois, September 15, 1754. Montchervaux's Company.
Durif, François Dominique	Discharged June 15, 1756.
Desclardins, Louis Benoit	Drowned in the river, February 12, 1754. Desmazellieres' Company.
Desmoulins, Louis	(H), May 4, 1756. Desmazellieres' Company.
Drouart, Denis	Discharged September 10, 1756.
Dromas, Joseph	Drowned in the river, March 5, 1754. Gramont's Company.
Dufossat, Guy	Cadet soldat. Died August 24, 1756. D'Aubry's Company.
Dupré, François	Deserted July 19, 1755.
Demany, Cazard	Deserted June 8, 1755.
Descom, Charles	Discharged June 14, 1756 and returned to France.

Dupré, Jean	Deserted June 8, 1755.
Duchef, Jean Baptiste	Discharged March 11, 1757.
Damar, Pierre	Drowned in the river, October 22, 1756. D'Artaud's Company.
Duplanac, Jean Pierre	Died February 25, 1756. Marentin's Company.
Danay, Jean Louis	Discharged April 18, 1756 and returned to France.
Defin, Jean	Died at Mobile, August 24, 1754. Grandmaison's Company.
Ducré, Armand Louis	Discharged October 30, 1756.
Danzin, Gaspard	Drowned in the river May 11, 1757. Chavoye's Company.
Delpart, Jean	Died in Arkansas, January 9, 1757. Reggio's Company.
Duchef, Jean Baptiste	Discharged March 11, 1757.
Donnant, Nicolas	
Dubuisson, Guilleaume	
Desorios, Sanetos	(H), December 19, 1758. See roll of June 1, 1760, folio 1.
Desjardins, André	Discharged December 31, 1764. (B), folio 29.
Duchesne, Louis	(A), folio 29.
Desmine, Claude	(A), folio 20.
Dupain, Pierre Emanuel Victor	Sergeant. (A), folio 13.
Daumé, Charles	
Dellerüe, Louis	(H), June 23, 1759. See roll of June 1, 1760, folio 1.
Dagnan, Guilleaume	
Delvac, Philippes	
Danicourt, André	(A), folio 5.
Danis, Honoré Martial	
Dareis, Pierre	Discharged November 30, 1769. (B), folio 41.
Diebeau or Dubeau, Claude Augustin	
Duvillard, Jacques	Discharged October 8, 1769. (B), folio 43.
Duffaud, Pierre	(A), folio 25.
Dufour, Nicolas	(H), September 26, 1769. (B), folio 44.
Destré, Nicolas	Roll of January 1, 1763, folio 45.
Desmortiers, Pierre	On half-pay of 6 livres. (C).
Danis, Jullien	
Des Gouttes, Jean	
Desportes, Louis	Discharged December 31, 1764. (B), folio 27.
Delayné, Nicolas Jean Baptiste	Discharged March 31, 1761. Roll of the same year, folio 13.
Desjardins, François	(A), folio 10.
Durand, Louis Antoine	(A), folio 6.

Dudoigt, Pierre François	Deserted November 15, 1761. See roll of the same year, folio 16.
Deschamps, Jean Baptiste	Corporal. On half-pay of 8 livres. (C).
Decarlin, Joseph Vincent	
Drugman, Jean Baptiste	On half-pay of 15 livres. (C). Sergeant. (A), folio 81.
Duperet, Claude Louis	(A), folio 12.
Delton, Silvain	
Devreigne, Louis	(H), March 11, 1758. See roll of June 1, 1760, folio 9.
Desmonts, Louis	
Dufaye, Etienne	Drowned February 7, 1766. (B), folio 33.
Desaigles, Jean	(A), folio 10.
Devin, Marin	
Doriot or Dauriaut, Jean François	(H), June 20, 1759. See roll of June 1, 1760, folio 6.
Ducuir, Laurent	
Dessouard, Jean	
Dupas, Jean	Died at Natchez, September 1, 1758. See roll of June 1, 1760, folio 8.
Duvardet, Claude	Deserted August 1, 1758. See roll of June 1, 1760, folio 8.
Douchy, Hubert Jean	Discharged November 30, 1769. (B), folio 41.
Demaneche, Blaize	Discharged and returned to France aboard the ship <u>Fortune</u>, January 1, 1759. See roll of June 1, 1760, folio 8. Name may also be spelled Demanêge.
Durand, Jacques	Discharged and returned to France on the <u>Fortune</u>, January 1, 1759. See roll of June 1, 1760, folio 8.
Dumesnil, Louis	
Durand, Jean	
Demay, Leger	Sergeant. Discharged September 15, 1763. On half-pay of 15 livres. (C).
Dubois, Jacques Joseph	
Dumain, François	Sergeant. On half-pay of 9 livres. Decision of November 30, 1764. Sent to the Bureau December 1, 1764. Discharged July 1, 1764.
D'Homer, Jerosme	
Desprez, Antoine	Deserted August 1, 1758. See roll of June 1, 1759, folio 9.

De Lage, Jean	Settled in Illinois. (B), folio 38.
Doyen, Louis	
Desmalle, Jean	Died at Balize, April 20, 1765. (B), folio 30.
Deszaize or Desraize, Jean	
Desnant, Jacques	
Desmoulins, Charles	Died suddenly at New Orleans, March 28, 1766. (B), folio 33.
Dubut, Jacques	On half-pay of 9 livres. Decision of June 11, 1764. Sent the Bureau the same day.
Demoly, Claude	
DeTroys, Joseph	
Didier, Gerard	
Doussin, Louis	Died May 2, 1758. See roll of June 1, 1760, folio 11.
Daux, Charles	Discharged March 31, 1761. See roll of the same year, folio 4.
Dufresne, Jean Ollivier	Discharged October 11, 1764. (B), folio 29.
Descrimes, Guilleaume	Discharged October 8, 1769. (B), folio 53.
Doucet, Pierre	(A), folio 4.
Desroches, Antoine	(A), folio 24.
Desgoulets, Jean	Deserted in Arkansas, October 26, 1759. See roll of June 1, 1760, folio 4.
Dubuisson, Dominique	Killed by gunshot at Balize, February 11, 1759. See roll of June 1, 1760, folio 4.
Deselle, Jean	Discharged June 1, 1764. (B), folio 26.
Decochiés, Gabriel	Discharged September 30, 1769. (B), folio 45.
Detron, Silvain	Discharged September 30, 1769. (B), folio 37.
Doussin, Maurice	
Dubuisson, François	
Desroziers, Jacques	
Dubois, Jean	Returned from prison in England. Arrived at Boulogne where his passport was validated June 9, 1763 for him to go to Rochefort. There he will take a ship to Louisiana to join his wife and children.
Delmasse, Jean	Discharged. See roll dated at Calais, May 2, 1763.

Dubois, Jean	Discharged, See roll of the same day, May 2, 1763.
Dauphin, Henry	On half-pay of 4 livres 10 sol. (C).
de Mante, Jacques	Sergeant. On half-pay of 15 livres. (C).
Desgait, Etienne	On half-pay of 9 livres. Decision of November 30, 1764. Sent to the Bureau December 1, 1764.
De Mante, Nicolas Marin	Corporal. On half-pay of 9 livres. (C). (A), folio 9.
Du Beau, Claude Augustin	On half-pay of 6 livres. (C).
Dautun, Edme	Soldier of d'Amelot's Company. (H), October 26, 1762. His death certificate was certified by M. Foucault and by M. le duc de Praslin and was sent to M. Camelin at Auxerre, July, 1769. It will be found in one of the cartons relating to Louisiana.
Dufort, Jean	Discharged November 20, 1769. On half-pay of 9 livres per month, decision of April 28, 1770.
Danis, Honoré Martial	and wife (P).
Durand, Antoine	(P).
Donnant, Nicolas	(P).
Delfin, Joannes	Swiss corporal. He and wife (P).
Destour, Le Sieur	Marchand de Lyon. (P).
Daux, Charles	Sergeant. Discharged February 6, 1770. On half-pay of 6 livres per month. Decision of April 28, 1770.
Durand, Jacques	Discharged February 6, 1770. On half-pay of 4 livres 10 sol. Decision of April 28, 1770.
Doyen, Louis	Discharged February 6, 1770. On half-pay of 4 livres 10 sol. Decision of April 28, 1770.
Delhaye, Henry Joseph	Corporal. Discharged February 6, 1770. On half-pay of 6 livres per month. Decision of April 28, 1770.
Dubois, Jacques Joseph	Discharged February 6, 1770. Duplessis' Company.
Diot, Thomas	Discharged February 6, 1770.
Dumoutier, Isaie	Discharged August 20, 1770. On half-pay of 6 livres. See the decision of September 8, 1776 in the carton of the half-pay soldiers dated June 9, 1777.

Duat, Guillaume	On half-pay of 6 livres per month. Decision of September 8, 1770.
D'Auphin, François	(A), folio 10.
Desnant, Jacques	(A), folio 25.
Dorel, Michel	Discharged July 1, 1765. (B).
Dupasquier, Henry	Discharged November 30, 1769. (B), folio 42.
Dutoy, Daniel	Departed for France on the <u>Samson</u>, October 1, 1769. (B), folio 45.
Dupré, Jean Baptiste	Enlisted in 1762. Discharged October 8, 1769. (B), folio 55.
Dardy, Jean Baptiste	Enlisted in 1762. (B), folio 56. Discharged October 8, 1769.
Darand, François	Enlisted in 1762. Discharged October 8, 1769. (B), folio 55.
Du Tillet, Le Sieur	Cadet. Died at sea on board the <u>Thëtis</u> while returning to France, June 4, 1770. The death certificate is in the Louisiana carton.

E

Erame, Louis	
Edeling, Jean	
Excrousailles, Antoine	Discharged April 18, 1756 and returned to France on the <u>Messager</u>.
Espinet, Jean Baptiste	Discharged November 30, 1769. (B), folio 44.
Escouder, Jacques	
Edouin, Antoine	(A), folio 8.
Emery, Jacques François	
Edme, Mathieu	(A), folio 12.
Elibon, Pierre	(A), folio 7.
Egand, Jean Baptiste	Discharged November 30, 1769. Settled at Natchitoches. (B), folio 48.
Edlé, François	Departed for France on the <u>Samson</u>, October 1, 1769. (B), folio 52.

F

Frédéric, Jean	Drummer.
Flechy, Pierre	Died January 8, 1746. Gauvret's Company.
Farineau, Martin	
Fenouillot, Jean Claude	

Ferrary, Prosper	
Ferrette, Marc	
Fiton, Mathieu	
Fonteneau, Pierre	(A), folio 5.
Fonteneau, Jean Louis	Died in Alabama, October 29, 1755. Grandchamp's Company.
Faye, Etienne François	Discharged August 18, 1751.
Felker, Jacques	Drowned while going down river from Natchez, October 28, 1754. Grandpré's Company.
Flambard, Pierre	
Ferre, François	Deserted April 28, 1730.
François, Pierre	Discharged due to injuries. Dorgon's Company.
Florés, Nicolas	
Faillard, Jean	
Fonteneau, Louis	
Fournier, Jean	Died March 10, 1751.
Fouré, Pierre	
Fontineau, Pierre	
Frechene, Victor	Died. Marest's Company. The date of his death is not on the roll sent to France.
Favelier, Antoine	
Foudoix, Jacques	
Fourqueux, Jean Baptiste	Discharged March 1, 1751. Settled in the colony.
Fouquet, Antoine	(H), October 13, 1756. Derneville's Company.
Filosa, Sylvain	
Finet, Joseph Hubert	(A), folio 4.
Favre, Pierre	(A), folio 5.
Fondeur, Jean Pierre	(A), folio 28.
Feraudon, Denis	Discharged August 18, 1751.
Faiffre, Jean	
Favre, Jean	
Fontaine, Antoine	
Ferraud, Fiacre	
Fournier, Jean	Died December 23, 1736.
Ferret, Francois	Died May 24, 1734.
Flamier, Joseph	Died September 1, 1738.
Flamand, Jean	Died October 31, 1735.
Ferret, Pierre	
Fiché, Joseph	Died September 15, 1750.
Fauché, Claude	Drowned and was found by the Indians, June 5, 1751.
Falconnet, Claude	Discharged June 25, 1751.
Failhet, Jacques	Drum major. Discharged August 18, 1751.
Fontinelle, Jean Baptiste	Died October 10, 1751.

Flaure, Joseph Laurent	Deserted July 17, 1751.
Fourriere, Jean Baptiste de	Died August 12, 1751.
Françure, Villers	Discharged April 30, 1751.
Fenouillou, Claude	Discharged July 26, 1756.
Flamant, Pierre	Sergeant. Hanged September 10, 1753. See the criminal proceedings in the Louisiana file.
Foltray, Antoine	
Floüard, Pierre	(A), folio 23.
Ferrant, Jean	
Feste, Joseph	Deserted August 30, 1761. See the roll for that year, folio 46.
Fritot, Michel	
Fitte, Jean	Discharged September 30, 1769. (B), folio 54.
Fourchet, Jean	Killed by the Indians, August 1, 1754. Dorgon's Company.
Freau, Jean Baptiste	Deserted in May, 1756.
Fabry, Louis Alexandre	Discharged May 1, 1754. Derneville's Company.
Felker, Jacques	Drowned while going down river from Natchez, October 28, 1754. Grandpré's Company.
Fouillot, Pierre	Departed for Cap Français on the <u>Concorde</u>, December 15, 1754.
Figuerre, Jean Baptiste	Deserted September 25, 1755.
Freint, Jean	Deserted July 17, 1755, and condemned to be hanged July 19, 1755.
Fauvin, François	(H), September 16, 1755. Montberault's Company.
Fosse, Robert	Deserted in Illinois, 1755.
Fontenay, Abraham	Died at Natchez, July 29, 1754. Gautraye's Company.
François, Louis	Condemned to the galleys for life, February 9, 1756.
Favier, Guilleaume	Discharged August 18, 1756 and returned to France.
Fort, Jean Pierre	Discharged July 16, 1756 and returned to France.
Ficher, Pierre	Sergeant.
Feré, Jean Firmin	Discharged March 1, 1764. (B), folio 30.
Flamien, François	(A), folio 20.
Falcon, Germain	Discharged November 30, 1769. (B), folio 53.
Forestier, Louis Nicolas	Discharged at Rochefort, June 6, 1761. Presented his discharge at the Bureau on September 11, 1761. On half-pay of 6 livres.

Ferret or Ferrette, Hyacinthe	Discharged June 30, 1768. (B), folio 36.
Fenard, Jean Pierre	Discharged July 31, 1764. (B), folio 27.
Fonteneau, Jean	
Fontaine, Henry	Discharged March 1, 1764. (B), folio 28.
Fromentin, Nicolas Pierre	Discharged March 1, 1764. (B), folio 29.
Fleury, Claude	
Forneret, Louis	(A), folio 10.
Faron, Pierre	(A), folio 8.
Fournier, Jean François	Died in Arkansas, May 28, 1759. See the roll of June 1, 1760, folio 5.
Fouré, Louis	(A), folio 9.
Figuerre, Jean Baptiste	Discharged and returned to France on the <u>Fortune</u>, January 1, 1759. See the roll of June 1, 1760, folio 5.
Foucault, Jacques	(A), folio 2. On half-pay of 9 livres. Decision of May 25, 1764. Sent to the Bureau the same day.
Foubert, François	(A), folio 22.
Ferrand, François	
François, Dominique	Died at New Orleans, January 19, 1758. (B), folio 35.
Foucault, Pierre	Discharged July 1, 1765. On half-pay of 6 livres. Decision of January 28, 1766. Sent to the Bureau on the 29th.
Frichard, Jean	(A), folio 22.
Frederik, Jean	Discharged September 15, 1763. On half-pay of 6 livres. (C).
Fontineau, Joseph	Discharged September 15, 1763. On half-pay of 4 livres 10 sol. Decision of June 11, 1764. Sent to the Bureau on the 12th.
Fauché, Antoine	Corporal. On half-pay of 8 livres. (C).
Fondeur or Fondair or Fondeux, Jean Pierre	On half-pay of 6 livres. Decision of March 22, 1765. Sent to the Bureau.
Fanton, Louis	Discharged November 30, 1769. (B), folio 49.
Foyer, Jean	
Fourcade, Bernard	
Fourchaud, François	Discharged December 31, 1764. (B), folio 28.

Fournier, Antoine	Discharged and returned to France on the *Fortune*, January 1, 1759. See the roll of June 1, 1760, folio 10.
Fresneau, Jean François	Discharged April 1, 1767. (B), folio 24.
Fonteneau, Henry	(A), folio 26.
Forgeur, Joseph	
Farquet, Aimée	Deserted at Balize, August 30, 1761. See roll of the same year, folio 43.
Fonteneau, Francois	Died at Mobile, January 16, 1759. See roll of June 1, 1760, folio 12.
Franc, Jean	
Faupied, Jean	Deserted June 19, 1758. See roll of June 1, 1760, folio 6.
Favre, Pierre	Corporal. On half-pay of 12 livres. Decision of April 26, 1766. Sent to the Bureau on the 27th.
Favet, Louis	
Filon, Mathieu	(A), folio 4. On half-pay of 6 livres. (C).
Fonteneau, Jean Louis	Enlisted January 1, 1743. (A), folio 11.
Fonteneau, Philippes	Discharged September 15, 1763. On half-pay of 6 livres. Decision of June 11, 1764. Sent the Bureau on the 12th.
Fontaine, Germain	(P).
Ferrare or Ferrarie, Prosper	Sergeant. Discharged September 15, 1763. On half-pay of 12 livres. (C).
Fol, Julien Denis	On half-pay of 6 livres. (C).
Favet, Louis	and wife and two children (P).
Ferrin, Michel Joseph	(P).
Fouré, Pierre	Corporal. Discharged February 6, 1770. On half-pay of 15 livres per month. Decision of April 28, 1770.
Fleury, Claude	Discharged February 6, 1770. On half-pay of 4 livres 10 sol per month. Decision of April 28, 1770.
Foyer, Jean	Discharged February 6, 1770. On half-pay of 4 livres 10 sol per month. Decision of April 28, 1770.
Fèrand, François	On half-pay of 4 livres 10 sol per month. Decision of April 28, 1770.

Fauss, Frédéric	Discharged February 6, 1770. Duplessis' Company.
Fabre, Pierre	(H), July 26, 1763. (B), folio 19.
Fizelle, Reynard	(H), June 26, 1765. (B), folio 32.
Felman, Laurent	Discharged September 30, 1769. (B), folio 45.

G

Genty, Jean	
Griel, Paul	
Gaillard, Jean	Drummer. (H), February 23, 1763. (B), folio 16.
Grimpel, Simon	
Guyot, Charles	Deserted February 28, 1750.
Guerin, Martin	
Grenouville, François	Discharged February 22, 1753 and settled in the colony.
Gaudet, Jean	Corporal. On half-pay of 9 livres, payable at Autun in Burgundy. (C).
Guerlot, Reme	
Guilmer, Jean Baptiste	(H), November 7, 1757. Dorgon's Company.
Gallet, Robert	
Gilbert, François	Died April 29, 1750.
Gautier, Antoine	Shot June 24, 1769. (B), folio 51.
Girault, René	
Gosselin, Jacques	
Gerard, Michel	Discharged May 1, 1751.
Giraud, Simon	
Goyaux, Nicolas	Drowned at Balize, January 10, 1754. Macarty's Company.
Grenade, Nicolas	Drummer. Discharged September 15, 1763. On half-pay of 6 livres. (C).
Glachaud or Glanchaud, Louis	
Gogué, Joseph	Discharged September 15, 1763. On half-pay of 6 livres. (C).
Guerin, Guillaume	Re-enlisted.
Giray, Jacques	Died at Mobile November 4, 1758. See the roll of June 1, 1760, folio 3.
Gasquin, Etienne Denis	
Geloix, Caesar	(H), July 16, 1756. Grandchamp's Company.
Guineau or Guinaud, Claude	(A), folio 11.

Germain, Etienne	Died April 17, 1751.
Grappe, Alexis	(A), folio 25.
Gautier, René ✓	Died April 25, 1758. See the roll of June 1, 1760, folio 3.
Grandchamp, Louis	
Guillard, Louis	Died December 17, 1750.
Guichard, Jacques	
Godin, André	Died December 25, 1750.
Gouffier, Jean François	
Garel, Charles	Grandchamp's Company. The date of his death is not on roll sent to France in 1747.
Gerard, Edme	Discharged September 15, 1743 (1763?). On half-pay of 6 livres. (C).
Grenier, Jean Baptiste	Discharged September 15, 1763, (B), folio 26.
Gibaut, Joseph	Died in Illinois, December 1, 1755. Marentin's Company.
Guerin, Jean	Discharged May 1, 1751.
Grenier, Pierre	Died October 17, 1750.
Guyot, René Jacques	Died July 8, 1745. Gauvry's Company.
Gilbert, Antoine	Died August 7, 1744. Membrede's Company.
Grevé or Grené, Vincent	Died July 26, 1734.
Grommée, Jean	Died October 2, 1735.
Gonisch, Claude	Died December 20, 1735.
Guidon, Joseph	Died September 10, 1734.
Guinet, Claude Augustin	Died September 5, 1734.
Grüel, Pierre	Died December 2, 1736.
Grafineau, Paul	Drowned November 1, 1738.
Goyeux, Jean	Deserted February 5, 1739.
Gonot, Jean	Deserted February 5, 1739.
Gouliat, Benoist	Deserted February 15, 1750.
Grison, Grançois	Died November 6, 1750.
Guilgau, Jean	Discharged August 1, 1760.
Gué, Joseph	Deserted July 13, 1750.
Gaudot, Agnan	Died December 29, 1751.
Gros, Barthélemy	Drowned August 1, 1751.
Gaulard, François Louis	Died September 14, 1751.
Guillemaire, François	Died October 16, 1751.
Gillet, François	Died September 14, 1751.
Gerbeau, Jacques	Discharged July 22, 1751.
Gremingue, Jerosme	Deserted April 29, 1751.
Gennevois, Jean	Deserted July 29, 1751.
Guay, Jean Baptiste	Died April 22, 1751.
Grillot or Grillaud, Lazarre	Discharged August 10, 1751.
Gangan, Louis	Died October 13, 1751.
Gerard, Louis	Died November 7, 1751.
Goutte, Pierre	Died August 27, 1751.
Gamin, Pierre	Died October 11, 1751.
Guillot, Pierre	Died October 18, 1751.

Grempel, Simon	Died October 21, 1751.
Guillard, Louis	Shot September 30, 1769. (B), folio 53.
Guinaud, F. Victor	
Gabriel, Charles	
Guerault, Bernard	Deserted September 17, 1756.
Georges, Jean Baptiste	Died July 30, 1755. Dorgon's Company.
Grenon, Michel Antoine	Discharged June 20, 1756.
Gary, Barthélemy	(H), December 13, 1756. Grandpré's Company.
Guerin, Jean Louis	Drowned in the river while going up to Natchez, December 19, 1754. Somme's Company.
Golesseau, Mathieu	Drowned at Tombecbe, April 27, 1755. Latour's Company.
Gesne, Toussaint	Discharged August 19, 1756. Latour's Company.
Guinet, Laurent	Deserted April 30, 1756.
Gerard, Joseph	Deserted September 27, 1754.
Guiot, François	(H), September 25, 1756. Desmazelliere's Company.
Gerard, Simon	Discharged September 1, 1756.
Giraud, Jean François	Drowned in the Wabash, November 10, 1756. Desmazelliere's Company.
Givry, Denis	Drowned in the river. See the roll sent December 24, 1758. It does not mention the year in which he drowned. Darazola's Company.
Garay, Barthélemy	Discharged July 26, 1756.
Galanne, Pierre	Deserted March 30, 1735.
Gallois, Michel	Discharged April 18, 1756 and returned to France.
Grassin, François	Drowned in the Arkansas River, February 14, 1755. Reggio's Company.
Grubillon, Pierre	Deserted September 17, 1754.
Gescote, François	(H), September 23, 1754. Trant's Company.
Guinault, Victor	Discharged July 16, 1754 and returned to France.
Guerrault, Bernard	Deserted September 17, 1756.
Graillot, Charles	Discharged April 18, 1756, and returned to France.
Georges, François	Deserted July 4, 1755.
Genty, Edme Romain	Drowned while going down river from Natchez, October 2, 1754. Artaud's Company.
Grisson, Joseph	Discharged July 17, 1756.

Gerbier, Etienne	Died May 15, 1755. Marentin's Company
Gaudin, Simon	Drowned at the Wabash Post, November 19, 1756. Macarty's Company.
Gillart, Sébastien	Deserted June 8, 1755
Guesnier, Gilles	Died in August, 1754. Mazan's Company.
Guerry, Pierre	Died in Arkansas, December 22, 1754. Mazan's Company.
Gabariau, Mathurin	Died November 9, 1754. Mazan's Company.
Gerard, Joseph	Killed at Mobile, July 11, 1757. Bellenos' Company.
Gros-Jacques, Jean Pierre	Killed by the Indians on the Cherokee River, July 4, 1757. Desvarennes' Company.
Girond, Pierre	Deserted August 29, 1757. Condemned, *in absentia*, to be shot. Verdict rendered April 24, 1758. See roll of June 1, 1760, folio 10.
Guillocheaud, Pierre	Discharged September 1, 1758 and returned to France on the *Fortune*, January 1, 1759. See the roll of June 1, 1760, folio 10.
Govare, Philippes Marie	
Goujard, François	Sergeant. Discharged September 15, 1763. On half-pay of 12 livres. (C).
Garillon, Blaize	
Grillet, Marin	
Gourlier, Antoine	(A), folio 19.
Gonin, Abraham	
Gotiffier, Claude	
Grognet, Antoine	
Gerard, Antoine	
Garnier, Laurent	
Galopeins, Antoine	
Glamet, François	
Grenet, Antoine	(A), folio 50.
Guilloteau, Jacques	Sergeant. Discharged March 31, 1761. See the roll of the same year, folio 12. On half-pay of 10 livres. (C).
Gabory, Sigisbert Léopol	
Guine[illegible], Pierre	
Gandois, Pierre	(H), May 31, 1766. (B), folio 33.
Gravetaut, Nicolas François	On half-pay of 6 livres. (C).
Guinchard, Etienne	Discharged October 31, 1769. (B), folio 38.
Guerpin, Jean Baptiste	
Gimmeval, Jean	
Guarbe, Joseph	(H), July 19, 1767. (B), folio 34.

Gaudier, François	Discharged October 18, 1764. (B), folio 27.
Gosson, Antoine	
Gaudier Prudhomme, Antoine	
Godart, Laurent	(A), folio 9.
Guilloton, François	Died April 17, 1763. (B), folio 9.
Goupy, Georges	
Goupy, Denis	Discharged at Havre in February, 1761. See the general roll of that port for February 22, 1761, folio 5.
Gonzalles, Antoine	(A), folio 10.
Gilbert, Jean	(A), folio 11.
Gerardin, Jean	(A), folio 22.
Germain, Jean	
Guerre, Joseph	
Gerard, Philippes	Discharged September 15, 1763. On half-pay of 6 livres. (C).
Guerin, Jean	Discharged October 31, 1769. (B), folio 46.
Guinard, Henry	On half-pay of 6 livres. (C).
Gremont, Simon	
Guenaut, Jacques Laurent	(A), folio 12.
Gautier, Nicolas	Corporal. Discharged September 15, 1763. On half-pay of 6 livres. (C).
Gabet, Claude François	Discharged May 1, 1767. (B), folio 35.
Guilleaume, Denis	Drowned in the river, July 22,1769. (B), folio 50.
Gonin, Jean	Died at New Orleans, March 22, 1768. (B), folio 35.
Genay or Genet, Joseph	(H), October 12, 1766. (B), folio 33.
Gilbert, Jerosme	(H), November 27, 1758. (B), folio 10.
Grandprés, Adrien	(A), folio 18.
Georges, Dominique	Hanged June 27, 1765. (B), folio 31.
Goiffard, Benoist	Discharged September 15, 1763. (B), folio 15.
Gollemart, Jean	
Garcin, François	Discharged September 15, 1763. On half-pay of 4 livres 10 sol. (C).
Guenon, Joseph	On half-pay of 6 livres. (C).
Guenon, Jean Baptiste	Died July 3, 1758. See roll of June 1, 1760, folio 10.
Guignon, Jacques	Died suddenly April 11, 1756. Murat's Company.

Gagnon, Philiberte	
Gauthier, François	
Grenier, Louis	Discharged September 15, 1763. On half-pay of 6 livres. (C).
Guillot, Ennemond	Discharged February 1, 1766. (B), folio 33.
Glaire, Abraham	Deserted August 30, 1761. See roll of the same year, folio 43.
Gallard, Etienne	
Genty, Claude	(A), folio 18.
Gisclair, Jean	(A), folio 18.
Gosselin, Jean	
Guesdon, Jean	Discharged July 25, 1768. (B), folio 36.
Gauvin, Jacques	
Guillet, Pierre	Discharged October 16, 1764. (B), folio 27.
Girond, Nicolas	(A), folio 1.
Gabory, Sigisbert Léopol	Discharged at Isle de Ré, August 20, 1770. On half-pay of 9 livres per month. Decision of October 17, 1770.
Guilloteau, Jacques Philipe	
Grosson or Gosson, Antoine	(A), folio 14.
Guesnon, Pierre	
Guerin, Guillaume	
Gruisses, Charles	Died September 28, 1769. (B), folio 54.
Gonord, Etienne	Taken prisoner by the English in 1754 while returning to Louisiana. He did not return to France until April 26, 1762. Discharged at Rochefort, May 16, 1762. Sergeant.
Garillon, Blaize	(P).
Gauthier, François	Corporal. Discharged February 6, 1770. On half-pay of 6 livres per month. Decision of April 28, 1770.
Gons, Joseph	Discharged February 6, 1770. Duplessis' Company.
Guigne, Pierre	Discharged February 6, 1770. Villiers' Company.
Gallart, Etienne	Discharged February 6, 1770. Villiers' Company.
Godart, Louis	See the list by M. de Repentigny dated February 6, 1770.
Guerpin, Jean Baptiste	Discharged August 20, 1770. On half-pay of 6 livres per month. Decision of October 17, 1770.

Germain, Jean — Fuselier. Discharged August 20, 1770. On half-pay of 6 livres per month.

Gaudet, Jean — Corporal. On half-pay of 9 livres per month. Decision of September 8, 1770.

Givoteau, Guillaume — (A), folio 5. See Pivoteau.

Groniete, Antoine — (A), folio 5.

Guinot, Joseph — (A), folio 10.

Guinaud, Henry — (A), folio 12.

Ganier, Louis — (A), folio 21.

Girard, André — Discharged July 1, 1767. (B), folio 34.

Georges, Jean — Discharged September 30, 1769. (B), folio 48.

Gourdon, Louis de — Entered the service April 1, 1769. Discharged November 30, 1769.

Gornoville, François — Entered the service June 1, 1769. Discharged November 30, 1769.

Grien, Frantz Thibault — Discharged September 30, 1769. (B), folio 54.

H

Hardy Noël Joseph

Hierle, François — Discharged July 1, 1750.

Husson, Claude — Died May 20, 1750.

Hippot, Jean

Hervy, Charles

Hodier, André — Discharged due to injuries.

Herier, Claude

Hube, Etienne

Hebreman, Georges

Hennane, Joseph

Hodable, Alexandre — See under l'O

Henry, Jacques

Hervieux, Claude

Harault, Pierre

Hervé, François

Hervy, Jacques — Died December 22, 1750.

Hurtebise, Guillaume — (H), September 19, 1757. Sommes' Company.

Helot, Louis

Huilleau, ? — Died September 5, 1738.

Huchette, Jean Baptiste Nicolas — Died October 6, 1734.

Hullir, René — Died in Arkansas November 4, 1738. Blanc's Company.

Hiby, Thibault — Deserted February 5, 1739.

Husson, Charles — Deserted June 30, 1750.

Horé, Jean	Died At Natchitoches March 3, 1755. Chabert's Company.
Hubert, François	Discharged June 1, 1751.
Harquet, Jean	Died October 11, 1751.
Havard, Louis	Died October 25, 1751.
Henry, Pascal	Shot July 30, 1751.
Herbelay, Hubert	(H), September 10, 1755. Grandpré's Company.
Houck, André	Deserted July 19, 1755 and condemned, *in absentia*, to be hanged.
Henry, Antoine	Died at Mobile December 4, 1756. Montberault's Company.
Hibou, Donat	Discharged August 10, 1756.
Henry, Jean	(H), September 5, 1755. Artaud's Company.
Hotz, Menard	Discharged July 16, 1754.
Husson, Gaspard	(A), folio 13.
Herbert, Jean	Killed or taken prisoner at Fort Wabash by the Cherokees or Chickasaws, November 9, 1757. Chabert's Company.
Hebert, Adrien	Discharged March 1, 1766. (B), folio 33.
Hirault, Jacques	Discharged March 1, 1766. (B), folio 6.
Hunaud, Pierre	Deserted April 20, 1761. See the roll for that year, folio 16.
Haquin, Jacques	
Hardy, Pierre	(A), folio 12.
Huard, Pierre	Carporal. Arrived in Louisiana in 1749 aboard the *Chimene*. Montchariaux's Company. See the general roll of troops dated June 1, 1760.
Hubert, Jacques	Discharged September 30, 1769. (B), folio 43.
Huard, Pierre	Arrived in Louisiana on the *Infante Victoire* in 1751. Neyon's Company. See the general roll of troops dated June 1, 1760. (H), September 30, 1759. See the roll of June 1, 1760, folio 6.
Hudain, Antoine Joseph	(A), folio 14.
Hersan, Jean François	Deserted October 17, 1765. Condemned as a deserter and sentenced, *in absentia*, to be shot. Sentence rendered October 17, 1765.
Housset, Pierre	(A), folio 14.

Haquet, Edme	(H), January 13, 1759. See roll of June 1, 1760, folio 10.
Homfroy, Charles Guillaume	
Harlay, Jean Baptiste	Discharged September 15, 1763. On half-pay of 6 livres. (C).
Huard, Pierre	This is the third Pierre Huard listed on the general roll of troops as of June 1, 1760. Discharged December 3, 1756. Reggio's Company.
Henry, Jean Baptiste	Sergeant. Served in artillery company in Louisiana. Discharged March 10, 1769. He presented his discharge at the Bureau and receives half-pay of 15 livres per month. Decision of June 18, 1769.
Harmenstrand, M.	(P). He was from London and was a Lieutenant Colonel in the British army.
Hirtz, Jean Pierre	Drummer. Discharged February 6, 1770. Desmasillieres' Company.
Helk, Michel	Discharged February 6, 1770. Vaugine's Company
Haidelai, François	Discharged February 6, 1770. Villiers' Company.
Hennequin, Nicolas	(A), folio 1.
Huart, Pierre	Enlisted in 1756. Discharged November 30, 1768. (B), folio 36.
Hann, François	Enlisted July 1, 1768. Discharged October 8, 1769. (B), folio 55.

I-J

Imbelle, Jean	Discharged May 31, 1756.
Janniau, Pierre	Fifer. On half-pay of 6 livres. (C).
Jacques, Jean Baptiste	(A), folio 5.
Jourdain, Edmé	
Joux, Denis	(A), folio 25.
Jamet, Simon	
Jouissianne, Pierre	
Jardelas	Discharged October 1, 1750.
Julie, René	
Jossard, François	
Jourdain, Jacques	Died August 6, 1744. Marest's Company.
Jolivet, François	Deserted February 5, 1739.
Jouglas, Barthélemy	Deserted March 12, 1751.

Jatiere, Étienne Jean	Died October 1, 1751.
Jourdan, Guilleaume	Died July 4, 1751.
Jolivet, Louis	Died November 9, 1751.
Jouette, Louis	Died May 14, 1751.
Jacob, Nicolas	Discharged July 29, 1756. Bentoist's Company.
Jacob, Jean Baptiste	Shot February 6, 1754. Pontalba's Company.
Jaquin, Jean	Discharged and returned to France on the <u>Rhinocéros</u>, July 10, 1754.
Jourdain, Nicolas	Discharged March 10, 1756. Re-enlisted.
Jouvenay, François poss. Duvernay	Drowned in the river, February, 12, 1754. His death certificate was sent to Mr. Jacques Poupardin, an officer of the King's army, on September 17, 1761.
Jouvenel, Barthélemy	Discharged April 18, 1756 and returned to France.
Julie, René	Discharged August 10, 1754.
Jean, Jean Antoine	Deserted November 20, 1756.
Julien, Roch	Discharged April 18, 1756.
Jamier, Pierre	Died at Fort Chartres, April 30, 1755. Villiers' Company.
Jean, Pierre Joseph	Died at Mobile, September 23, 1754. Grandmaison's Company.
Jacquelin, Michel	Discharged November 30, 1769. Roll of January 1, 1763, folio 47.
Jacquemard, Jean	
Jourdain, Joseph	(A), folio 4.
Jacques, François	(A), folio 18.
Jolivet, Thomas	(A), folio 6.
Juillet, Michel	Discharged February 6, 1770. On half-pay of 12 livres per month. Decision of April 28, 1770. Sergeant.
Josseux, Jean Baptiste	(A), folio 6.
Jossé, Antoine	(A), folio 6.
Jacquemin, Jean Baptiste	
Jupin, Jean Baptiste	(A), folio 22.
Joubert, Pierre	
Jamin, Philippes	Deserted at New Orleans, January 26, 1761. See roll of the same year, folio 40.
Jably, Laurent	Discharged and returned to France on the <u>Fortune</u>, January 1, 1759. See roll of June 1, 1760, folio 12.

Jacques, Jean	(P).
Jourdain, Nicolas	(A), folio 10.
Jardins, Pierre Maurice	Deserted October 14, 1765. Condemned, <u>in absentia</u>, following the proceedings conducted in Louisiana, October 17, 1765. Trudeau's Company.
Jacques, Le Né (Negro)	(P). M. Aubry's servant.
Jamin, Jean Baptiste	Discharged August 20, 1770. On half-pay of 12 livres 10 sol per month. Decision of October 17, 1770.
Jagnau, Pierre	(A), folio 9.
Jarre, Jean François	Deserted October 30, 1766. (B), folio 33.
Jaquet, Charles	Enlisted in 1768. Deserted September 10, 1769.
Jean, Jacques	Banished September 30, 1769. (B), folio 55.

K

Kolb, Henry	
Kenik, Jean	Died January 11, 1751.
Kel, Jacques	
Kemer, Michel	Condemned, <u>in absentia</u>, for desertion. See the proceedings of September 30, 1753.
Kremer, Frederick	Corporal in Hallwyll's Swiss regiment. On half-pay of 12 livres per month. Decision of October 25, 1769. Sent to the Bureau on the 27th.
Kestre, George	See under Q.
Kerner, Antoirek	Discharged August 1, 1768.

L

Le Tueur, Guillaume	
La Ville, Jean	
Le Clerc, Jean Baptiste	Died at Balize, August 1, 1746.
Lacour, Jacques	(H), August 23, 1756. Chabert's Company.
Le Roy, Denis	Discharged July 1, 1751.
Le Comte, Charles	Drowned in Illinois, July 7, 1755. Chabert's Company.
Laurent, Jacques	
La Boulaye, Mathurin	
Le Clerc, Patrice	
La Couture, Arnoult	Discharged June 1, 1751.

La Roche, Jacques	(A), folio 22.
La Fosse, Jacques	
La Chambre, René de	
Lexcellent, Charles	Corporal. On half-pay of 9 livres. (C).
Le Grand, Jacques	Discharged October 1, 1751.
Le Brun, Jacques	
La Grange, Louis	
La Vigne, Pierre	Died at Mobile.
La Caze, Jacques	Discharged May 1, 1750.
Langlois, Jacques	Discharged June 1, 1751.
Luquet, Pierre	Discharged September 15, 1763. On half-pay of 9 livres. Decision of June 11, 1764. Sent to the Bureau the same day.
Laurendine, Pierre	(A), folio 4.
Le Grain, Louis Pierre	Died April 6, 1746. Sergeant in Blanc's Company.
Lambert, Nicolas	
Labrosse, Nicolas de	
Le Mecsle, André	(H), March 11, 1759. See roll of June 1, 1760, folio 9.
Lefort, Pierre	Discharged July 1, 1750
Le Brun, Jacques	See below.
Laubiere, Pierre	
Le Guerné, Pierre	
Leijster, Thomas	
Le Blocq, Thomas	
Lebreton, Antoine	Died December 25, 1745. Benoist's Company.
La Ville, Thomas	
Le Comte, Clement	Died March 9, 1746. Sergeant in Dorgon's Company.
Launay, Charles	Died at Natchitoches, January 19, 1765. Roll of January 1, 1763, folio 31.
Laroze, Benoit	On half-pay of 9 livres. Decision of April 4, 1764. Sent to the Bureau on the 5th.
Lescombe, Joseph André	
Laurent, Louis	(A), folio 8.
Lamarre, Pierre	
L'Hiver, Pierre	(A), folio 7.
Lebrun, Charles	Died October 1, 1751.
Lehut, Jean	
Langlois, Pierre	Died at New Orleans, December 10, 1757 (1767?). Grandchamp's Company.
Lobel, Jean Baptiste	
Laurençon, Jean	
Le Flot, Jean Baptiste	

Le Roy, Etienne	
Loison, Michel	(H), September 18, 1754. Grandchamp's Company.
L'Homme, Claude	
Longuemare, François	
La Fleur, Pierre André	(A), folio 7.
La Renaudiere, Charles	Discharged February 1, 1751.
La Vertu, Louis	
La Marre, Jean François	Discharged July 1, 1750.
Le Vegue, François	
Lemoyne, Jean	
Le Masle, Jean	Died. Grandpré's Company. The date of his death is not indicated on the roll submitted.
Laloüette, Jacques	Discharged July 10, 1754 and returned to France on the Rhinocéros.
Leblanc, Jean	Died in Illinois, December 15, 1745. Le Verrier's Company.
Le Grand, Pierre	Corporal. On half-pay of 12 livres. Decision of November 19, 1765.
La Riviere, Charles	Died January 20, 1750.
Lefebvre, René	Died April 10, 1745. Gauvry's Company.
Le Vacher, Edmé François	Died August 15, 1745. Gauvry's Company.
La Rochelle, Simon	
Lobel, Jean	
Lavus, Jacques	Discharged October 1, 1750.
Lannier, Martin	Deserted September 30, 1738 LeBlanc's Company.
Le Blanc, Paul Guilleaume	Died November 4, 1751.
La Pluye, Pierre	Died September 25, 1751.
Le Vasseur, Jean	Died May 6, 1738.
Le Boulanger, François	Died June 26, 1736.
Le Cuit, Pierre	Died April 28, 1734.
Legal, Henry Louis	Died November 1, 1737.
Legal, Thomas	Died May 8, 1738.
Linerale, Blaise	Died October 22, 1738.
Le Moyne, François	Died January 4, 1737.
Le Comte, Louis	Died March 27, 1738.
Le Jeune, Pierre	Died May 29, 1735.
La Roche, Jacques	Died October 23, 1737.
La Vallée, Jean	Died October 15, 1737.
Langloiserie, Jacques Ste. Thereze de	Died September 21, 1737.
Lefevre, Rodolphe	Died January 27, 1739. Buissonniere's Company.
Lafontaine, Claude	Died June 14, 1750.

La Bruyere Blaize	Died September 26, 1751.
La Garde, Bernard	Died March 7, 1751.
La Ribardiere, Charles	Discharged May 1, 1751.
Le Fort, Jean	Died September 6, 1751.
Le Prestre, Jacques	Died December 10, 1751.
Lallemand, Joseph	Condemned to the galleys, May 6, 1751.
Lorea, Jerosme	Died November 16, 1751.
La Saigne, Léonard	Discharged September 1, 1751.
Le Comte, Louis	Died December 26, 1751.
Le Mineur, Louis	Discharged July 23, 1751.
La Marque, Pierre	Died December 18, 1751.
Legarnier, Pierre	Drowned March 14, 1751.
La Neuville, Thomas	Died March 12, 1751.
Lassaigne, Claude	(H), April 10, 1754 Macarty's Company.
Levreau, Jerosme	
Le Guenec, Guillaume	
La Glenc, Jacques	Deserted July 4, 1756.
La Ville, Pierre	(A), folio 4.
Labbé, Pierre	
Lacaze, Pierre	
Lescouyer, Thomas	
Laroquette, Jean	Deserted October 14, 1765. Condemned, <u>in absentia</u>. The verdict was rendered in Louisiana, October 17, 1765. Villiers' Company.
Le Masson, Mathurin	
La Court, Pierre	
La Haye, Jacques	
Loquies, Antoine	
Le Caze, Antoine	
La Touette, Jacques	
La Porte, Jean	Discharged August 31, 1756. Derneville's Company.
La Barre, Joseph	Cadet Soldat. Died September 5, 1754. Montchervaux's Company.
Le Blanc, Antoine	Shot February 9, 1756. Montchervaux's Company.
Lebas, Joseph Robert	Died while returning from Illinois, December 15, 1755. Montchervaux's Company.
Lardat, Jean	Discharged June 1, 1756.
Lefevre, Antoine	Died at Mobile, February 21, 1754. Bonnille's Company.
La Vannerie, Antoine	Deserted September 1, 1754.
Lane, Pierre	Deserted September 27, 1756.
La Haye, François Laurent de	Died in Illinois, January 15, 1754. Montberault's Company.
Le Blanc, Guilleaume	Died at Tombecbe, January 14, 1754. Villermont's Company.

Le Tevet, Antoine	Drowned in the river, October 17, 1755. D'Aubry's Company.
Le Nez, Jean	Drowned in the river, January 10, 1754. D'Aubry's Company.
Langeront, Etienne	Deserted April 15, 1755.
L'Ecluse (?), Jacques François Joseph de	Discharged April 18, 1756 and returned to France.
La Haye, Jacques	Discharged July 16, 1756 and returned to France.
Lefevre, Jean	Discharged May 21, 1756.
Lhermand, Pierre	Discharged July 16, 1754.
Loquin, Antoine	Deserted September 18, 1756.
La Motte, Jean François	(H), June 11, 1754. Du Tillet's Company.
Leurasque, Paul Antoine	Discharged June 21, 1756.
Landez, Jean	Discharged April 18, 1756 and returned to France.
Le Grand, Charles	Deserted June 4, 1756.
Lhommon, Jean	Discharged July 10, 1756 and returned to France.
Lhommeau, Jean Baptiste	Drowned while going down river from Natchez, October 2, 1754. Mazan's Company.
La Seigne, Léonard	Discharged October 1, 1754.
Lhormand, Pierre	Discharged July 16, 1754 and returned to France.
Le Leu, Louis	Discharged and settled in the colony, May 1, 1752.
La Chaise, François	Died at New Orleans, January 4, 1757. Grandpré's Company.
Le Comte, François	Shot April 6, 1757. Grandpré's Company.
Lançon, Pierre	Discharged and settled in the colony, January 2, 1751.
Loiseau, François	Died at Vincennes' post, March 31, 1757. Hazeur's Company.
Laval, Pierre	Deserted July 11, 1757.
Ligerboult, Frédéric	Died at the Tunica post, August 4, 1757. Gramont's Company.
Ladurantée, Jean	Died October 30, 1757. Pontalba's Company.
L'Ecuyer, Etienne	
La Maitre, Jean	Drowned in Illinois, June 25, 1757. Gourdon's Company.
Le Gaud, Mathieu	Discharged and settled in the colony, February 12, 1753.
Langlois, Jean Baptiste	Deserted June 24, 1757 at Vera Cruz. See roll of June 1, 1761, folio 10.
La Croix, Pierre	Discharged (A).
Labory, Jean	Deserted July 27, 1759 and shot the following September 13th. See roll of June 1, 1760, folio 1.

Louvigny, Jacques	
Le Comte, Joseph	(H), March 10, 1767. See roll of January 1, 1763, folio 34.
Le Tier, François	See Thiers below. (A), folio 20.
Le Gauffre, Pierre	(A), folio 21.
La Poule, Claude François	Discharged November 16, 1769. (B), folio 46.
Le Comte, Jean Baptiste	
Le Long, Barthélemy	(A), folio 19.
Lainé, Jean Charles	
Leger, Charles	Discharged September 15, 1763. On half-pay of 4 livres 10 sol. (C).
Lhuillier, Joseph	
La Cour, Antoine	
Lestang, Jean	(A), folio 4.
Lattier, Joseph	
La Goutte, Jean	(A), folio 5. On half-pay of 6livres. Decision of April 1, 1764. Amount raised by 6 livres. Decision of April 30, 1772.
Le Fevre, Joseph	
√Lambert, Pierre Joseph	Discharged June 1, 1765. (B), folio 31.
Le Rat, Pierre Georges	Deserted in Arkansas, October 26, 1759. See roll of June 1, 1760.
La Fontaine, Joseph	(A), folio 25.
La Grange, Jean	(A), folio 7. On half-pay of 4 livres 10 sol. Decision of June 11, 1764. Sent to the Bureau on the 12th.
Le Blond, Pierre	
Lamy, Jacques	
Le Coq, Georges	Deserted June 27; arrested July 7 and condemned to be shot July 24, 1758. See roll of June 1, 1760, folio 3.
La Valle, Sébastien	
La Perine, Pierre	Discharged November 30, 1769. (B), folio 49.
Labau, Charles	
Lavau, Antoine	
Le Curon, Guilleaume	(A), folio 6.
Lancien, Jean	Discharged at Havre in February, 1761. On half-pay of 6 livres. Decision of October 22, 1772. See the general roll of discharges made at Havre on February 22, 1761, folio 5.

Lousnard, François	
✓Lambert, Jean Louis	Discharged July 8, 1758. See roll of June 1, 1760, folio 5.
Landrony, Joseph	Invalid. Settled in Arkansas, December 31, 1769. (B), folio 52.
Lorette, Charles	Deserted in Arkansas, October 26, 1759. See roll of June 1, 1760, folio 5.
Le Teurs, Guilleaume	Corporal. Discharged September 15, 1763. On half-pay of 9 livres, payable at Rouen. (C).
Labatte, Jacques	(A), folio 14.
Le Coeur, Gabriel	Deserted October 14, 1765. Condemned, in absentia. The verdict was rendered in Louisiana, October 17, 1765.
Lafargue, Jean	
Le Grand, Jean	Discharged May 21, 1761. Considered unworthy to serve the king. See roll of the same year, folio 32.
La Forest, Claude	(A), folio 8.
La Fleur, Jacques	(A), folio 9.
Landry, Jean Baptiste Simon	
La Fleur, Jean Baptiste	On half-pay of 6 livres. Decision of June 11, 1764. Sent to the Bureau on the 12th.
La Carié, François	Discharged September 15, 1763. Died at the hospital at Niort, November 26, 1764.
Lambert, Jean Baptiste	On half-pay of 4 livres 10 sol. Decision of June 11, 1764. Sent to the Bureau on the 12th.
Leblanç, Charles	(A), folio 2.
Le Maure, Michel	(H), February 7, 1759. See the roll of June 1, 1760, folio 6.
Le Nez, François	On half-pay of 4 livres 10 sol. Decision of October 10, 1764. Sent to the Bureau June 1, 1764 (?).
Laurent, Claude	(A), folio 24.
Lallemand, Joseph	(A), folio 21.
Lefort, Jean Antoine	Drowned in Bayou St. John, June 23, 1765. (B), folio 31.
L'Eternel, Noël	
Le Cointre, Jean François	
L'Ecuyer, Etienne	Discharged January 2, 1766. Roll of January 1, 1766, folio 32.
La Lanne, Jean	

Lagé, Jean Amand	(H), January 11, 1758. See roll of June 1, 1760, folio 8.
Logis, Nicolas	
Le Turc, Jean Baptiste	(H), January 20, 1767. (B), folio 34.
Lefevre, Simon Claude	
Logis, Nicolas	
La Ronce, François Gilles Germain	(A), folio 14.
Larriere, Nicolas	
Le Fevre, Nicolas	
Larmond, Pierre	Discharged October 31, 1769. (B), folio 43.
Lancelot, Louis	
Le Guay, Jean Gabriel	
Longuay, Pierre	(A), folio 2. On half-pay of 8 livres. Decision of November 19, 1765. Sent to the Bureau on the 20th.
Le Grand, Jean Baptiste	Discharged October 1, 1769. Roll of January 1, 1763, folio 47.
Louis, Henry	Discharged September 30, 1769. (B), folio 47.
Le Gué, René	(A), folio 26.
La Grange, Henry	
La Martiniere, Jean Baptiste	
L'Eff, Henry	(A), folio 16.
Le Court, Jacques	On half-pay of 6 livres. (C).
La Voize	(A), folio 16.
Laye, Henry Joseph de	
La Cou, Jean Joseph	Soldat Reformé. Died on board the *Thëtis* while returning to France, June 4, 1770.
Le Maire, Philip Joseph	(H), February 9, 1759. See roll of June 1, 1760, folio 11.
Leon, Gaspart	Died at Natchitoches, March 31, 1769. (B), folio 47.
Loriot, Mathieu	
Le Brun, Jacques	
Lequarre, Jean	Departed for France on the *Père de Famille*, September 24, 1769. (B), folio 37.
Laporte, Joseph	(A), folio 17
Lamendé or Lamante, Joseph François	(A), folio 17.
Laborie, Guilleaume	Discharged November 30, 1769. (B), folio, 39.
Le Comte, Jean Etienne	
Le Hèrant, Jacques	Discharged October 31, 1769. Roll of January 1, 1763, folio 47.
Le Comte, Jean Baptiste	(A), folio 19.

Lefevre, Nicolas Martin	
Lamy, Jacques	Sergeant. Discharged September 15, 1763. On half-pay of 9 livres. (C). (P).
Le Bouché, Rene	(A), folio 1.
Langlois, François	Discharged November 30, 1769. (B), folio 45.
Laval, Pierre	Deserted at Vera Cruz, July 11, 1757. See roll of June 1, 1760, folio 4.
Le Maitre, Jean	Drowned in Illinois, June 25, 1757. See roll of June 1, 1760, folio 8.
Lefevre, Nicolas	Deserted at Pointe Coupée, December 17, 1758. Chavoye's Company. See general roll of June 1, 1760, folio 10. Discharged September 15, 1763.
Lemêle, André	
Lusseau, Pierre	Died in Illinois, December 19, 1763. (B), folio 11.
Lalaine, Jean	
Laubel, Jean Baptiste	
Lamarre, Pierre	Discharged September 15, 1763. On half-pay of 9 livres. Decision of June 11, 1764. Sent to the Bureau on the 12th.
Lacou, Paul	
La Pierre, François	(A), folio 10. On half-pay of 6 livres per month. (C).
Lardin, Jacques	
La Roziere, Guillaume Bernard	Discharged February 6, 1770. On half-pay of 4 livres 10 sol per month. Decision of April 28, 1770.
Larriere, Nicolas	Discharged September 15, 1763. On half-pay of 16 livres. (C).
Lacou, Jean	Discharged September 15, 1763. On half-pay of 16 livres. (C).
Lancelot, Bernard	Taken prisoner from the <u>Fortune</u> while enroute to Louisiana in 1756. He was imprisoned in England from whence he returned on May 1, 1763. He arrived at Boulogne where he received his discharge.
Le Coursonnier, Charles François	Discharged. See roll dated at Calais, May 2, 1763.
Louis, Jean	On half-pay of 4 livres 10 sol. Decision of June 11, 1764. Sent to the Bureau on the 12th.

La Combe, Etienne	On half-pay of 2 livres. Decision of September 22, 1763. Sent to the Bureau on the 23rd. Discharged from the Canadian troops with half-pay of 8 livres 2 sol.
La Ribardiere, Charles	On half-pay of 6 livres per month, payable at Paris. He had served since 1720. His discharge was delivered at New Orleans, March 12, 1768. In the margin of his discharge is written, "He has served in this colony since 1720, and obtained half-pay of 6 livres per month in 1751. By order of La Cour."
Lexcellent, Charles	Corporal. Discharged September 10, 1763, after having served 26 years. On half-pay of 9 livres per month, payable at Chatillon-sur-Seine in Bourgogne.
Libster, Jean	Corporal in Hallwyll's Swiss Regiment. Discharged September 31 (sic) 1763 after having served 264 months. On half-pay of 12 livres, payable in Alsace.
La Pierre, Antoine	Artilleryman. Discharged October 8, 1769. (P).
L'Eternel, Noël	(P).
LeBlond, Pierre	(P).
Le Comte, Louis	Discharged February 6, 1770. On half-pay of 9 livres per month. Decision of April 28, 1770.
Laval, Sébastien	Corporal. Discharged February 6, 1770. On half-pay of 15 livres. Decision of April 28, 1770. Died at the hospital in La Rochelle, February 2, 1770.
Lhomme, Claude	Discharged February 6, 1770. On half-pay of 6 livres per month. Decision of April 28, 1770.
Loumar, François	Discharged February 6, 1770. On half-pay of 4 livres 10 sol. Decision of April 28, 1770.

Legai, Jean Gabriel	Sergeant. Discharged February 6, 1770. On half-pay of 12 livres per month. Decision of April 28, 1770.
Lancelot, Louis	Discharged February 6, 1770. La Periere's Company.
Laigle, Nicolas	Discharged February 6, 1770. Trudeau's Company.
Lequerce or Le Thiers, François	See M. de Repentigny's list of February 6, 1770.
Loriau, Mathieu	Fusilier. Discharged August 20, 1770. On half-pay of 6 livres per month. Decision of October 17, 1770.
La Brosse, Nicolas	Discharged August 20, 1770. On half-pay of 6 livres. Decision of November 2, 1770.
La Para, Guillaume	(A), folio 1.
Lorine, Jacques	(A), folio 1.
Le Caû, Mathurin	(A), folio 16.
Le Cointre, Etienne	(A), folio 19.
La Rose, Benoist	(A), folio 23.
Luquet, Pierre	(A), folio 25.
Laporte, François	Discharged August 1, 1765. (B), folio 31.
Legrand, Pierre	Discharged August 1, 1765. (B), folio 32.
Lahure, Nicolas	Discharged August 1, 1766. (B), folio 34.
La Salle, François	Deserted December 26, 1767. (B), folio 34.
Lamy, Jacques	Died October 27, 1769. (B), folio 39.
La Sage, Pierre	Discharged September 30, 1769. (B), folio 35.
La Porte, André	Discharged and settled in Arkansas, September 30, 1769. (B), folio 51.
La Forge, François	Deserted September 22, 1769. (B), folio 51.
Leyne, Jean	Enlisted in 1764. Discharged September 30, 1769. (B), folio 54.
Layete, Nicolas	Departed for France on the _Samson_, October 1, 1769, folio 54.
Lavigne, Laurent de	Artilleryman. Enlisted April 1, 1765. Departed for France on the _Père de Famille_, October 8 1769. (B), folio 55.

M

Marmotte, Pellerin	Drowned September 3, 1750.
Mercier, René	
Marette, Nicolas	Discharged March 1, 1751.
Manot, Alexis	
Mouton, Philippes	(A), folio 19.
Magny, Jean	Drowned February 20, 1763. (B), folio 23.
Maître, Joseph	Condemned, <u>in absentia</u>, for desertion. See the criminal proceedings of September 30, 1753.
Messin, Nicolas Antoine	Died June 18, 1751.
Mouchette, Eugène	Died.
Mathieu, Nicolas	Died December 8, 1745. Blanc's Company.
Marlier, Charles	Discharged May 31, 1761. See roll of same year, folio 5.
Martin, Henry	On half-pay of 8 livres. Decision of September 22, 1765. Sent to the Bureau on the 25th.
Maquignon, Claude	Died in Illinois, December 15, 1745. Macarty's Company.
Maigros, Jacques	Discharged June 1, 1750.
Moreau, Jean Baptiste	Died September 18, 1761. See roll of same year, folio 24.
Monquoir, François	
Mondion, Pierre	
Maigros, Antoine	Died at Natchitoches, January 31, 1765. See roll of January 1, 1763, folio 31.
Miodonet, Jean	
Mantet, Jean Pierre	(A), folio 17.
Monet, Mathieu	
Morandy, Jean	Discharged September 1, 1751.
Motta, Anastase	
Martin, Jean Louis	
Moreau, Pierre	Discharged February 1, 1751.
Martin, Thomas	Shot August 11, 1751.
Maurice, Pierre	On half-pay of 9 livres. Decision of June 11, 1764. Sent tb the Bureau on the 12th.
Monteche, Dominique	Discharged April 1, 1750.
Marmellon, Jacques Daniel	Deserted December 12, 1745, at Natchitoches.
Menard, Gilbert	Died January 21, 1754. Villiers' Company.
Maitonneuve, Charles	Died December 26, 1755. D'Artaud's Company.

Maire, Jean	
Marchand, François	Died January 26, 1746. Marest's Company.
Manelle, Jacques	(H), September 6, 1757. Villier's Company.
Moreau, Paul	Discharged July 1, 1750.
Mercier, Jean	Discharged September 15, 1763. On half-pay of 6 livres. (C).
Macteau, Jacques	Died January 10, 1757. d'Hauterive's Company.
Mannequin, André	
Metivel, Jean Baptiste	Died at the hospital in Mobile, December 6, 1754. de Marentin's Company.
Morel, André	Discharged August 1, 1755.
Moniot, Pierre	
Manime, Jean Baptiste	Discharged June 1, 1751.
Monget, Jean Michel	
Mathieu, François	Died December 6, 1750.
Moloret, Emmond Thomas	Discharged March 1, 1750.
Marc, François	Died November 4, 1751.
Martin, François	Died July 25, 1751.
Menagé, Louis Etienne	
Montenol, François	Died October 24, 1738.
Mazero, Jean	Died May 24, 1738.
Mingué, Guilleaume	Died January 22, 1738.
Morion, Jean	King's carpenter. Died August 8, 1738.
Manard, Jean François	Died January 7, 1737.
Meliers, Pierre	Died July 21, 1736.
Marchand, François	Died December 26, 1736.
Milory, Jean	Died September 19, 1734.
Moreau, Théodore	Deserted January 21, 1738. Buissonniere's Company.
Macée, Pierre	Deserted February 5, 1739.
Masson, Guilleaume	Died October 2, 1751.
Menard, Guilleaume	Died May 17, 1751.
Martin, Hellaire	Died February 5, 1751.
Mirel, Joachim	Banished March 22, 1751.
Marquet, Jean Baptiste	Died June 25, 1751.
Michaud, Jacques	Died April 10, 1751.
Marié, Jean Baptiste	Died July 20, 1751.
Meunier, Louis	Died October 26, 1751.
Mikel, Michel	Shot February 27, 1751.
Morel, Nicolas	Died September 17, 1751.
Morin, Pierre	Died November 8, 1751.
Murat, Claude	Deserted July 17, 1755.
Mandré, Henry	
Mainard, Pierre	
Macard, Joseph	
Michel, Louis	

Malagée, Jean	
Mousseau, François	(H), January 11, 1759. See roll of June 1, 1760, folio 4.
Martre or Marthre, Joseph	Deserted October 21, 1759. See roll of June 1, 1760, folio 11.
Mercier, Gilbert	Deserted January 26, 1761. See roll of same year, folio 16.
Massent, Barthélemy	
Mamclair, Jacques Louis	(A), folio 26. On half-pay of 6 livres. Decision of March 22, 1765. Sent to the Bureau on the 23rd.
Moulins, Louis	
Moreau, Alexandre	
Monget, Jean	
Marchu, Guilleaume	
Maréschal, Claude	Discharged July 16, 1754.
Mathieu, Joseph	Deserted May 14, 1758. Derneville's Company.
Menelet, Nicolas	Discharged January 12, 1754.
Molard, Claude	(H), January 9, 1755. Montberault's Company.
Mabire, Jean	Died September 11, 1755. Montberault's Company.
Massé, Georges	Drowned while going down river from Natchez, October 2, 1754. Montberault's Company.
Mansecourt, Jean	Died in Illinois, January 18, 1755. de la Houssaye's Company.
Mansard, Pierre	(H), January 10, 1756. de la Houssaye's Company.
Maury, Pierre	(H), February 3, 1756. Desmazelliers's Company.
Maillard, Jean	(H), January 13, 1755. Darazola's Company.
Massy, Pierre	Drowned while going down river from Natchez, October 2, 1754. Gramont's Company.
Mignardin, Jacques	Discharged July 16, 1756 and returned to France.
Magnanaut, Vincent	Deserted in 1754.
Mazurre, Pierre	(H), January 1, 1756. Desvarennes' Company.
Maçon, Henry	Deserted July 4, 1755.
Mervillon, René	Deserted June 15, 1756.
Marcantel, François	Discharged October 30, 1756.
Menou, Jacques	Discharged April 1, 1756.
Mozaque, Etienne	Discharged June 1, 1756.
Masson, Jullien	Deserted July 17, 1755.
Muret, Coezard	Deserted June 15, 1756.

Moreau, Bidau Vidal	Drowned at the Wabash post, November 10, 1756. Villier's Company.
Michel, Louis	Discharged April 18, 1756 and returned to France.
Maste, Jean Jacques	Died in the German village, November 16, 1757. Hazeur's Company.
Mauchatillon, Jean	Discharged May 1, 1757. Settled in the colony.
Mesnard, Gabriel	Deserted in Arkansas, October 26, 1759. See roll of June 1, 1760, folio 4.
Magny, Nicolas	Discharged October 1, 1757.
Moreau, Pierre	Deserted June 3, 1757.
Marcelle, Jean	Drummer. Benoist's Company. Discharged October 1, 1764. (B), folio 28.
Mantel, Jean	
Minier, François	
Mathieu, Joseph	
Midon, Claude	
Mauger, Jean	(H), March 26, 1761. See roll of the same year, folio 6.
Margotta, Jacques	On half-pay of 6 livres. Decision of June 11, 1764. Sent to the Bureau on the 12th.
Meusnier, Pierre	(A), folio 5.
Morgat, Pierre	
Mignot, Pierre	(H), March 10, 1767. (B), folio 34.
Martin, Nicolas	(A), folio 7.
Mandoxa, Felix	Discharged July 1, 1764. (B), folio 28.
Menant, Pierre	On half-pay of 8 livres 10 sol. Decision of August 22, 1764. Sent to the Bureau on the 5th(?).
Martenne, Claude	Discharged and returned to France on the Fortune, January 1, 1759. See roll of June 1, 1760, folio 3.
Martin, Jean	
Manjard or Mangeard, Nicolas	(A), folio 10.
Mezieres, Claude	Died at Mobile, April 24, 1758. See roll of June 1, 1760, folio4.
Manassa, Jean Baptiste	
Marié, Alexis	(A), folio 7.
Millot, Charles	Discharged December 1, 1764. (B), folio 26.

Marche, Jean	(A), folio 7.
Matagrin, André	Drowned April 17, 1764. (B), folio 28.
Mirandole, Pierre	(A), folio 14.
Martin, Pierre	(A), folio 9.
Merice, Jean	(A), folio 9. On half pay of 9 livres. Decision of June 11, 1764. Sent to the Bureau on the 12th.
Mancelle, Alexis	Discharged at Calais, Octcber 13, 1762. Decision of April 15, 1767.
Mignot, Nicolas	Discharged June 1, 1764. (B), folio 28.
Meudre, Claude	Discharged at Calais, October 13, 1762. On half-pay of 9 livres. See the roll of the same date.
Mouza or Moussa, Pierre	(A), folio 10.
Manata, Jean Baptiste	
Masson, François Joseph	(A). On half-pay of 6 livres. (C).
Marchand, Bernard	Discharged March 1, 1765. (B), folio 31.
Marchand, Pierre	
Montaroy, Pierre	Settled in Illinois. (B), folio 46.
Mayer, Nicolas	
Marais, Nicolas	(A), folio 12.
Moreau, Pierre Jean	Discharged August 31, 1763. (B), folio 12.
Meure, Etienne	Discharged and returned to France on the king's ship <u>Fortune</u>, January 1, 1759. See the roll of June 1, 1760, folio 7.
Mercier, Philippes	(H), May 1, 1766. (B), folio 33.
Missonniere, Jean Baptiste	Discharged February 1, 1764. (B), folio 26.
Mongenay, Jean	
Massolle, Laurent	(A), folio 14.
Massé, Louis	
Maugna, Joseph	(A), folio 18.
Memin, Louis	Sergeant. Discharged September 15, 1763. On half-pay of 12 livres. (C).
Michaud, Louis	Discharged May 1, 1764. (B), folio 29.
Marchand, Jean Nicolas	(A), folio 2.
Morel, Jean	Sergeant. Discharged July 1, 1764. Gautray's Company. On half-pay of 12 livres. Decision of November 30, 1764. Sent to the Bureau the next day.

Milsan, Jean François	
Marc, François	
Maillard, Jean Jacques	(A), folio 16.
Moullard, François	Discharged September 15, 1763. On half pay of 6 livres. (C).
Mortalle, Jean Claude	(A), folio 17.
Menager, Jean	(A), folio 23.
Maréchal, Jean	Discharged September 30, 1769. (B), folio 53.
Mercier, Pierre	
Millot, Nicolas	Discharged March 1, 1765. On half-pay of 4 livres 10 sol. Decision of March 22, 1765.
Maugin, Simon	
Millan, Claude	(A), folio 17.
Mantel, Pierre	
Mafré, Claude	
Manciau, Denis	Departed for France on the <u>Samson</u>, October 1, 1769. (B), folio 50.
Manjeau, Denis	
Metoyer, Pierre	Died February 27, 1764. (B), folio 19.
Mauregat, Jean	
Moguin, Simon	Deserted August 1, 1758. See roll of June 1, 1760, folio 11.
Maugein, Denis	
Martin, Jean Louis	Discharged November 30, 1768. On half-pay of 6 livres. Decision of June 18, 1769.
Maillard, Pierre	
Marchand, Louis	Discharged October 8, 1769. (B), folio 49.
Martier, Pierre	
Morare, François	(A), folio 18.
Metailles, Jacques	(A), folio 23.
Maire, Joseph	
Morelle, André	Discharged November 30, 1769. Roll of January 1, 1763, folio 23.
Metzer, Philippe	Discharged November 30, 1769. (B), folio 42. On half-pay of 12 livres 10 sol. (C). On September 15, 1763, he was discharged from the company of artillery in which he was a corporal.
Maurice, Simon	On half pay of 4 livres 10 sol. Decision of June 11, 1764. Sent the Bureau on the 12th.
Missuer, François	On half-pay of 6 livres. (C).

Marsant, Bernard	On half-pay of 6 livres. Decision of June 24, 1765. Sent to the Bureau on the 25th.
Mang, Christian	Discharged January 31, 1764 after having served 330 months. On half-pay of 12 livres per month, payable in Alsace. He served as a corporal in Hallwyll's Swiss Company.
Montel, Pierre	Soldier in Grandmaison's Company. Discharged January 10, 1764. On half-pay of 9 livres per month. Decision of October 25, 1769. Sent to the Bureau on the 27th.
Morin, Marc Antoine	Sergeant. Morin, wife, and daughter (P).
Mernos, Antoine	Discharged November 20, 1769 and returned to France on the _Père de Famille_. Sergeant. On half-pay of 12 livres per month. Decision of April 28, 1770.
Maugein, Simon	(P).
Marc (Negro)	Islander. (P). Servant of M. La Forest de Laumont, Lieutenant of Infantry.
Martin, Jean	Discharged February 6, 1770. On half-pay of 4 livres 10 sol. Decision of April 28, 1770.
Massan, Barthélemy	Discharged February 6, 1770. Desmazilliere's Company.
Monesta, Jean Baptiste	Discharged February 6, 1770. Duplessis' Company.
Moulard, Jean	Discharged February 6, 1770. On half-pay of 4 livres 10 sol, payable at Paris. Decision of July 16, 1771. Vaugine's Company.
Monjenet, Jean	Discharged February 6, 1770. Villiers' Company.
Mangin, Denis	Discharged February 6, 1770. Villiers' Company.
Mercier, Pierre	Discharged February 6, 1770. Villiers' Company.
Metzger, Jean Philippe	(A), folio 3.
Maynot, Charles	Departed for Santo Domingo, July 22, 1763, on the frigate _Aigrette_. (B), folio 3.
Madal, Jean	(A), folio 20.

Malice, Michel	Discharged February 1, 1764. (B), folio 30.
Morga, Pierre	(A), folio 25.
Monhard, Pierre	(H), August 11, 1765. (B), folio 30.
Macrohon, Cornelius	Discharged September 30, 1768. (B), folio 36.
Martin, Pierre	Enlisted April 1, 1769. Discharged October 8, 1769. Roll of January 1, 1763, folio 39.
Mirold, Joseph Antoine	Discharged September 30, 1769. (B), folio 42.
Marquis, Joseph	Discharged October 16, 1769. (B), folio 45.
Métayer, Jacques	Discharged September 30, 1769. (B), folio 51.
Miller, Jean Georges	Discharged October 8, 1769. (B), folio 55.
Maire, Nicolas	(A), folio 3.

N

Nabot, Jean	
Noyel, François	Died April 15, 1754. Desvarennes' Company.
Nicolle, Jean	Killed by the Indians, April 20, 1750.
Nicolle, Louis	Died February 8, 1751.
Nicaise, Jean Baptiste	Discharged May 1, 1750.
Nugnot, Julien	
Nezair, Charles	Condemned to the galleys, June 3, 1750.
Naud, Emery	Deserted June 30, 1750.
Narcis, Denis	Died October 24, 1751.
Noizet, Hubert	Discharged October 17, 1751.
Noiret, Joseph	Died October 14, 1751.
Nivoix, Honoré Sébastien	Died October 14, 1751.
Neveux, François	
Nouiller, Joseph	Strangled in prison, March 15, 1756. La Tour's Company.
Neyon, (?)	Cadet Soldat. Died October, 1755. de Neyon's Company.
Nibouillet, Antoine	Deserted April 15, 1755.
Norritte, François	(H), December 15, 1754. Villier's Company.
Nesick, Mathieu	Died in Illinois, November 20, 1754. Neyon's Company.
Niolon, Jean	Hanged June 4, 1756. Mazan's Company.
Normand, Pierre	Deserted January 1, 1757.

Neveu, Jullien	Died at New Orleans, September 4, 1757. Chabert's Company.
Nouspaon, Louis	Drummer. On half-pay of 6 livres. (C).
Nicolas, Jean	
Neyrand, Antoine	(A), folio 40.
Neveu, Claude	(P).
Navaron, François	Corporal. (P).
Nollet, François	Discharged September 30, 1769. (B), folio 50.
Nicolas, Joseph	
Nantais, François	
Nauvac, Jean Baptiste	Discharged October 8, 1769. (B), folio 43.
Nadal, Jean	
Nouveau, Louis	Discharged October 31, 1769. (B), folio 46.
Navet, Jullien	
Nyerre, Pierre François	Sergeant. Discharged March 4, 1769. On half-pay of 10 livres, payable at Valenciennes. Decision of September 3, 1769. He is from Bouchaim.
Nonotte, Charles Vincent	Died at the hospital, January 24, 1758. See roll of June 1, 1760, folio 8.
Nicolas, Hugues	
Nombre, Jean Antoine	Discharged September 15, 1763. On half-pay of 6 livres. (C).
Nicoleau, Louis	(P).
Nourry, André	Died in Illinois, January 15, 1765. (B), folio 31.
Nemingre or Neminger, Antoine	(A), folio 17.
Nicolet, Joseph	Died in New Orleans, February 9, 1766. (B), folio 34.
Nemingre, André	
Nicolet, Jean	Called La Roze. Corporal. Reggio's Company. Killed while going to Arkansas under the name of Jean Baptiste Bernard, a soldier of the same company. Bernard has since obtained a pardon from Governor Kerlerec. See the Governor's letter of September 12, 1756.
Niolet, Pierre	Discharged November 6, 1769. Roll of January 1, 1769, folio 40.
Navet, Julien	Corporal. (P).
Noir, Michel Joseph	(P).
Neveu, François	Discharged February 6, 1770. Duplessis' Company.
Narbonne, Antoine	(A), folio 37.

O

Oldrin, Pierre
Oudel, Thiery — Deserted from Terrepuy's Company.
Oré, Jean
Obreville, Pierre
Oüallé, Antoine
Ontra, Joseph — Died August 16, 1736.
Oudable, Alexandre — Discharged July 1, 1751.
Ouriez, Louis — Discharged June 1, 1751.
Ouardier, Louis — Died in Arkansas, March 25, 1757. Reggio's Company. (A), folio 24.
Ollivier, Jean
Ollivier, Joseph
Ollivier, Nicolas — (H), November 20, 1766. (B), folio 33.
Ovel, Jean Baptiste — Discharged June 1, 1764. (B), folio 28.
Onfroy, Charles Guillaume — Drowned in Bayou St. John, January 31, 1769. (B), folio 38.
Ornsteinn, Servais — Discharged October 31, 1769. (B), folio 45.
Ock, Michel — Departed for France on the Samson, October 31, 1769, (B), folio 48.

P

Pirion, Mathieu — Shot July 31, 1750.
Perrier, Paul
Perraut, Joseph
Philibert, Etienne
Pignon, Claude
Paulet, Antoine — Discharged May 1, 1750.
Picard, Jacques — Died September 15, 1745. Blanc's Company.
Pasquier, Charles Théodore.
Phelypeaux, Jean Baptiste
Polmanne, Georges — Sergeant. Discharged September 15, 1763. On half-pay of 15 livres. (C).
Ployard, Nicolas — Drowned at the Wabash post, November 10, 1756. Gautreye's Company.
Panquinet, Louis
Parisy, Pierre — Died at New Orleans, April 19, 1757. de la Houssaye's Company.
Poirson, Jean Baptiste
Perchel, Pierre
Pastor, François
Pouliquinx or Policain, Jacques (A), folio 7.

Paron, Gabriel	
Prudhomme, Pierre	Discharged April 1, 1750.
Prudhomme, Jacques	
Paul, Charles	Discharged November 30, 1751.
Pajot or Pagot, Louis	(H), November 13, 1766. (B), folio 33.
Pommard, Jacques	
Pelusset, Joseph	Died December 7, 1754. Macarty's Company.
Pauleret, Pierre	
Paboeuf, François	
Pien, Mathurin	
Pamel, François	
Pajot, Marin	Died August 13, 1745. Membrede's Company.
Perron, Louis	
Pichon, Julien	Died December 21, 1737.
Papion, Jac	Died April 10, 1738.
Palis, François	Died August 4, 1738.
Pajot or Pajet, Jean	Died December 6, 1738.
Poussel, Etienne	Died July 20, 1737.
Pellerin, Girard	Died April 9, 1737.
Pajet or Paget, François	Died July 25, 1735.
Peja, Jean	Died in 1738. Benoist's Company.
Prevost, Jean	Died October 4, 1750.
Paquin, Jean	Deserted June 30, 1750.
Pentinette, Louis	Discharged September 1, 1750.
Plottier, Louis	Died September 23, 1750.
Picottin, Charles	Died October 28, 1751.
Pernous, Claude	Discharged August 18, 1751.
Perette, Claude	Died September 3, 1751.
Perrin, David Jean	Died November 19, 1751.
Proux, Nicolas	Corporal. Died September 4, 1753. Died of a wound he received the same day. See the criminal proceedings against Pierre Flamant in the Louisiana carton.
Pellerin, Charles	Condemned, *in absentia*, for desertion. See the proceedings of September 30, 1753.
Porson, Jean Baptiste	Died February 18, 1751.
Plesmin, Jean	Discharged August 18, 1751.
Progin, Jacques	Died October 8, 1751.
Poulin, Jean	Died March 29, 1751.
Pier, Jean	Died October 20, 1751.
Paquier, Jean	Died June 24, 1751.
Pierril, Lazarre	Discharged June 1, 1751.
Perigois, Michel	Died October 10, 1751.
Pesche, Pierre	Discharged June 30, 1751.
Pinget, Pierre	Shot September 6, 1751.

Poulin, Pierre	Discharged July 22, 1751.
Pain, Hugues	Deserted October 21, 1751.
Penne, Jean	Died at Mobile, December 19, 1754. Grandchamp's Company.
Pharamond, Pierre	Died at Natchez, September 30, 1754. Montberault's Company.
Perdigaux, Jean	
Pottin, François	
Perieo, Guilleaume	Deserted March 1, 1763. (B), folio 22.
Padet, Jean	
Parmentier, Dominique	Shot at Mobile, September 6, 1757. Paupulus' Company.
Pousin, Jean Lambert	Departed for France on the <u>Samson</u>, October 1, 1769. (B), folio 52.
Perelle, Mathurin	
Prevost, Antoine	
Perrette or Parret, Jean Claude	Died March 22, 1768. (B), folio 36.
Pincemail, Louis Noël Paul	Discharged Septmeber 1, 1764. (B), folio 26. Re-enlisted in 1767; discharged October 8, 1769.
Perriers, Pierre	Drowned at Natchez, November 19, 1754. Grandchamp's Company.
Prevost, Michel	Died at Arkansas post, July 20, 1754. La Tour's Company.
Poitier, René	(H), June 10, 1754. Derneville's Company.
Poiré, Edmé Lucien	Sent to France to be discharged. Died there.
Petaut, Guilleaume	(H), September 15, 1755. Chavois' Company.
Patrice, Jacques	Discharged April 18, 1756 and returned to France on the <u>Messager</u>.
Perdrigaux, Jean	Died at the hospital, May 14, 1754. Chavois' Company.
Petit, Foelix	Died at Pointe Coupée, September 5, 1754. Grandpré's Company.
Pitel, Jacques Etienne	Drowned while going down river from Natchez, October 2, 1754. Hazeur's Company.
Prevost, Simon	Drowned while going up river to Pointe Coupée, March 4, 1754. Villemont's Company.
Parisy, Claude	Died at Mobile, September 8, 1754. Villemont's Company.
Petit Louche, Bertrand	Discharged August 16, 1756.
Peltier, Nicolas	Discharged April 18, 1756 and returned to France.

Perault, Jean François	Died at Mobile, October 9, 1755. Gautraye's Company.
Perchette, Pierre	Discharged May 24, 1756.
Pelissier, Etienne	(H), May 24, 1754. D'Arazola's Company.
Pommand, Jacques	Discharged July 16, 1756.
Pernay, Jean	Drowned in the river, August 26, 1756. Neyon's Company.
Picon, Joseph	Died at the Arkansas post, April 11, 1756. Murat's Company.
Persignac, François	Drowned while going down river from Natchez, October 2, 1754. Murat's Company.
Parăud, Nicolas	Deserted June 8, 1756.
Pineau, Jean	Died October 6, 1756. D'Artaud's Company.
Pignana, Diego	Deserted April 26, 1755.
Pillevert, Jullien	Deserted in 1754.
Pian, Mathieu	Discharged August 10, 1754.
Payer, Jean	(H), February 19, 1757. Bellenos' Company.
Perichaud, Léonard	Discharged and settled in the colony, August 5, 1753.
Privée, Denis	Killed or taken prisoner by the Cherokees or the Chicasaws at Fort Wabash, November 9, 1757. Trant's Company.
Poussingre, Léopol	
Portay, François	(A), folio 16.
Perioux, Jacques	Discharged and settled in the colony, June 1, 1754.
Pasquier, Jean François	
Perdignan, Jacques	Fifer in Benoist's Company. Died November 12, 1764. (B), folio 26.
Pannier, Louis	On half-pay of 4 livres 10 sol. (C).
Poiré, Antoine	Discharged December 31, 1764. (B), folio 26.
Pesche, Urbain	Discharged November 11, 1758. See roll of June 1, 1760, folio 2.
Petit Jean, Martin	On half-pay of 6 livres. (C).
Puelle, Victor	Discharged June 30, 1768. (B), folio 36.
Pivoteau, Guilleaume	(A), folio 5. On half-pay of 4 livres 10 sol. Decision of June 11, 1764. Sent to the Bureau on the 12th.
Prou, François	
Peujat, François	Discharged June 1, 1764. (B), folio 27.

Piot, François	Deserted in September, 1769. (B), folio 37.
Pontmaire or Poulmaire, Jean	On half-pay of 4 livres 10 sol. (C).
Papillon, Jacques	
Portier, Mathieu	
Peignier, François	(H), March 6, 1767. (B), folio 34.
Prudhomme, Pierre Sébastien	(A), folio 8.
Prié, Antoine	
Portron, André	(H), October 27, 1759. See roll of June 1, 1760, folio 5.
Prudhomme, Antoine Gaudier	Listed under "G".
Poret, Jean	(A), folio 14.
Pongé, Jean	(A), folio 14.
Poirier, Jean Etienne	Died at Mobile, December 9, 1759. See roll of June 1, 1760. Bonnille's Company.
Panet, Mathieu	
Paul, Jean	
Paillet, Guilleaume	(A), folio 22.
Pidoleau, Pierre	(A), folio 24.
Picard, Jean François	
Peligaud, André	
Paraud, Benoist	
Pusseau, Pierre	
Pillé, Pierre	Discharged and returned to France on the <u>Fortune</u>, January 1, 1759. See roll of June 1, 1760, folio 7.
Prou, Jean	(H), August 14, 1758. See roll of June 1, 1760, folio 7.
Portiers, Pierre	
Periche, Philippes	(A), folio 14.
Poitevin, René	Discharged September 15, 1763. On half-pay of 6 livres. (C).
Pilliau or Pilliot, Abel	Returned to France on the <u>Samson</u>, October 1, 1769. (B), folio 47.
Pauré or Poiray, Eugene	Discharged at Havre. See the general roll of February 22, 1761. His baptismal certificate indicates his name to be Eugene Joseph Pourée.
Prisser or Priesler, Joseph	(A), folio 18.
Pesciquemane, Cantelip	
Petit, Eugene	Corporal. (P).
Poisson, Jacques	Drowned July 27, 1764. (B), folio 27.
Perrette, Pierre	(A), folio 23.

Pasquier, Jean François	Died at Balize, September 30, 1767. (B), folio 35.
Pagès, Guilleaume	(A), folio 2.
Perolet, Antoine	
Pouillard, Jacques Joseph	(A), folio 26.
Pilliau, Léopol	(H), October 22, 1769. (B), folio 50.
Plantin, Thomas	(H), June 4, 1764. (B), folio 29.
Parpillaud, Charles	Deserted April 27, 1761. See roll of same year, folio 12.
Pepin, Jean	Discharged March 1, 1764. (B), folio 29.
Picard, Louis	Discharged at Havre. See the general roll of February 22, 1761. Placed on half-pay.
Pascal, Léonard	
Prades, Jean	Discharged September 30, 1769. (B), folio 54.
Prioux, Michel	
Paradis, Marin	(A), folio 1.
Polian, Coezar	Deserted October 15, 1751. See roll of the same year, folio 46.
Paindavoine, Nicolas Joseph Jérémie	Died December 31, 1765. (B), folio 31.
Pontif or Pontis, François	Handed over to the land forces. See the letter of Berryer to M. Hocquart at Brest dated October 31, 1760.
Parisy, Pierre	(H), April 19, 1757. See roll of June 1, 1760, folio 2.
Prevost, Claude Antoine	Died at the Arkansas post, May 23, 1759. See the roll of June 1, 1760, folio 10.
Peltier, André	(A), folio 6.
Prudhomme, Jean	(A), folio 18.
Piochet, Jean Baptiste	
Petit, Jude	Discharged February 6, 1770. Duplessis' Company.
Prout, Louis Barthélemé	Discharged October 1, 1768. (B), folio 33.
Prevost, Claude Antoine	
Perret, Pierre	
Polian, Jacques	
Pradier, Joseph	
Perrin, Claude	Discharged. See the roll dated at Calais, May 2, 1763.
Petit Didier, Claude	Corporal. (A), folio 4. On half-pay of 9 livres. (C).

Peille, Antoine	Sergeant. On half-pay of 20 livres. (C).
Piaut, Abel	Died at Isle de Ré, January 30, 1770. See M. Giraud's roll of Isle de Ré for the month of January, 1770. Vaugine's Company.
Picard, Jean	Corporal (P).
Potier, Pierre	(P).
Paraud, Benoist	(P).
Pastor, François	Discharged February 16, 1770. On half-pay of 12 livres. Decision of April 28, 1770. He died at the hospital at La Rochelle, March 1, 1770.
Pottier, Mathurin	Sargeant, Discharged February 6, 1770. On half-pay of 9 livres. Decision of April 28, 1770.
Poussain, Jean Lambert	Sergeant. Discharged February 6, 1770. On half-pay of 12 livres. Decision of April 28, 1770.
Peret, Pierre	Discharged February 6, 1770. On half-pay of 4 livres 10 sol.
Peron, François	Discharged February 6, 1770. Villier's Company.
Parlat, Jean	(A), folio 2.
Paussé Jean	(A), folio 3.
Puigrand, Antoine	Departed for Santo Domingo on the _Aigrette_, July 22, 1763. (B), folio 3.
Poulman, Jean	(A), folio 6.
Plumet, François	Discharged August 1, 1765. (B), folio 31.
Perot, Etienne Joseph	(H), April 1, 1767. (B), folio 35.
Placet, Antoine	Discharged December 1, 1767. (B), folio 35.
Pajot, François	Discharged October 8, 1769. (B), folio 38.
Pinter, Joseph	Deserted September 28, 1769. (B), folio 52.
Paillet, Jean	Artilleryman. Enlisted in 1767. Discharged September 30, 1769. (B), folio 55.

Q

Quellier, Francois	Died April 20, 1751.

Questre, Georges	Discharged April 1, 1765. Roll of January 1, 1763, folio 32.
Quenet, Pierre	
Quentel, Pierre	Corporal. On half-pay of 12 livres. (C).
Quartier, Jean Pierre	On half pay of 6 livres. (C).

R

Raoul, Jean	Discharged May 1, 1751.
Rossy or Roussy, Jean Baptiste	Sergeant. Discharged September 15, 1763. On half-pay of 16 livres. Decision of June 26, 1765. Sent to the Bureau on the 25th (?).
Rambin, André	
Renauda, Antoine	Died July 21, 1756. D'Aubry's Company.
Roussel, Jean	
Rousseau, Pierre	Died August 14, 1746. Gauvrit's Company.
Rolland, Charles Guillaume	Died December 6, 1745. Membrede's Company.
Renardy, Joseph	
Renoire, Jean Louis	Deserted June 21, 1751.
Requiem. Charles	Died March 12, 1750.
Robinot, René	Died December 23, 1754. DeBarennes' Company.
Roland, Jean	
Roland or Rollin, Michel	Discharged May 1, 1751.
Ragon, Guillaume	
Riot, Jean	
Remy, François	(H), November 22, 1757. Chabert's Company.
Regnier, Charles	
Riquoy, Simon	
Rosty, Antoine	Terrepuy's Company. Date of death was not on the roll sent to France.
Reblingue, Jean	Killed August 14, 1746. Terrepuy's Company.
Remy, Jean	
Rachal, Jean	
Rachal, Pierre	Died at Natchez, April 19, 1756. Desmazellieres' Company.
Rachal, Louis	(A), folio 24.
Raclot, Claude	Sergeant. On half-pay of 15 livres. (C). (A), folio 4.
Regnard, Jean Baptiste	
Roucheteau, René Aymé	Discharged July 23, 1751.

Rouget, Etienne	
Renaud, Jean Baptiste	(A), folio 19.
Rouyeuse, Claude	
Roussel, Paul	
Reyne, Jean Baptiste	
Rivarde, Jean Baptiste	
Royer, Pierre	
Riol, François	Died May 15, 1745. Chavois' Company.
Rachal, Barthélemy	(A), folio 12.
Roy, Jean	Died August 19, 1736.
Renault, Claude Joseph	Died June 3, 1738.
Rondelon, François	Died September 30, 1738.
Rigolet, Joseph	Died October 16, 1735.
Rohan, Antoine	Shot for desertation, January 27, 1741. See the procès-verbal attached to the letter of M. Scimars de Belleisle of April 28, 1741.
Richard, Jacques	Died November 27, 1750.
Roeabois, Antoine	Died December 26, 1751.
Rets, Charles de	Died November 25, 1751.
Rombdiere, François	Discharged June 1, 1751.
Roux, Jacques	Died September 18, 1751.
Redon, Guillaume	Condemned, in absentia, for desertion. See the proceedings of September 30, 1753.
Royer, Jean	Died September 23, 1751.
Romain, Lambert	Discharged June 1, 1751.
Raverdy, Marc	Died October 24, 1751.
Raffine, Jean	Deserted November 20, 1761. See the roll of the same year, folio 5.
Rozier, Léonard	
Roubeau, Joseph	
Rousselot, Antoine	
Remegaud, Simon	
Renard, François	
Rondet, Pierre Joseph	(H), November 12, 1757. Benoist's Company.
Royer, Jean Baptiste	Deserted November 3, 1754. Derneville's Company.
Raby, Pierre	Discharged April 1, 1756.
Roy, Claude Joseph	(H), June 8, 1754. Somme's Company.
Rolin, Pierre	Shipwrecked at Balize, January 10, 1754. La Tour's Company.
Rochet, Philippes	Discharged July 10, 1755 and returned to France on the *Rhinocéros*.

Roujot, Louis	(H), August 15, 1755. Bonnille's Company.
Richard, Pierre	Drowned in the river, July 27, 1754. Favrot's Company.
Rolein, Jean Claude	Deserted September 1, 1754.
Robine, Julien	Discharged April 18, 1756 and returned to France.
Renaud, Jean Joseph	(H), October 27, 1756. Darazola's Company.
Rangé, Jacques	Drowned while going down river from Natchez, October 2, 1754. Gaumont's Company.
Regnier, Louis	Drowned in the river, June 20, 1755. D'Aubry's Company.
Royer, Claude	Deserted July 19, 1755.
Robaille, Jean	Discharged July 16, 1756 and returned to France.
Renaud, Jean Louis Denis	Deserted April 26, 1755.
Renaud, Jacques	Drowned while going down river from Natchez, October 2, 1754. Macarty's Company.
Robert, Gabriel	Died December 31, 1754. Chabert's Company.
Riché, Maurice	Killed or taken prisoner at Fort Wabash by the Cherokees or Chickasaws, November 19, 1757. D'Aubry's Company.
Ricortier, Jean	Condemned, <u>in absentia</u>, to be broken on the wheel for having assassinated his commanding officer, June 7, 1757. Gourdon's Company.
Ripaire, Nicolas François	Discharged February 1, 1764. (B), folio 29.
Rabigo, Jean Louis	(A), folio 21.
Rochefort, Pierre	(H), October 26, 1765. (B), folio 30.
Reaux or Raux, Pierre	(A), folio 20.
Robert, Jean	
Roussel, Denis	On half-pay of 4 livres 10 sol. (C).
Reaux, Pierre	
Royer, Nicolas	(A), folio 8.
Royaux, Alexandre	Discharged October 8, 1769. (B), folio 47.
Rambaud, Pierre	(A), folio 5.
Raison, Jean	
Roche, Claude	
Robert, François	
Rondeau, René	
Rennepont, Etienne	

Roger, Jean	
Rocher, Jean	(A), folio 8.
Richard, Jean	(A), folio 8.
Rollet, Henry	(A), folio 14.
Renaud, Pierre	(A), folio 9.
Roy, Pierre	On half-pay of 9 livres. Decision rendered at Compiegne, July 19, 1764. Sent to the Bureau on the 24th.
Roussel, François	
Ramelot, Lambert	(A), folio 21.
Roze, Jacques	On half-pay of 6 livres. (C).
Rolet, Michel	
Robier, Jean	Discharged October 31, 1769. (B), folio 51.
Roes or Rose, Jacques	(A), folio 12.
Richard, Georges	
Raymond, Pierre	(A), folio 16.
Royer, Pierre	On half-pay of 6 livres. (C)
Renal, Jean	
Redon, Pierre	Discharged and returned to France on the <u>Fortune</u>, January 1, 1759. See roll of June 1, 1760, folio 12.
Raymond, François	
Robinet, François Louis	
Riquet, Pierre	Corporal. Discharged July 1, 1764. On half-pay of 9 livres. Decision of December 12, 1764. Sent to the Bureau the same day.
Ringaud, Marc	Discharged February 6, 1770. On half-pay of 4 livres 10 sol. Decision of April 28, 1770.
Ruffier, François	Sergeant. Discharged September 15, 1763. On half-pay of 15 livres. (C).
Retz, Pierre Louis	(A), folio 23.
Rouriere, Jean	(A), folio 19.
Rouence, Claude	
Rissé, Jean	(A), folio 24.
Roussel, Jean	(A), folio 2. Sergeant. On half-pay of 12 livres. (C).
Royer, Jean	(A), folio 7.
Rousseve, Jean Baptiste Maurice	
Raingot, Simon	(H), October 24, 1769. (B), folio 38.
Rodes, Jacques	(A) folio 14.
Richard, Georges	
Reste, Pierre Louis	
Rasseret, Jean	Died at Mobile, February 26, 1756. Bonnille's Company.

Renands, Jean Baptiste	
Robinet, François	On half-pay of 9 livres. Decision of September 22, 1763. Sent to the Bureau on the 23rd.
Richaume, Georges	Discharged February 6, 1770. On half-pay of 4 livres 10 sol. Decision of April 28, 1770.
Robert, François	Discharged February 6, 1770. On half-pay of 4 livres 10 sol. Decision of April 28, 1770.
Rozier, Léonard	Corporal. Discharged February 6, 1770. On half-pay of 6 livres. Decision of April 28, 1770.
Raux, Pierre	Discharged February 6, 1770. On half-pay of 6 livres. Decision of April 28, 1770. (H) at Isle de Ré, April 29, 1770.
Renal, Jean	Discharged February 6, 1770. On half-pay of 6 livres. Decision of April 28, 1770.
Rondeau, René	Discharged February 6, 1770. Desmazellieres' Company.
Ringard, Augustin	Discharged February 6, 1770. Desmazellieres' Company.
Raison, Jean	Discharged February 6, 1770. Desmazellieres' Company.
Roussel, Jean	(A), folio 5.
Roubelais, Jean	(A), folio 18.
Roche, Jean Jacques	Departed for France, October 1, 1763. (B), folio 26.
Rondeau, René	Departed for France on the <u>Samson</u>, October 1, 1769. (B), folio 38.
Repmenter, Abraham	Discharged October 8, 1769. (B), folio 35.
Rivois, Jean	Discharged and settled in Arkansas, November 30, 1769. (B), folio 48.
Roussel, Claude	Discharged October 8, 1769. (B), folio 49.
Roulland, Pierre Joseph	Discharged November 30, 1769. (B), folio 51.

S

Sibilot, Jean	(H), August 29, 1756. Macarty's Company.
Siberfing, Martin	

Sabatier, Joseph	Discharged May 1, 1751.
Serignot, Anne	Died February 13, 1746. Membrede's Company.
Steigre, Joseph	Died November 29, 1750.
Simon, Thomas	
Sylvestre, Claude	On half-pay of 9 livres. Decision of June 11, 1764. Sent to the Bureau on the 12th.
Seringe, Nicolas	
Scheneberck, Maurice	
Servin, Pierre	
Saunier, Pierre	
St. Pierre, ?	Died March 19, 1744. Le Verrier's Company.
Sarrazin, François	
Speigle, Alexandre	Drummer. Discharged because of injuries. Grandpré's Company.
St. Germain, Pierre	Died January 27, 1739.
Staulive, Noël	Died April 26, 1735.
Sénéchal, Jean Gland	Died November 20, 1736.
Saunier, François	Died September 2, 1731.
Simonneau, François	Deserted April 14, 1750.
Siffet, Louis	Condemned to the galleys, June 3, 1750.
Saver, Jean Philippes	Died October 1, 1751.
Soyard, Pierre	Died October 9, 1751.
Saussard, Pierre Claude Malo	Died September 7, 1751.
Stuard, Guillaume André	
Saramiaque, Renaud	(A), folio 1.
Sorin, Louis	
Schemitt, Hubert	Died at Kaskaskia, May 5, 1756. Favrot's Company.
Suisser, Paul	(H), November 3, 1754. De la Houssaye's Company.
Soulard, Gabriel	Died October 25, 1754. Murat's Company.
Sautrau, Claude	Deserted June 8, 1755.
Suppé, Jean	(H), November 7, 1756. Gourdon's Company.
Sirogue, Martin	Discharged April 18, 1756 and returned to France.
Savant, Mathieu	Discharged March 19, 1755.
Saulet, Louis François	
Setier, Paul	Discharged September 15, 1763. On half-pay of 6 livres. (C).
Sénéchal, Pierre	
Santier or Saintier, François	(A), folio 25.
Sambolt or Saubolt, Benoist	(A), folio 51.
Sanville, Claude	

Sarlat, Jean	
Souillot, Jean Pierre	
Samuël, Jean Baptiste	Discharged October 1, 1764. (B), folio 29.
Simonet, Joseph	
Sabotte or Sobot, Guillaume Etienne	(A), folio 10.
Serano, Thomas	Discharged November 30, 1769. (B), folio 41.
Scouijer, Thomas	
Selle, Jean de	
Sibillot, Michel	(P).
Siret, Jean	
St. Jullien, Louis	On half-pay of 6 livres. (C).
Schemitz, Abraham	Discharged November 16, 1769. (B), folio 49.
Sénéchal, Jean Joseph	Discharged March 31, 1761. (B), folio 22.
Simon, Jean	(H), April 16, 1763. (B), folio 24.
Sautrais, François	(A), folio 21.
Salvin, Jean	
St. Dizier, Etienne	
Santé, Jean	Died at New Orleans, March 26, 1765. (B), folio 31.
Seguin, Jean	
Saussé, Jean	On half-pay of 9 livres. Accorded April 9, 1772.
Sellier, Toussaint	
Sabattier, Jean	(P).
Scellier, Charles	Discharged March 31, 1761. See roll of the same year, folio 36.
Saucier, François	
St. Agnès, Pierre	
Soriaux, André	(H), March 7, 1761. See the roll of same year, folio 4.
Soriaux, Pierre	
Sonsois, Louis	Sergeant. Discharged July 1, 1764. On half-pay of 12 livres. Decision of November 30, 1764. Sent to the Bureau on December 1. Murat's Company.
Salins or Salem, Mathieu	(A), folio 22.
Santré, François	
Salvan, Jean	Discharged September 30, 1769. Roll of January 1, 1763, folio 37.
Sequin, Jean	
St. Aigne, Pierre	Deserted August 30, 1761. See roll of the same year, folio 40.
Savy, Jean	Discharged. See roll dated at Calais, May 2, 1763.

St. Jacques, ?	On half-pay of 9 livres. Decision of June 11, 1764. Sent to the Bureau on the 12.
Soudan, Joseph	Soldier. Deserted October 17, 1765. Condemned, <u>in absentia</u>, following trial, October 17, 1765.
Souillot, Jean Pierre	(P).
Scheleger, Joseph	Discharged February 6, 1770. On half-pay of 4 livres 10 sol. Decision of April 28, 1770.
Simonet, Joseph	Discharged February 6, 1770. On half-pay of 4 livres 10 sol. Decision of April 28, 1770.
Scouder, Jacques	Discharged February 6, 1770. On half-pay of 4 livres 10 sol. Decision of April 28, 1770.
Sénécal or Sénéchal, Pierre	Discharged February 6, 1770. Duplessis' Company.
Schmitz, Antoine	Discharged February 6, 1770, on half-pay. Decision of April 27, 1751 (?). Sent to the Bureau on the 28th. Vaugine's Company.
Scoulier, Thomas	Discharged February 6, 1770. On half-pay of 4 livres 10 sol. Decision of April 28, 1770.
Sanville, Claude	Drummer. Discharged August 20, 1770. On half-pay of 9 livres. Decision of October 17, 1770.
Servraise, Claude	(A), folio 16.
Servraise, Joseph	(A), folio 17.
Serville, Michel	Discharged February 1, 1764. (B), folio 30.
Simate, Georges	Banished July 27, 1769. (B), folio 37.
Schtorm, Augustin	Banished May 25, 1769. (B), folio 38.

T

Theris, Mathieu	Discharged in 1745 and returned to France.
Thierre, Nicolas	Discharged November 15, 1769. (B), folio 41.
Terion, François	Died December 28, 1751.
Triboulet, Jean	Deserted March 15, 1746.
Tasseau, Jean Jacques	Drowned November 28, 1751.
Turpot, Jacques	Discharged November 15, 1769. (B), folio 40.
Tournier, Guillaume	(H), May 13, 1756. Montberault's Company.

Treville, François	Killed or taken prisoner by the Cherokees or Chickasaws, November 9, 1757. Somme's Company.
Tetard, François	
Thomas, Pierre	
Tourbier, François	On half-pay of 9 livres. (C). Discharged September 15, 1763.
Toutin, Charles	Discharged November 1, 1750.
Tessier, Gabriel	
Tourtillé, Jacques	
Tual, Guillaume André	
Tumerman, Joseph	Discharged September 1, 1751.
Thomas, René	Died at Natchez, February 1, 1756. Gourdon's Company.
Timon, Nizier	Discharged August 18, 1751.
Thibault, Jean	Died February 28, 1751.
Tison, Antoine	Shot July 14, 1745 for rebellion. Marest's Company.
Trancha, Alexis	Died October 11, 1734.
Thuillier, Adrien	Died September 1, 1735.
Travers, Thomas	Deserted February 5, 1739.
Tortillé, Jacques	Died August 20, 1751.
Tristan, Pierre	Condemned, <u>in absentia</u>, for desertion. See the proceedings of September 30, 1753.
Theriau, Raymond	Deserted August 1, 1750.
Tousel, Etienne Joseph	Died August 9, 1751.
Tisserand, Joseph	Died September 14, 1751.
Terrier, Pierre	Died September 6, 1751.
Taqueda, Pierre	Deserted April 27, 1751.
Tiercelin, Philippe Joseph	Died July 31, 1751.
Tournier, Jean	
Tellier, Jean	Deserted August 30, 1761. See roll of same year, folio 43.
Texier, Pierre	Condemned to the galleys for life, February 9, 1756. D'Aubry's Company.
Taillou, Jean	Discharged October 8, 1769. (B), folio 50.
Taillandier, Michel	Drowned November 18, 1756. Benoist's Company.
Travaux, Louis Charles	Died September 16, 1754. Dorgon's Company.
Tiesset, Louis	Discharged November 1, 1756.
Tardieu, Louis	Discharged August 1, 1754.
Tuyau, Pierre Nicolas	Deserted or lost at the end of April, 1755. Gautraye's Company.

Tendre, Jean	Drowned in the river, October 2, 1754. Desmazellieres' Company.
Tronquet, Pierre	Discharged August 16, 1756.
Touvenel, Robert	Deserted June 8, 1756.
Ton, Pierre	(H), February 25, 1754. Gourdon's Company.
Trapé, Michel	
Thouin, René	Discharged July 16, 1756 and returned to France.
Trudel, Jean Etienne	Discharged December 14, 1754.
Touzé, Louis	Died at Natchez, October 6, 1754. Chabert's Company.
Tassin, Pierre	Settled in the colony, June 1, 1751.
Toffin, Pierre	(H), August 4, 1757. Trant's Company.
Taillefer, Jean François	
Thibeaudau, Michel	(A), folio 21.
Ternier, Etienne	(A), folio 4.
Tardioet, Charles	
Thomassin, Antoine	
Tardy, Renard	
Tampier, Etienne	
Touchard, Jean	On half-pay of 6 livres. Decision of April 4, 1764. Sent to the Bureau on the 5th.
Tatton, Jean Jullien	
Terrenoire, Jean Joseph	(A), folio 2.
Truchet, François	
Tixerand, Gerard	Deserted in June, 1759. See roll of June 1, 1760, folio 4.
Tamoineau, Pierre	Deserted at the Arkansas post, October 26, 1759. See roll of June 1, 1760, folio 4.
Tavernier, Jean	Discharged and settled in Illinois. (B), folio 38.
Texier, Jacques	
Troncy, Benoist	
Tenard, François	Corporal. On half-pay of 8 livres. (C).
Testot, Claude	On half-pay of 8 livres. (C).
Touchée, Pierre	
Tevenot, Jean	Sergeant. On half-pay of 10 livres. (C).
Tardy, Pierre	Corporal. Discharged February 6, 1770. On half-pay of 6 livres. Decision of April 28, 1770.
Thiot, Gilles	(A), folio 18.
Truchon, Denis François	
Tinon, Claude	
Thibault, Nicolas	Discharged December 31, 1764. (B), folio 29.
Trudeau, Rosalie	

Tirguit or Tirquit, Antoine	Died April 4, 1761. Roll of the same year, folio 46.
Thierry, Louis	(A), folio 1.
Tudeau, François	Discharged November 30, 1769, after having served 21 years. On half-pay of 7 livres 10 sol. Decision of July 2, 1769.
Tessier, Gabriel	
Tagot, Jacques François	Discharged December 30, 1769. (B), folio 52.
Thiers, François	On half-pay of 6 livres. (C).
Tardivet, Charles	(P).
Tual, Guillaume André	Wounded soldier. (A), folio 4. (P).
Tessier, Gabriel	Discharged February 6, 1770. Duplessis' Company.
Tual, Guillaume	Fusilier. On half-pay of 6 livres, payable at Dol in Brittany. Decision of September 8, 1770. Sent to the Bureau on the 14th.
Trufflot, Louis Jacques	(A), folio 16.
Talon, Jean Julien	(H), July 26, 1767. (B), folio 35.
Taurich, Faye	Discharged November 16, 1769. (B), folio 52. He enlisted in 1764.
Torel, Michel	Discharged November 16, 1769. (B), folio 52.

V

Villeret, Jean Mathieu	On half-pay of 6 livres, payable at Besançon. Decision of September 8, 1770. Sent to the Bureau on the 14th.
Vauquiere, Eloy	
Voltre, Mathieu	
Vallé, Maurice	
Vignon, Jean René	Discharged August 10, 1754.
Vilmenaye, Joseph	Died at Natchez,in 1745 or 1746.
Vigueroux, Charles	
Veores, Philipes Adam	Discharged July 1, 1750.
Vitrequin, Gatien	Discharged April 1, 1750
Vally, André	Died February 20, 1751.
Vivier, François	
Vilmane, Jacques	Died February 11, 1745. Gauvry's Company.
Versiau, André	Died September 27, 1738.
Villeroux, François	Died November 6, 1750.
Vindos, Henry	Drowned November 20, 1750.

Vié, Antoine	Died August 25, 1751.
Vigoureux, Cornil Joseph	Shot June 16, 1751.
Viala, François	Died October 1, 1751.
Vachelier, Gilbert	Died October 15, 1751.
Vírauvancourt, Pierre	Died October 6, 1751.
Vidal, Pascal	Condemned to the galleys, May 6, 1751.
Vitcoq, Pierre	Died October 31, 1751.
Vincent, Pierre	Drowned December 30, 1751.
Violon, Pierre	Discharged February 1, 1751. Re-enlisted, see below.
Virard, Pierre	
Vaudois, Nicolas	
Vivien, Louis	
Vhaud, Jean	Discharged July 10, 1754 and returned to France on the <u>Rhinocéros</u>.
Vanquiere, Eloy	(H), July 19, 1755. Grandpré's Company.
Vaspy, Antoine	Deserted in Alabama, January 15, 1755.
Vigroux, Charles Philippes	Discharged by order of the court, 1754.
Vernon, Joseph Thomas	Discharged July 10, 1756, in order to return to France.
Villiers, Claude	Discharged April 18, 1756 and returned to France on the <u>Rhinocéros</u>.
Varé, François	Shot February 9, 1756. De Neyon's Company.
Vergnon, Gabriel	Deserted at Camp Campeachy in 1755 or 1756.
Vergeront, François	Drowned in the Wabash River, November 10, 1756. Mazan's Company.
Verouil, Nicolas	(H), March 19, 1757. Bellinos' Company.
Vial, Joseph Marie	On half-pay of 9 livres. Decision of May 25, 1764. (A), folio 2.
Verdette, François	
Voiseau, Claude François	
Villet, François	
Vieux, Pierre	(A), folio 5.
Verdier, Pierre	Sergeant. (P).
Verrier, Etienne	Drowned while returning from Alabama, October 1, 1759. See roll of June 1, 1760, folio 2.
Vascocu, Antoine	(A), folio 6.
Varette, Henry	
Vaché, Antoine	
Vincent, Jean	(A), folio 22.

Valis, Antoine	(H), November 25, 1768. (B), folio 36.
Viart, Laurent François	(A), folio 14.
Vinet, François	Discharged February 16, 1764. (B), folio 27.
Viel, Antoine	Discharged February 6, 1770. Duplessis' Company.
Verron, Etienne	
Vialand, Pierre	Discharged November 16, 1769. (B), folio 48.
Voisin, Jean Pierre	(H), November 9, 1765. (B), folio 31.
Viollon, Pierre	Discharged February 6, 1770. On half-pay of 4 livres 10 sol. Decision of April 28, 1770.
Verdet, Joseph	(P).
Voignier, Jean	Sergeant. Discharged September 15, 1763. On half-pay of 12 livres. (C).
Vaillant, Louis Nicolas	(H), June 9, 1767. (B), folio 35.
Vasseron, Bernard Joseph	
Verron, François	Returned to France on the <u>Samson</u>, October 1, 1769. (B), folio 50.
Vatonne, Barthélemy	(A), folio 17.
Vidoux, François	(A), folio 14.
Verdel, François Louis	
Villanis, Jean François	Discharged February 6, 1770. On half-pay of 4 livres 10 sol. Decision of April 28, 1770.
Vilcain, Jean François	Discharged. See the roll dated at Calais May 2, 1763.
Villot, François	Artilleryman. (P).
Vachez, Antoine	Discharged February 6, 1770. On half-pay of 6 livres per month. Decision of April 28, 1770.
Vtois, Samuël	Discharged February 6, 1770. Duplessis' Company.
Vasseron, Bernard Joseph	Discharged February 6, 1770. Villiers' Company.
Villeret, Jean Martin	Discharged September 1, 1764. On half-pay of 6 livres. Decision of September 8, 1770.
Viet, François	(A), folio 24.
Viter, Pierre	Discharged August 1, 1766. (B), folio 32.
Vincent, Augustin Nicolas	Enlisted March 16, 1769. Discharged October 8, 1769. (B), folio 55.

W

Wourne, Joseph	(A), folio 14.
Willaume, Antoine	
Wourne, Joseph	On half-pay of 6 livres. (C).
Woua, Jean	(H), August 29, 1757. Trant's Company.

Y

Yentzen, Guibert	
You, Simon	

Z

Zizany, François	Died October 27, 1751.

www.ingramcontent.com/pod-product-compliance
Lightning Source LLC
Chambersburg PA
CBHW061835260326
41914CB00005B/1002
* 9 7 8 0 8 7 5 1 1 3 5 5 5 *